FOOTPRINTS
AND OTHER PLAYS

Family Albums
A Geometric Tragedy

Arrowheads
The paths not taken

Credit Titles
The Draft Blowing In

Home Movies
Second to None

Footprints
The future of the past

Vitasta
LET KNOWLEDGE SPREAD

BANGALORE LITTLE THEATRE

COMMENTS ON THE PUBLICATIONS

Bangalore Little Theatre deserves hearty congratulations on the publication of Indian classics adapted for the contemporary stage. This work is not only important for India, it also makes plays from Indian writing known across the world. We can all look forward eagerly to the series of volumes planned. It is a very important and necessary project.

Ursula Werdenberg
Dramaturg-Playwright,
Secretary General of The International Playwrights' Forum

There is a hunger for strong dramatic texts in India, where theatre production has grown far more rapidly than playwriting. In that context, these volumes will be seen as yet another precious gift that BLT has given to the theatre community.

Anmol Vellani
Theatre Director and past Founder-Director
of India Foundation for the Arts

This initiative would allow theatre practitioners from other parts of the world to access this work and look at the possibilities of staging these plays in multiple languages and in multiple cultural contexts.

Vidyanidhi Vanarase
Founder-Dirtector, International Association
for Performing Arts and Research

These are a valued resource...they celebrate authors past and present and their translators as well, making the local, global.

Richard Crane
Playwright-Director,
Co-founder of Brighton Theatre

We have eagerly awaited the publication of these volumes. They have finally arrived. They will reach performers and audiences right across national borders and far beyond.

Sai Paranjpye
Theatre personality and award winning film director

An international leader in our field, especially its serious investment in new play development, including the publication series that can benefit all of us theater makers across the world.

Bill Rauch
Artistic Director, Perelman Performing Arts Center
at the World Trade Center, New York City

The new publication series produced by the Bangalore Little Theatre are an important and most welcome addition to world theater knowledge. Bravo!

Arthur Giron
Founding Member of Ensemble Studio Theatre, New York, formerly
Head, Graduate Playwriting Program, Carnegie Mellon University

I am delighted that you are presenting all these plays that are at one and the same time enjoyable, revealing and memorable!

Roddam Narasimha
Science Historian and Professor,
Jawaharlal Nehru Centre for Advanced Scientific Research

Bangalore Little Theatre has reached veteran status in Indian theatre with their powerful theatrical interventions in the community, spanning 60 years...these volumes enrich our understanding of the capacity of theatre to create spaces for potent ideas, that demand our engagement.

Yvette Hardie
President: ASSITEJ (International Association for Theatre for Children and Young People)

Your contribution to the goals of the International Playwrights' Forum, to the artistic treasures of your country, as well as for universal culture in general is indescribable indeed.

Gad Kaynar (Kissinger)
Professor, International Theatre Institute
The Yolanda and David Katz Faculty of the Arts, Tel Aviv University

My warmest congratulations. This is a significant milestone and a wonderful achievement that gives readers an opportunity to think about our pasts and our presents through a history of ideas.

Anuradha Kapur
Past Director, National School of Drama

ये नाम केचिदिह नः प्रथयन्त्यवज्ञां
जानन्ति ते किमपि तान्प्रति नैष यत्नः ।
उत्पत्स्यते तु मम कोऽपि समानधर्म
कालो ह्ययं निरवधिर्विपुला च पृथ्वी ॥

Those who deride or ignore my work –
let them know: my efforts are not for them.
There will come along someone who shares my spirit:
the world is vast, and time endless.

– ***Bhavabhuti***

Bangalore Little Theatre is privileged to receive a substantial grant from ***Kusum*** *and* ***Mohandas Pai*** *towards education and institutional development programmes, which include the publication of these plays.*

Published by,
Renu Kaul Verma
Vitasta Publishing Pvt Ltd
2/15, Ansari Road, Daryaganj
New Delhi 110002
info@vitastapublishing.com

ISBN 978-93-90961-10-8

MRP ₹450
First Edition 2022

Editors: Kanagam King, Papri Sen Sri Raman
Layout: Deepak Mote
Illustrations: Supriya Kannan
Printer: Vikas Computer and Printers

CONTENTS

FOREWORD TO THE SERIES

Bangalore Little Theatre is an enormous exercise in imagination. It remains an aspiration for theatre performers and a source of inspiration for practitioners. The passion, perseverance, toil and grace is the hallmark of this intimate Institution, which has embarked on many pathbreaking initiatives, programmes and productions. If the History of Ideas programme was unique, the translation and adaptation of Indian classics in English is a huge service. In the programme Vijay Padaki has presented a pertinent model, wherein the play scripts transcend the cultural specificity and period in time to speak in a universal language that addresses our contemporary concerns. Although we read the text in English, we experience the content in the original. A truly remarkable feat.

BLT has had a strong play development programme for a long time. It is most appropriate that the plays are being published now. Several volumes of plays can be expected in print very soon. This is a huge contribution to the institution of theatre in India. We can be sure they will be received with enthusiasm world-wide.

Feroz Abbas Khan
Theatre director and award winning film maker

SPECIAL MESSAGE

For nearly 60 years, Bangalore Little Theatre has been instrumental in promoting theatre arts in Bengaluru and across the country. The ambitious project of publishing their most successful plays in a multi-volume anthology marks a great point in their story – another marker of the tremendous success they have attained.

In translating to English and adapting the plays for the modern stage, Mr Vijay Padaki (BLT) is conserving the best of Indian theatre. Each play is especially relevant to contemporary situations, from environmental concerns to resurgent regional identities, to introspecting the carnage of wars and finally the complexities of court politics.

I am certain that such a project provides us the perfect opportunity to understand, perhaps for the first time in recent years, the sheer wealth of Indian theatre spanning different cultural and linguistic traditions in the subcontinent. In producing such plays, and putting them together in this volume, BLT has undertaken a public service, one which every Indian living in the 21st century can profit from, for a long time to come.

With this, I wish BLT the very best for this and their many future endeavours.

Shashi Tharoor
Member of Parliament for Thiruvananthapuram

PUBLISHER'S NOTE

We were very enthusiastic when we first associated ourselves with Bangalore Little Theatre and became a participant in their theatre book publishing project in July 2019. We had envisioned a series of ten books by December 2020. But this has been a classic case of what man proposes, god disposes.

By divine grace we did manage to publish the first three volumes in December 2019 and we were happy to participate in the very smooth launch function that theatre lovers in Bangalore got to witness. All seemed well. Until March 2020, when a tiny little flu' virus disrupted our lives.

The pandemic hit small businesses most and the lockdown resulted in shut shops and heavy job losses. Books were the last concern of people and the publishing industry was among the worst hit. But we overcame the first wave of the Corona pandemic. Vitasta survived. True we were not able to promote and sell our first three volumes of theatre books due to market forces being negative, but by the end of 2020 we were convinced that we were not abandoning ship. A year later, despite circumstances that are globally disruptive and beyond our control, Vitasta decided to go ahead and publish the next three volumes of the theatre book series. And here we are with the first book this year, Volume 4, titled Footprints.

In this set of plays, the family is at the core of all the stories. Perhaps keeping with the dystopian times, the playwright here systematically goes about de-constructing the family bit by bit, very unlike Indian cinema and literature where the 'family' is the nucleus that holds disparate elements together. The plays were mostly written through the 1980s and '90s, times of great socio-economic change in the country. Burning of brides with the help of kerosine stoves was an international scandal. 1992 also saw a mass movement against the Dunkel Draft, the Intellectual Property Rights protocol India signed. It was also the era when retroviral drug production for HIV-AIDS became a rights issue, as did commercialisation of in-vitro fertilisation which came into focus. The vanishing of plant and animal species, climate change, burden on the earth, carbon footprints, everything received attention. The last story on the 65-million year cycle of apocalypse and the kidnapping of the writer from the nest, says it all.

Perhaps, this set of plays will help clarify for audiences and readers, how small the framework of the family is, how vulnerable and fragile, and push towards a less petty and more global mindspace.

As our very own poet Rabindranath Tagore said:

Where the mind is without fear and the head is held high;
Where knowledge is free;
Where the world has not been broken up into fragments
by narrow domestic walls;
Where words come out from the depth of truth;
Where tireless striving stretches its arms towards perfection...

Read on... about the imperfection of the world and then think what the definition of perfection should be.

SALUTATIONS

Volumes 1-3 of the publication project were pushed through in very little time to meet the deadline of 17 December 2019, kicking off the Diamond Jubilee year of BLT. It was on that date in 1960 that BLT had its first public performance. From the original plan of a token release of one volume we went on to release three volumes! The people who went out of the way to make this happen were Papri Sen Sri Raman, Kanagam King and their team at Vitasta Publishing. BLT commissioned the publication of six volumes of plays to Vitasta. It has been a great pleasure working with the Vitasta team, ever meticulous in editorial inputs and ever patient with the BLT team. It has been a great learning experience working with Papri and her team.

It is well known that the huge collection of play scripts in BLT had remained unpublished for years. We are thankful to the Managing Committee of BLT to take on the publication task with determination in 2019 – and for pushing us into its execution. There has been an even more powerful hand behind the publications project, invisible but relentless in drive over several years. Rupande Padaki, known to all of us as Rupa, was in many ways responsible for the publications to be taken up. She succeeded at last.

Deepak Mote • Vijay Padaki

PREFACE TO THE VOLUME

Bangalore Little Theatre (BLT) was restructured in 2008. A public charitable trust was created with a non-profit status. *Theatre development* activities, which were pursued in an on-and-off manner till then, were now placed in a newly created Academy of Theatre Arts.

The planning process identified several well-planned and long-term programme 'thrusts'. They may also be seen as 'verticals' in the mission. The verticals are served by some cross-cutting activities, with their own plans and commitments – some of long standing within BLT and some adopted afresh in the ATA plan.

For example,

- *Methodology Development*, training methods, including trainer-training and training directors.
- *Play Development*, in which BLT has had a long track record.
- *Partnership Development*, reinforcing the organisation's commitment to collaboration.
- *Competence Development*, promoting talent in the theatre for new writing, new directors, new artists – both on stage and off stage.

New play development is thus a major commitment in the long-term plans of BLT. More recently, BLT created an entirely new programme called NEW VOICES. It includes the creation of a Writers Forum and the creation of opportunities for play scripts to be performed. The programme thrust is extended to colleges and universities, organising theatre festivals of only new and original plays.

In the early years of play development, a great deal of the new writing came from my desk. Ah, but very few of them were turned into theatre productions by BLT! As a highly-democratised set-up, the group had clear criteria for the selection of plays for performance, and the process was driven by the twin principles of governance – participative decisions and transparency.

I wrote for the enjoyment of writing, not for inflicting the scripts on BLT, and with no desire to be seen as a playwright. At the end of each writing project, I shared the script with a few friends whose opinion I valued, and that was it. I went on to the next writing project. Seeing the play scripts published was never the objective.

In 2019, I stepped down from all management responsibilities in BLT, continuing simply as a Trustee. The Managing Committee of BLT decided to felicitate me for the long years of service to the organisation. First, they put together a Festival of my plays, spread over the months of May-September 2019. If that was not enough to increase my hat size by two inches, they overwhelmed me next with the project to publish all my plays.

A team within the Committee took charge, worked out the arrangement with Vitasta Publishers, and here we are! We have play scripts in a whole publication series from Bangalore Little Theatre.

I succeeded in persuading the publications team to position the series as Plays from *Bangalore Little Theatre*. It is, after all, the character of BLT that has promoted new writing for the stage, and created the conditions for me to write. Play development has been led by me over many years in BLT. I sincerely hope the NEW VOICES programme will carry forward this nurturance.

In this preface, it would be appropriate to reproduce one section of the preface to Volume 1, published in December 2019.

> Bangalore Little Theatre (BLT) was created in 1960. In its very first three years, English language theatre moved out of the Cantonment to reach all of Bangalore. BLT very decisively sought an alternative theatre experience in a post-colonial social context. Reaching out to those active in the Kannada theatre in the city, they created a truly inclusive theatre society. BLT was influenced greatly by the Little Theatre movement of the 'fifties in the UK, decentralising theatre activity from London, disseminating high-quality theatre widely through training, outreach, and community involvement.
>
> Within a year of inception, BLT arrived at a character and identity for itself: to maintain pride in its strictly amateur status, but to conduct its affairs in a thoroughly professional manner. The group gave itself a constitution and, through that, a participatory style of functioning. The group was seen as belonging to a membership, and therefore, to be managed by a transparently elected management committee. The founding members were the first to give way to younger members to take the group forward.
>
> Of special significance was the group's positioning as *Community Theatre*, relating to the Indian socio-economic reality. In sum, within a short space of five years BLT was:
>
> - an *Indian* theatre group with a global outlook.
> - assimilating the best of British theatre traditions in a new Indian environment.
> - relating to Kannada and all other regional language theatre groups – actively assisting them.
>
> Related to the last point is one other indisputably important feature of BLT. It is the only English language theatre group in Bangalore (perhaps one of very few anywhere in India) with strong links to the local-regional theatre, building bridges across language divides. Many of the stalwarts on the Kannada stage and screen

have been either life members of BLT or have been prominently involved in some capacity or the other. Indeed, BLT has been a substantial support to Kannada theatre groups in their start-up stages.

* * * * *

The plays included in this volume are different from the first three volumes in one important respect. They are not thematically compiled. These plays were written in the period 1986 to 2002 and represent explorations in combining form with content. We know, of course, that form without content is mere indulgence. (It is so in all of the arts.) I can say with some confidence that in my writing, it has always been the content that drove the form. Is there something about the content that holds the five plays together? Perhaps, yes – and perhaps without my being aware of it until now. Looking back, putting the plays together for this publication, I see a humanistic undercurrent in the plays, *an affirmation of the human spirit*, the innate ability to question the given, so often remaining suppressed, and the ability to find alternatives.

It is known that a lot of my writing has been influenced by field experiences in my professional engagements. The content of the play has often (not always) begun as a case study, intriguing in itself, but demanding an alternative perspective. The alternative perspectives have provided the raw material for the play scripts. There should be no need to explain this further. The plays should explain themselves.

Before *Credit Titles* I wrote mainly for the enjoyment of writing. *The Hindu* award did the damage of getting me to see myself as a playwright. The original script of *Credit Titles* required an 'Author's Note'. An excerpt from that might be worth reproducing here:

> The danger in winning a prize for a play script is, of course, the precipitation of the belief that one is a playwright. Of course, I am not. I enjoy writing plays, as I enjoy working with wood, but that does not make me a playwright. Or a carpenter. The truth is I enjoy working on lots of different things. That only makes me a lot of a dabbler. The truth I have to accept is that there is a lot more to a craft than displaying a toolkit. It is most deceptive when there is also a recognisable body of takers. Why, even as a schoolboy, I had an indulgent audience. Even takers for the misshapen stools and bookends that I turned out regularly. My accountant gives me one more good reason not to call myself a playwright: *The Hindu* award is then deemed an income. …I am referring to what was rather special for me in *Credit Titles*: the enjoyment was almost

> entirely in the act of writing itself, and who cares what happens to the script afterwards! With no producer or audience in mind, with little thought to how the finished product might be received, with nothing to prove to anybody, it was easier to be accepted by the characters in the play, to get their permission to sit in a corner and watch them at play, to submit to their play.

Many thanks to Asha Mathew, Minti Jain and Murtuza Khetty for the help in editing the manuscripts for this Volume.

Vijay Padaki
Series Editor

STAGE DIRECTIONS
with the actor facing the audience

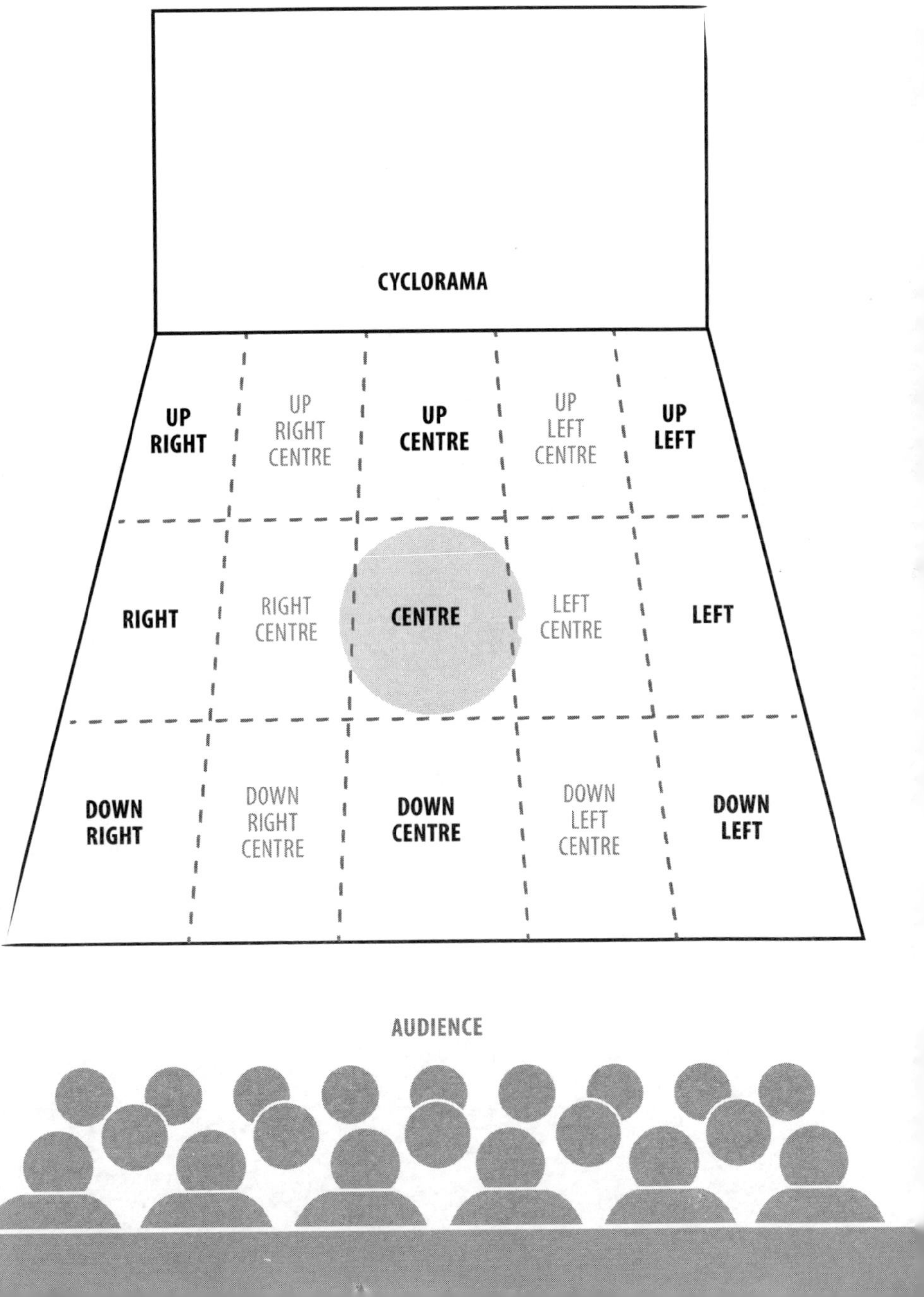

Family Albums

A Geometric Tragedy
Vijay Padaki

FOR
MS THIMMAPPA

CHARACTERS IN THE PLAY

INDU .... *Dr Indira Mahesh-Dixit, twenty-nine, psychiatrist, highly respected at the Institute and in the profession.*

LAKSHMI .... *Twenty-eight, a degree in home science and a writing diploma under her belt. Now a housewife, after several pocket money jobs.*

VIC .... *Vikram S Dixit, thirty-two, Indu's husband, chartered accountant. Recently made partner of the firm.*

HEMANT .... *Lakshmi's husband, thirty.*

POPS .... *Shankar L Dixit, father of Vic. Took an early retirement from a Calcutta based trading company to set up an agency business of his own.*

BABA .... *Kedarnath Prabhu, Hemant's father. Depot Manager in a public sector corporation, which he joined as an apprentice thirty years ago.*

AMMAJI .... *Hemant's mother, efficient manager of the Prabhu household.*

MAMA .... *Mrs SL Dixit, affectionate mother, patient wife, and hostess. Gives free baking lessons on Saturdays.*

DASH .... *Darshan Sheth, Vic's friend from college days. Son of family friends, buys and sells cars and accessories.*

BUDDHOO .... *Gautam, Hemant's friend. Lecturer in an Arts and Science College.*

MINOO .... *Hemant's sister. In junior college.*

MINTY .... *Vic's sister. Occupation – student. Difficult to say in what subjects.*

The following parts must be doubled in casting, with four actors playing two parts each:

1. Ammaji and Mama
2. Pops and Baba
3. Buddhoo and Dash
4. Minty and Minoo

The doubling is best done through contrasts in acting, resorting to only the barest essentials in costuming or personal props.

INTRODUCTION

Formerly, when religion was strong and science was weak, men mistook magic for medicine. Now, when science is strong and religion is weak, men mistake medicine for magic.

From the programme playbill

The story of Lakshmi is based on an actual case of a woman who was sucked into the vortex of a self-fulfilling prophecy, ending in institutionalised psychiatric treatment. The substance of the case has been retained. The circumstances have been fictionalised to serve the purpose of dramatisation.

The platform for the play script is the work of Thomas Szasz and reveals the underlying concerns in the play about the precipitation of mental illness by the very act of psychiatric diagnosis and intervention. Szasz, a respected psychiatrist himself, questioned the bona fides of the 'mental illness industry' in his classic publications, *The Myth of Mental Illness and The Manufacture of Madness*. The humanistic perspective in Szasz is revealed in the sub-title to the book: *Foundations of a Theory of Personal Conduct*. Taking the cue, we might, in fact, benefit from a re-examination of all forms of dogma and all institutionalised faiths – especially the way they might be perpetrating problematic behaviours towards their own indispensability.

The play works on the story of Lakshmi, a young, vivacious, newly-married woman, who is systematically broken down into a 'classic' psychiatric syndrome. We have no difficulty in recognising her condition as a mental illness, nor in giving the condition an appropriate label. But we do not easily see how the steadily deteriorating condition might be on account of the label itself. The human spirit resists the intrusion, but it is an unequal match against the temple. The resistance can become another symptom, and thus a liability, inviting upon herself more attention, more 'treatment'.

In the play, the counterpoint to Lakshmi's passage is provided by Indu, Dr Indira Mahesh-Dixit, the psychiatrist, who is rapidly gaining international recognition for her pioneering work in new therapy models, and who undertakes Lakshmi's case. As a newly-married woman herself, she is not without trials in her own period of adjustment. And she has her own ways to deal with them.

The performance

By design, the other characters in the two households are played by the same actors, helping to interweave the events in their lives into a recognisable mosaic. Some territoriality in the use of the acting areas should be useful. For example, the sweep from Up-centre to Down-left for the psychiatrist, her clinic, home, study; the arc at stage centre from

Down-left-centre to Down-right-centre for neutral and public spaces; the sweep from Up-centre to Down-right for Lakshmi, her kitchen, her room.

Language Notes

Adat nahin hai na: Not used to it, you see
Arati: Ritual with an oil lamp
Kumkum: Vermillion powder, also used in ritual
Buddhoo (Gautam's name): Epithet to mean dopey, goofy
He, his, him: In orthodox custom, women are not expected to speak their husbands' names
Zaroor: Sure, of course
LAKSHMI
Goddess of wealth
Saraswati: Goddess of learning
Agarbatti: Incense sticks
Pudina: Mint
Lahore: City in Pakistan. Families in both countries continue to refer to friends/relatives in the other place
Jalebi: Fried sweet dish
Bahu: Daughter-in-law
Badam: Almond
Calmpose: Brand name for relaxant/sleeping pill (like Valium)
Bhabhi: Brother's wife
Didi: Older sister
Puglee: Nut, crazy girl (affectionately)
Haldi-kumkum: Turmeric powder and vermilion powder, used with grains of rice in arati
Puja/Pooja: Worship ritual
Budtameez: Ill-mannered
Patidev: Husband-lord
Lakh: A hundred thousand
Pariah: Pie dog, mongrel. Used to mean a low-caste person
Bhoot (bangla): Ghost (haunted house)
Khandan: Clan, family tree
Palak sag: Spinach
Rishi: Heavenly sage in mythology
Chinar: Himalayan pine tree
Chandan: Fragrant paste from sandalwood, used in worship
Rudraksh: Seed from Himalayan tree, used to make prayer beads, rosary
Nani: Grandmother (maternal)
Nada: Drawstring, as in pajamas

FIRST PERFORMED

By Bangalore Little Theatre at the Deccan Herald Theatre Festival in Bangalore, September 1989.

Indu .... SHUBA RAO-ABRAHAM
Lakshmi .... AARTI KARMARKAR
Vikram .... ROHIT JAISINGH
Hemant .... SHIVAKUMAR BELAWADI
Pops and Baba .... UK JAYADEV
Ammaji and Mama .... POILE SENGUPTA
Dash and Buddhoo .... SAROSH SHERIFF
Minoo and Minty .... KUMUDA RAO
Stage .... SHAILESH RUDRA, JAYANT RUDRA, DEEPAK PADAKI
Lighting .... KN JAYANTH, PRADEEP BELAWADI, KARTHIK
Property .... KESHWAR SAHAR, MADHAVI RAO, ASHWINI TAMBE
Costumes .... KIRTI KARMARKAR, YVETTE MONTEIRO
Sound .... CHATURA PADAKI
Make up .... SUJATHA BELAWADI
Designed and directed by .... VIJAY PADAKI

SCENE 1

Indu in her study, Left. She is rapidly checking out a tray of slide transparencies, stopping occasionally to make notes in the margins of a manuscript. She is barely visible. Presently her voice fades in over the audio system, as she continues to work silently.

INDU'S VOICE

The evidence before us was devastatingly significant. Chemotherapeutic options had produced uniformly weak, transient, and unreliable results, and were indeed to be viewed as counterproductive. Psychotherapeutic procedures were contra-indicated, with the attendant risk of reinforcing the delusion states. ECT was ruled out at the very start. There were, in other words, no interactive or confounding effects on the data for sixteen weeks of the Intensive Cognitive Restructuring programme. The shifts in every one of the criterial clinical variables have been significant and far beyond any earlier record.

Towards the end of the statement, Indu turns in her seat, facing the audience, sitting demurely with hands on her lap. A single spot picks her up momentarily and goes out.

She shifts to a seat Down-centre. The post-conference interview.

A spot picks up Indu. She is cool, and answers questions from several interviewers with professional care.

INDU

On the contrary, our experience in the revised programme has shown that the total time in the ICR is actually less, provided the inputs at each stage are as per schedule... A good question. I wish I had the original graphs with me here, but the attrition rates have been consistently significant... Yes, categorically yes... I would have no hesitation in coordinating or even simply taking part in such a cross-cultural project... You are right. The ICR model suggests several other applications beyond the psychiatric clinic. Yes, the implications of our Intensive Cognitive Restructuring programme are far reaching... Yes, I am. He is in a chartered accountancy firm, he has been made a partner recently... No, we don't have any... At my husband's parents... We are a society in transition, you know. We are rapidly moving away from the physical structure of a joint family system, but the emotional basis remains in such arrangements... It has been an exhilarating experience. I am glad I was able to make it... It came as a surprise. I had no idea my paper was being considered for the award. I felt honoured when I heard the citation being read... Well, back to work, I suppose. Yes, certainly. The research in this field has just begun... Thank you, too, for your kind hospitality. It has been a very enjoyable visit. My best wishes to your readers.

She sits straight, hands in her lap. The lights turn dazzling bright a few times and fade out. A spot picks up Lakshmi, seated alone Down-right, a diary and a pen in her hands. She remains still.

Crossfade to Indu's study, Left. She picks up the telephone receiver.

INDU

Dr Mahesh-Dixit... ah, Dr Sharma's case... good... not surprising, good... I'll see her, but there's no need to rush it... another day or two... please do that. Thank you for calling. Good night.

Crossfade to Lakshmi, in the same position as before, as Indu crosses over to her, a clip-board in hand. Lakshmi rises, smiles faintly, as she closes her diary.

LAKSHMI

Good morning.

INDU

(Speaking as she examines Lakshmi's case papers) Good morning. Are you eating well now? Appetite okay? Sleeping all right? *(Leading her to the seat Down-centre.)* What do you do in the reading room?

LAKSHMI

Newspapers...

INDU

Uh... um... We have magazines, books, short stories... Sit down. *(Lakshmi sits)* You are writing too?

LAKSHMI

Yes.

INDU

Have you written to anybody at home?

LAKSHMI

No, not yet.

INDU

Do you like writing?

LAKSHMI

It's just a diary.

INDU

How nice – will you show me? *(Pause)* No hurry. Whenever you feel like it. Feel free to spend more time in the reading room – whenever you want to.

LAKSHMI

Yes.

INDU

We also have a hobby room, you know. First floor, on the right side.

LAKSHMI

Yes... Thank you.

INDU

Well, you must be thinking of all that you'll be doing when you get back. *(Pause)* It will be very soon, you know. I'm going to recommend that it should be as soon as possible. There are just a few small formalities. *(Pause)*

Are you looking forward to going back? *(Lakshmi smiles just a bit)*

Good, I'm sure you are. You go ahead with what you were doing now. I'll see you tomorrow in the morning.

Indu pats Lakshmi and crosses to Left with the case papers. Lakshmi remains seated, opens her diary, and looks up. Crossfade to Left, Indu at telephone.

INDU

P443. ... Prabhu, Lakshmi... Reference Dr PK Sharma... Remission satisfactory... Discharge Monday 10:00 am... No, it won't be necessary. I've examined her myself... I'm sending the papers to your room... Thank you, sister... One more thing, please ask the operator to book a fixed time call to Dr Raymond Simpson in London... 11:30 pm... I'll take the call on my home number... That will be all.

Crossfade to Down-centre

SCENE 2

Lakshmi, in the seat Down-centre, looking radiant. She is joined by Hemant, standing above, to one side. A photo shoot. The lights turn dazzling bright two to three times through the following passage. Both continue to face forward as they talk, freezing briefly when the lights brighten.

LAKSHMI

Who invented the myth that women take longer to dress?

HEMANT

Adat nahin hai na. The trouble with this suit business, Nina, is that...

LAKSHMI

Lakshmi. Your mother has given me the name. Change of name with change of surname.

HEMANT

Anyway, the real problem is the tie. I can never get the length right.

LAKSHMI

You should get a clip-on tie. Have you seen one of those things?

HEMANT

It can fall off. Imagine the tie falling off when I am signing the register in the hotel.

LAKSHMI

Or tipping the room boys.

HEMANT

Imagine it happening last week at the reception.

LAKSHMI

When we were asked to feed each other ice cream.

HEMANT

That was fun, wasn't it?

LAKSHMI

It was funny. Doing it for the cameras was funny.

HEMANT

Let's go. We have only another day before getting home.

LAKSHMI

Did you tell him the number of copies?

(Crossfade to Right, the Prabhu home. Minoo is peering eagerly out front.)

MINOO

They've arrived! They're here! Ammaji, they have arrived!

(Ammaji, Baba, and Buddhoo rush in and wait at the entrance. Hemant and Lakshmi cross over to enter the house.)

AMMAJI

One minute, one minute. Not so fast.

(She does the arati, banishes the evil eye, applies kumkum on Lakshmi's forehead, and gives her a flower for her hair.)

Now, knock down this pot of rice as you step in.

LAKSHMI

(Entering) And on every grain is carved the name of one yet unbegotten.

(General cheer. Lakshmi touches the feet of Ammaji and Baba, hugs Minoo, who thereafter holds on to Lakshmi's hand. Hemant moves away to Buddhoo, begins to take off his coat and tie.)

BABA

You had no problems with the reservations, I hope.

HEMANT

No, no problems. So, how are things here, Buddhoo?

(Buddhoo shrugs, helps Hemant with the coat and tie.)

BABA

Mishraji assured us there was nothing to worry about. He had taken care of everything.

LAKSHMI

Except for the name on the reservation chart. They spelt Hemant's name...

AMMAJI

(Gently but firmly) No matter how they spell his name, he will always be him. Isn't that so, Lakshmi dear?

LAKSHMI

Oh yes, he hasn't had his name changed. *(The others laugh, Minoo excitedly.)*

AMMAJI

All right, you people change and get some rest. We have the whole day to talk about your travel adventures. Come on, Minoo, you can help me with the fruit salad. You must join us for lunch, Buddhoo.

BUDDHOO

Zaroor, I'll come.

MINOO

Can I help you unpack?

LAKSHMI

Of course, you can.

AMMAJI

You can help them later. Come now.

Ammaji, Minoo, and Baba step Down-right, as Lakshmi and Hemant move away. Buddhoo exits.

MINOO

I'll get the fruit out of the fridge.

AMMAJI

You do that. *(Minoo exits. Pause.)*

BABA

Well, you got the boy to marry after all.

AMMAJI

He's fond of her.

BABA

And you succeeded where I failed. You managed to bring Lakshmi into this house. *(Laughs at his own joke)*

AMMAJI

I do hope he'll be happy with her.

BABA

Of course he'll be happy.

AMMAJI

What do you think of her?

BABA

What do I think of her? You're asking me that now?

AMMAJI

Tell me what you think of her.

BABA
I'll tell you. She might not be much in the Lakshmi department, but she is strong in the Saraswati department.

AMMAJI
She talks a lot.

BABA
She is bright.

AMMAJI
Maybe.

BABA
Don't you... aren't you fond of her too?

AMMAJI
Of course I'm fond of her.

Fade out

Lakshmi Up-right-centre, humming to herself as she does the last of her unpacking. Hemant helps putting the empty bags away. Lakshmi collects her diary, writing pads, moves to a seat.

HEMANT
How many diaries do you have?

LAKSHMI
They are not all diaries.

HEMANT
Aren't they?

LAKSHMI
They are different things. Different papers for different things.

HEMANT
Like office files.

LAKSHMI
Different files for different jobs.

HEMANT
Different matters.

LAKSHMI
Different misadventures.

HEMANT
Different people.

LAKSHMI
Different pests.

HEMANT
Alphabetical codes.

LAKSHMI

Colour codes.

HEMANT

What are they anyway?

LAKSHMI

No secrets. These are prose, these poetry, and these for jotting ideas and notes for working on later.

HEMANT

And there's a new one I see.

LAKSHMI

Opened last week! A new pad, with lemon coloured imported onionskin paper, for the new chapter in life.

HEMANT

What do you do better? Writing or jabbering?

LAKSHMI

(Tossing a towel at him as he skips away) Go for your bath, you! *(He exits. Lakshmi calls after him)*

What about you? What's lacking in word, do you make up in deed?

Lakshmi picks up her new pad, moves to a seat. Fade to low. She is barely visible. Presently Lakshmi's voice comes in over the audio system.

LAKSHMI

I saw a wandering minstrel
His woman
Metered steps behind
The babe in her arms
The tear in her eye contained

I saw a barefoot traveller
His burden
A book of dreams
Shred small and blown each morn
Each night each page regained

I saw two infants on the street
One cried
Fondled in harness
Led home by German shepherds on leash
The other entertained
Fade out

SCENE 3

Dash is seen in the seat Down-centre, facing forward, a TV remote in his hand. Indu enters, notices Dash, stops. She has returned from a trip.

INDU
Dash! What are you doing here?

DASH
Ditto. What are you doing here?

INDU
I live here now, you know.

DASH
Oh! Terribly sorry. I'm leaving. As soon as I finish this drink, and clean up the mess in the kitchen, and switch off the video, and turn on the fan for you, and...

INDU
Oh, shut up Dash. Nobody's throwing you out.

DASH
I've answered your question. You haven't answered mine. *(Pause)* You were expected back only tomorrow. Pops and Mama are out at Cookie's estate. There is no grub in the house except in the aquarium. And, anyway, where's Vic?

INDU
He got off on the way.

DASH
How was the trip?

INDU
Oh, good. It was good.

DASH
What do you mean – got off on the way? *(Indu looks at Dash and smiles.)* Jumped off the plane?

INDU
He was bored. We were both bored. A jungle resort log cabin is fine for one day and one night. Stretch it to two days. And one night. What do you do after you've counted all the flintlock muskets on the walls and memorised the zoological names of all the wild beasts supposedly crawling all over the park – that you never got to see anyway?

DASH
So you quit the log cabin, stripped to your Tarzan outfits and moved into a woodpecker's nest?

INDU

We just took a room in a hotel in Mysore city, and decided to catch up on some reading.

DASH

Reading!

INDU

Well, I had my reading and he had his.

DASH

Daintily bookmarked his and hers.

INDU

Mostly the post-budget analyses. What else on the first day of March? That's when we realised that we could read better if we got back home.

DASH

And home is where... Vic is not.

INDU

He got off at the office. It was on the way. He's picking up some papers, which he just remembered.

DASH

Should I ring Cookie's place to inform...

INDU

No, don't. Let them take their time.

DASH

They might be upset that there wasn't a proper reception on your arrival.

INDU

You can pour me a drink, can't you?

DASH

Sure. I'm sorry, I should have asked.

INDU

And you can do the needful on behalf of the household, can't you?

Through the following passage, Indu leaves her bags Up-centre, perhaps with Dash's help, moves to desk Left, takes out a figurine from her handbag, places it carefully on the desk, takes out two agarbattis, moves to Dash to get them lighted, returns to the desk, places the agarbattis before the figurine – all in a matter-of-fact way. She then takes out a cologne freshener and dabs her forehead and face with it.

DASH

As long as I have a latch-key to the front door.

INDU

And the kitchen door is unlocked.

DASH
Thank god the bar is not locked.

INDU
How is business?

DASH
Business? Oh, okay.

INDU
Will the budget affect your business?

DASH
Indirectly, yes. It will mean a different class of customers. But no real effect on... you know... things will still sell. As long as people need cars, they will be sold.

INDU
You'll still afford scotch?

DASH
Why not? When things cost more, people have to pay more. If some have to drop out of the race, there are always others joining in.

INDU
What is the plan for tomorrow?

DASH
You mean...

INDU
The reception do.

DASH
Oh, there was to be a small group for cocktails about the time you arrived. You are not supposed to be back yet, you know. Then we'd all drive up to a slightly bigger crowd invited at the club lawns. Then Vic and you would – you know – you'd be expected to...

INDU
How exciting. A surprise cocktails and dinner evening by the Dixits!

DASH
I don't think you meant that.

INDU
Where's that drink?

DASH
Oh, I'll get it. Sit down. I'll get it in a minute.

Dash exits. Lights fade out and in quickly. Indu sits Down-centre, facing forward, freezes. Vic, Pops, Mama enter briskly and position themselves beside and above Indu. Dash stands aside Down-left with a drink in his hand. A photo shoot. The lights turn dazzling bright a few times through the following passage. The group continues to talk and face forward, freezing briefly when the lights brighten.

MAMA

Thank goodness you didn't have the video people coming here.

VIC

Not here, certainly not. They'll be there at the club.

MAMA

They can do what they like on the lawn out there. It'll be the manager's headache.

POPS

Where's Minty?

VIC

She must be around somewhere. I haven't seen her since we got back.

MAMA

I haven't seen her in twenty years.

POPS

She should be here. Somebody look for her.

VIC

Minty! You should be here! Minty!!

INDU

How did she get the name?

VIC

Minty? I don't remember.

DASH

She fell into a cauldron of pudina chutney when she was a baby.

POPS

I don't remember either.

DASH

She's never brushed her teeth since then.

VIC

Isn't it something about the radio jingle she always kept chirping?

MAMA

Raj uncle gave her the name.

VIC

Raj uncle? You mean the radio jingle came later?

MAMA

He said she reminded him of the parakeet by that name in his mother's bungalow.

POPS
In Lahore. Raj's mother in Lahore.

MAMA
Where on earth could she be?

VIC
Minty!

POPS
Why don't you get Darshan for one or two?

DASH
No, no...

MAMA
Yes, Darshan. Come and stand here.

POPS
I don't suppose the two of us are needed any longer.

Mama and Pops push Dash towards Vic and Indu, and take his place Down-left. Dash, Indu, and Vic stand in front of the seat. The lights brighten momentarily. All others exit abruptly. Indu left standing. Presently she sits. Crossfade to Minty at Left, curled over the telephone.

MINTY
Look, nobody asked me... no, you couldn't assume that... nobody takes me for granted, okay... not even you... Well, get lost then. Don't let me see your pricky face again. Prick! Arsehole!

She hangs up, buries her head in her arms. Indu crosses over quietly, notices Minty, and moves above her. Minty becomes aware of her presence, sits up.

INDU
You must be Minty.

MINTY
Yeah. Hi... you are Indira...

INDU
Hi.

MINTY
I'm sorry. I was just... like... I was just resting.

INDU
It's all right. *(Pause)* You can call me Indu.

MINTY
I'm sorry, I missed all the receptions and parties. I missed something.

INDU
We missed you.

MINTY
I heard they were grand.

INDU

Did you? They must have been, then.

MINTY

Weren't they? I saw the pictures. They looked grand.

INDU

They took lots of pictures. *(Pause)* When did you...

MINTY

Oh, just now... a little while ago.

INDU

You got back today.

MINTY

Yeah... when did you move in?

INDU

It's been – let me see – just over a week now.

MINTY

You came in straight from the...

INDU

Exactly a week yesterday. Yes, we came here straight.

MINTY

I was planning to be back in time. It just...

INDU

That's all right.

MINTY

I'm sorry.

INDU

Back from where?

MINTY

Oh, I signed up for the E&E last month – you know the environment and ecology awareness course at St. Xavier's...

INDU

Environment and ecology?

MINTY

Yeah, it's a summer course for two months. It includes a ten-day trek in the Western Ghats. Like, I wasn't getting anywhere in the conversational French classes – and my evenings were all getting blocked – so I thought what the hell, this looks good, and I joined up.

INDU

And you dropped French.

MINTY

Yeah, I had to. This was so much more important, you know. Like, with the forests disappearing in the Western Ghats, the cost of butter on your dining table goes up. Did you know that?

INDU

Is that why you took the course?

MINTY

There's so much – so much, so much – to be done. This planet will just end up like burnt toast if we don't do something about our environment.

INDU

Somebody should put the mains off.

MINTY

Yeah, that's right. That's good. Somebody must put the mains off! *(Pause)* Have you... settled down? Are you comfortable?

INDU

Quite comfortable, thank you. Were you busy? Am I intruding?

MINTY

No, not at all. Actually, Mama told me this was going to be your study. I was just trying to make a call.

INDU

Go right ahead.

MINTY

No, I'll try later. There's something wrong with the line I think.

INDU

Anytime you want to...

MINTY

(Abruptly) When did you meet Vic?

INDU

What?

MINTY

When did you two first meet?

INDU

Oh, I'm sorry... I didn't know you meant... well, let's say about three months ago.

MINTY

I guessed that. About three months ago.

INDU

You did? How clever!

MINTY

It was about three months ago that he first started talking about psychiatry and mental illness and mental health, and all that.

INDU

It's pronounced psychiatry.

MINTY

Psychiatry. Vic even showed me the announcement of a course in personality development.

INDU

Where was that?

MINTY

It was called just that. The Institute of Personality Development. It had a course director, who had a degree from some famous place in California. Dr... what was it... shit, I can't remember... It was a Shah, I think. Dr something-or-other Shah.

INDU

What did you learn there?

MINTY

I didn't join. I couldn't. Like, I already had the computer course going, and the tuitions for chemistry... Mama was very strict about the chemistry tuition. (She grins) My weak subject.

INDU

You probably gained a lot by not joining the course.

MINTY

Two girls from my class joined up. They said it was fun. There was a lot of stuff about knowing yourself and all that.

INDU

And what did they find out about themselves?

MINTY

Like, for instance, there was an exercise called The Blind Men of Hindustan. You got different descriptions of yourself from different people. They were all – you know – bits and pieces, like snapshots. Some were way out and really funny. Like Ayesha, my girlfriend who was there, was told by a guy that she was like an empty room freshly painted. And they all had to see what meaning Ayesha could get out of it.

INDU

What did she make of it finally?

MINTY

She wouldn't tell. She said it was all about relationships, and love, and the need to reach out to people... you know, things like that. *(Pause. They exchange smiles.)* Was it love at first sight?

INDU
You mean...

MINTY
Yeah, Vic and you. How did you decide to splice up?

INDU
Well, I thought I could do with a proper accountant...

MINTY
And he could do with a psychiatrist! *(They laugh)* Honestly, woman to woman, did you fall for him? Thuppokk – on your nose?

INDU
What's that supposed to mean?

MINTY
You know, did you want him madly, wildly, passionately?

INDU
Minty, Minty, where on earth did you get these mad – wild, passionate – ideas? It doesn't happen that way. Except in Mills & Boon.

MINTY
Of course, it does! You're just saying that to change the topic. Love is grand. It's the greatest force in nature.

INDU
Have you been in love? Are you in love?

MINTY
No! I'm not in love with anybody – not right now.

INDU
Oh...

MINTY
Earlier maybe. Like there was this Coorgi guy, I knew last year.

INDU
Was that the first time?

MINTY
No. *(Long pause)*

INDU
Do you want to say something?

MINTY
No! Yes, I want to... I think you're lying about Vic and you.

INDU
Minty, listen to me. The greatest force in nature has nothing to do with love as you see it – as we all want to see it. Nature's masterpiece creation is gender. Just that. Male and female.

MINTY

It can't be. The human brain is... how do you say it... we are not cockroaches. We have love on our side.

INDU

The only real attraction between male and female is in the emission of scents – if and when emitted. Everything else is a vocabulary of pure rubbish, romanticised ceaselessly over thousands of years because of the limitless capacity for mischief in the human brain.

MINTY

You mean you don't love Vic that way? You don't want each other madly?

INDU

Of course we love each other. Not madly, thank goodness.

MINTY

I don't think I like this conversation.

INDU

Well, it wasn't actually a conversation, was it? More like a discussion.

MINTY

I don't think I liked the fucking discussion.

INDU

Minty, I think... is there something troubling you?

MINTY

I don't think I'm going to like you.

INDU

Oh, did I say something wrong?

MINTY

You're so... what is it?

INDU

It's not unusual for young girls at this age to have a head full of romantic fantasies.

MINTY

Why must you talk with a mouth full of shit?

INDU

You think I'm talking nonsense?

MINTY

Shit. I think you're talking shit. You've put your alimentary drive in reverse.

INDU

And I think you are saying that to test me.

MINTY

What? Test you for what?

INDU

Like, am I trustworthy? Whose side am I on? (Pause) Will I tell on you?

MINTY

You wouldn't dare...

INDU

I don't have to. The true story of the week's extension in camp to collect data on tribal migration... that's what it was, we'll be told – data collection on tribal migration... the true story will out some time or the other.

MINTY

Nothing happened, you hear? Nothing happened between Chander and me. Whatever you might have heard...

INDU

Chander? That's a new one. As I have it, it was the young man – from the Trivandrum Institute – the authority on primates in tropical rain forests.

MINTY

Ohhh! *(She bursts into tears, burying her head in her arms at the table)*

INDU

Minty, Minty, get a hold on yourself. It didn't concern me. I wasn't going to talk about it to anybody. You must trust me. You can talk to me anytime, about anything you ever want to.

Blackout

SCENE 4

Baba at seat Down-centre, alone. Ammaji enters, crosses to him.

BABA

What did he say?

AMMAJI

He asked about your diabetes. Am I still passing you jalebis under the table, he asked.

BABA

He's been our family doctor for thirty years after all. What did he say about Lakshmi?

AMMAJI

He told me many things.

BABA

He told you?

AMMAJI

He told me how foolish it was to change to fluoride toothpaste, he told me that President Zia's plane crash was engineered by a Buddhist monk in exile, I was told that from now on, he would get his hair cut once in two months because the cost of a haircut had increased by five rupees. But he didn't say much about our bahu.

BABA

Then it couldn't have been serious.

AMMAJI

He says it is common for newly married girls to be a little nervous and anxious.

BABA

She doesn't appear anxious.

AMMAJI

Different people express their anxiety in different ways, he says. Some become quiet. Some talk more, he says.

BABA

Since she has studied much more, and has been working and all, she may be a bit...

AMMAJI

'She may be trying to please you.' That's what he said.

BABA

So, what are you supposed to do?

AMMAJI

Nothing. Just hot milk with drinking chocolate at night, or badam if we can afford it.

BABA

Did you tell him about the lights being on late at night – twelve o'clock, one o'clock?

AMMAJI

'All part of the same thing. Nothing to do but relax.' She can safely take half a Calmpose after dinner if she is restless. If necessary, one full tablet. *(Pause)*

BABA

What do you think?

AMMAJI

I think there is something more, but he is not telling us.

BABA

Well, she has been with us three months... If there's anything like that, you will know, I suppose.

AMMAJI

'Anything like that' is probably what she needs. A bahu is a bahu only after the first baby has arrived. Instead of all this reading and writing and talking-talking – all the time. No, I think we should consult somebody else. We will have to do it sooner or later it seems.

Crossfade to Right. Minoo and Lakshmi are having a chat.

MINOO

Just like that? You pick up a pen, and it just comes?

LAKSHMI

That can happen only with magic pens. Without those, there must be something to feed the pen.

MINOO

Experiences.

LAKSHMI

Not just experiences. Yes, that, to start with, but something else that mixes with it and catches fire, and lets off sparks, so that you are forced to look at it.

MINOO

I know, I know, I read about it somewhere. It's called something – the fourth eye or something, a poet's special way of looking at things. Like being able to see dragonflies dancing on top of Qutub Minar from the ground below.

LAKSHMI

That's a clever one!

MINOO

Or like Xray vision – seeing through a heart of stone.

LAKSHMI

Or like soda bottle myopia – not seeing beyond the pimple on one's nose. *(They laugh)*

MINOO

You're... you're so sweet, bhabhi. I don't know what to call you – didi or bhabhi or what.

LAKSHMI

I'll tell you what you can call me, shall I?

MINOO

Uh... huh.

LAKSHMI

Because we are going to be very special friends, it can be a secret just between the two of us. You can call me Nina.

MINOO

I couldn't call you that!

LAKSHMI

Better still, you can call me Ninoo. It will rhyme with Minoo. *(Minoo is overwhelmed. She caresses Lakshmi's cheeks gently, cautiously, and takes her hands in her own.)*

MINOO

You're so... Oh, I'm so happy!

LAKSHMI

And I am happy too – with you. *(Pause)*

MINOO

Can I ask you for something? *(Lakshmi smiles and nods)* Will you... will you help me with my lessons?

LAKSHMI

Of course, Minoo.

MINOO

I'm such a dud in the arts subjects, especially literature.

LAKSHMI

How can anybody have eyes like yours and be called a dud?

MINOO

I don't know...

LAKSHMI

You've done all right so far I can see.

MINOO

I've pestered Buddhoo for help. *(She stops short and giggles.)* You know Gautam, Hemant's friend. I've taken his help now and then.

LAKSHMI

How nice of him.

MINOO

He is a lecturer in MV Arts & Science. He is very helpful, but... you know, I think it's really a question of developing an interest in the subject.

LAKSHMI

Is Buddhoo a childhood nickname?

MINOO

No, believe it or not, I was responsible for that. I gave him the name.

LAKSHMI

You, Minoo?

MINOO

We were having dinner. I was quite small then – eight or nine, I am told. The family was at dinner, and the conversation must have turned to Hemant's dear friend, and I referred to him as Gautama the Buddhoo. Everybody laughed – except Ammaji – and a nickname was born.

LAKSHMI

And it stuck.

MINOO

It stuck. Even Ammaji calls him Buddhoo now.

LAKSHMI

Ammaji... is she...

MINOO

Yes?

LAKSHMI

Nothing... It's all right.

MINOO

Then, they asked me to give Hemant a nickname. But I just couldn't get one.

LAKSHMI

So, Hemant has remained Hemant.

MINOO

I just couldn't produce a sticker for him. Hemant just didn't... you know... I didn't even try after some time.

LAKSHMI

Minoo, is Ammaji very health conscious in the house?

MINOO

I don't know about health, specially, but she is very particular about many things around the house. Everything in order, everything to plan. She is very happy when guests praise her housekeeping. I suppose she is particular about hygiene and diet too... Things like that... You know. *(Pause)* Why do you ask?

LAKSHMI

For some time now she has been insisting that I drink a glass of milk every night.

MINOO

Milk is good, isn't it?

LAKSHMI

I don't have the habit. I gave up drinking milk years ago. And she gives me a vitamin tablet with it. *(Minoo giggles)* What's the matter? What's so funny?

MINOO

Maybe there is some good news in the family!

LAKSHMI

Puglee! There is no such thing. And if something like that happens, I will tell you myself. Okay?

MINOO

Then she is just fussing over her daughter-in-law.

LAKSHMI

It doesn't quite feel like that. It's more like some kind of...

MINOO

I know, that is Ammaji's nature. She talks in a business-like way... abrupt, sometimes blunt, rough...

LAKSHMI

No explanations. She doesn't even let me keep the tablets in my room.

MINOO

Has it made any difference?

LAKSHMI

I didn't like it in the beginning. I couldn't read or write at night. I couldn't concentrate, I would just doze off.

MINOO

Well, milk and badam can be very heavy.

LAKSHMI

Especially if you are not used to it. But later I found that my mornings were much nicer. I felt brighter, more alert. I could chirp with the birds through the kitchen window while getting breakfast ready.

MINOO

You are writing more these days.

LAKSHMI

I am. I see new things. I feel new things.

MINOO

Can I... May I read some of it?

LAKSHMI

Certainly. Here, I just finished this yesterday.

Ammaji has entered. A short, awkward pause. Minoo greets her pleasantly. Lakshmi rises.

AMMAJI

Lakshmi, I'd like to see you for a minute, if you don't mind.

LAKSHMI

Certainly...

AMMAJI

Wait for me. I'll be with you soon. *(Lakshmi exits)* Minoo, isn't it time you started paying more attention to your studies?

MINOO

But I was just going to...

AMMAJI
Instead of wasting your time here and there?

MINOO
Lakshmi bhabhi said she would help me. She is good in...

AMMAJI
I'm talking about studies – not this kind of idle chatter. Take care.

Ammaji exits. Minoo remains silent. She looks at the sheaf in her hands, holds it close to her, and slowly wipes a tear from her eye.

SCENE 5

Lakshmi in seat Down-centre. Buddhoo is with her. She is agitated.

LAKSHMI
Who is Dr PK Sharma? Why must I see him? They are not telling me anything.

BUDDHOO
Please Lakshmi, keep calm.

LAKSHMI
Keep calm? You too, Buddhoo? You want me to keep calm?

BUDDHOO
Lakshmi, I was only trying to...

LAKSHMI
They are obsessed with that. Is it not enough, they are drugging me every night like baddies in a C-grade film? Now, they want me to be examined by a specialist. For what? Specialist in what?

BUDDHOO
They told you about the sleeping pills?

LAKSHMI
You'd think they had the guts to tell me? Vitamins! Vitamin tablets for undernourished, overworked, underdeveloped Lakshmi.

BUDDHOO
You knew? And you continued?

LAKSHMI
What do you take me for? When Minoo told me about it – yes, sweet Minoo, poor Minoo – when she blurted it out one evening, I was dazed. But not so stupid to go on with the act.

BUDDHOO
What about Minoo? Was she...

LAKSHMI

What could I do? I didn't want Minoo harmed in any way. She would be hounded and clawed the rest of her life. *(Pause)* I played my own B-grade script against them. I asked Hemant to have the little pink pill one night. *(She laughs)* You should have seen his face. I was feeling a bit uneasy, I said, and I might throw up the milk and vitamins. Why waste it? Go on, it will enhance your masculine powers, your brute charm. Take it, you brute! He was terrified. Like summer tempest came his confession, the explanation, the apologies. I told him to come out with me to meet Ammaji. *(Pause. Suddenly bitter again.)* More apologies, more explanation!

BUDDHOO

Hemant didn't... didn't he...

LAKSHMI

Hemant didn't. Period.

BUDDHOO

And Ammaji? How did you... how did she...

LAKSHMI

How did she come to know that I came to know? I confronted her. The next morning I tiptoed down to the kitchen before Hemant could get up, greeted her as politely and demurely as ever, and while she was going on about the cheek of the newspaper boy leaving the gate open, day after day after day, and how she was going to set a trap for him one day, I took out glass tumblers from the cabinet and made a pyramid with them at her place at the dining table. You know... ten glasses and a pyramid like that, 4321. On the single glass on top, I put a pinch of haldi, a dash of kumkum, a few grains of rice, and cradled on them was the little pinky. Enter Ammaji – pause – then the bang of a teacup on the table, A-grade dialogue. Ammaji – what is this? Lakshmi – morning puja. Ammaji – what is this budtameezi? Have you gone mad? Lakshmi – I almost did. But I was saved by my patidev. Saved in the nick of time. Ammaji – to cut a long story short – exit huffing and puffing.

BUDDHOO

You know, they think you are...

LAKSHMI

Say it! Say it, dammit! They think I'm nuts, don't they? How much? This much? That much? What is Dr Sharma going to find out about me? That I have some kind of hormonal excess that sends signals to my tongue? That my grand aunt from Jabalpur used to lock me up in the toilet when I was six? Or is he going to find a worm crawling about somewhere in the cauliflower up here? What label are they going to put on me? What do you think, huh?

BUDDHOO

Lakshmi, I don't think it's anything serious – nothing that serious. I don't think there is any need to...

LAKSHMI

Not that serious! How serious? Serious enough to be brought here by force. They didn't use a rope, thank goodness, they haven't done that yet. But without a word, without warning?

BUDDHOO

You didn't know about today's appointment?

LAKSHMI

Today's arraignment! Buddhoo, you've been put here on duty as the trustworthy Jack-of-all in the Prabhu family. You'd better keep a tight watch on me. Any moment now I'm going to start smashing windows. *(She laughs)* It's what they expect me to do, isn't it? So they'll be proved right! *(Pause. She quietens.)*

BUDDHOO

I'm sorry. I don't know how to... I'm so sorry this is happening to you.

LAKSHMI

Buddhoo, Buddhoo – what can I tell you about all that's really happened in the short space of a fortnight. How do I tell you?

BUDDHOO

I don't know what to say – what to do.

LAKSHMI

What can you do? You're one of them.

Enter Ammaji and Hemant from Right, followed by Baba. They position themselves around and above Lakshmi's seat. They speak from their positions. Buddhoo watches from aside Down-left.

AMMAJI

Dr Sharma heard everything.

HEMANT

He saw too.

AMMAJI

Through the one-way screen.

HEMANT

It was quite clear.

BABA

It was clear.

AMMAJI

Agitated speech.

HEMANT
Florid, fluent, but fantasised speech.

AMMAJI
Disproportionate verbosity.

HEMANT
The signs were quite clear.

BABA
The signs were clear.

HEMANT
Flights of fancy.

AMMAJI
Retreat into flights of fancy.

HEMANT
Attention-seeking devices.

AMMAJI
Retreat to attention-seeking devices.

HEMANT
Histrionic appeal.

AMMAJI
Retreat, retreat, retreat.

HEMANT
They were all there.

BABA
Quite clear.

AMMAJI
And the laughter.

HEMANT
And the laughter.

AMMAJI
Dissociated from the speech.

HEMANT
Dissociated from the content of speech.

AMMAJI
Dissociated from the context of speech.

HEMANT
Dissociated.

BABA
Quite.

AMMAJI
Take her in.

LAKSHMI
No!!!

AMMAJI
Did you hear that?

ALL THREE
Did you see that?

AMMAJI
Take her in!
Blackout

A TRIP

After a moment, in the dark, an extended hiss. It is followed by other hisses, first, one after the other, then, tumbling over one another, unrelenting. A tight spot picks up Lakshmi lying still, sedated, while the rest of the cast makes choreographed patterns around her. They are barely visible, in outline, rather than in full body. Their hisses have changed imperceptibly in intensity, held low. A slow fade out. The hissing stops abruptly.

Spot on Minoo Down-centre. She is holding Lakshmi's poems as last seen. She reads.

MINOO
I saw two infants on the street
One cried
Fondled in harness
Led home by German Shepherds on leash
The other entertained
I saw myself in an old cafe
The poison
In my veins, the stale breath
Purged by the stroke of a whisper
A love, a faith unstained.
I saw a wandering minstrel...
She stops, stares vacantly ahead.
Fade out

SCENE 6

The Dixit home Left. Pops is seated, making notes while Indu is serving him tea, helping herself, and tidying up.

POPS

You will also have to tell me what Regical tablets are. It comes up again and again in this book, and it says the chemical compound is metabisulphite – $K_2S_2O_4$.

INDU

Regical is probably a brand name, Pops. Metabisulphite, as far as I can make out, is a preservative... you know the sort of thing you add to juices and jams. Mama will be able to tell you.

POPS

Shhh! Not a word to Mama. Not yet. This is not like her Saturday afternoon group – half the cakes smelly, the other half like sand castles. Did you see the garlic bread they turned out last week? Rid the whole neighbourhood of mosquitos.

INDU

Pops, you're mean!

POPS

Drove me out of the house for the rest of the day!

INDU

You can probably get the stuff at the supermarket. Or the local Food Craft Institute. If you draw a blank, I'll put one of our research assistants on the job.

POPS

Aha! That's what we need – research staff.

INDU

Anyway, what made you turn to wine making?

POPS

Oh, this and that.

INDU

When did you start?

POPS

Three months ago.

INDU

Just three months? That's good progress! The last sample you gave me to taste was not bad at all.

POPS

When I asked those people at Ericsons for a dealership, you know what they told me? Sorry, no go, because my selling experience in laminations and binders, they said, was unsuitable for handling their range of liquors. At least that's what they said officially. Crooks! Don't I know their game? They would like me to block three lakhs in a deposit with them.

INDU

I suppose it would be a prestigious dealership if you got it.

POPS

Nah! It's not worth it. It might help a bit in coping with the liquor bills in this house, but I was not going to be bullied into their terms. But that's how I got interested in finding out more about alcohol.

INDU

You would have the wine and drink it too.

POPS

Oh, more than that, much more than that, I can tell you. In a couple of years, I'll be selling the stuff and making good profits too.

INDU

That sounds more serious than kite flying.

POPS

Of course, I'm serious. Ericsons will come to me then, begging for an agency!

INDU

There's nothing like being on your own, is there?

POPS

There's nothing like being your own boss. You are absolutely right. That's what I have always said to Vicky. That's what I have been telling you too. It is all right to keep the post at the Institute for some time. But you must aim at setting up your own clinic. The sooner the better.

INDU

Actually I am very much on my own. I get my salary through the Institute, but the money for that and everything else in my unit comes from outside grants. I can take it all wherever I want to, whenever I want to.

POPS

Good. That's very good. I like your independence. I wish you could drive some sense into that husband of yours.

INDU

He seems content enough.

POPS

What kind of work is that? Office timings! Paperwork! My god, you should see the paperwork. Have you been to his office? Piles and piles of papers – wall to wall papering. And what is it all about? Somebody else's bloody paperwork! Somebody else's profits! Somebody else's taxes!

INDU

Still, he's a partner now. Not an employee.

POPS

Actually, that's one thing I don't like about your work too.

INDU

Oh?

POPS

What is the stuff you deal in? Other people's problems. That's the raw material for your work. Whatever you achieve in life depends on that. You survive and grow only on somebody else's problems.

INDU

As long as there are problems in the world, there will be a need for help to solve the problems and a need for professionals to help solve them.

POPS

(Laughs) Indu, I've been a salesman all my life. The gut of my job has always been to convince people that they have a problem – for which I have the solution.

INDU

So what are you proving?

POPS

Tomorrow, I'm going to convince people that their problem is, they haven't had enough wine – and I have the solution to the problem.

INDU

So what are you proving?

POPS

At least I'll be peddling my wares with the full knowledge that it's the game of peddling. As always. As in all things I've peddled. The buyer and the seller are equals. If they engage in the game of wits, it is with full knowledge of the consequences of losing.

INDU

I see.

POPS

Don't take it to heart, Indu. It is just a personal view. I have come a long way from the days I was travelling twenty-five days a month to earn my silver stars in the company's record books.

INDU

That was over thirty years ago, wasn't it?

POPS

I don't think psychiatrists were invented in those days. Maybe that's why we didn't have problems of that kind. *(Laughs)* At least, not at the rate you see today.

INDU

Were you always in Calcutta?

POPS

Most of the time. It was always the base. I had short postings in the mofussil depots once in a while. Otherwise, good old Cal. *(A pause)* Why did you ask?

INDU

There was a Mr Chatterjee in your company.

POPS

The city is full of Chatterjees.

INDU

This was SN Chatterjee. Sudipto was his name, I think.

POPS

Head of the Commercial Unit! How do you know him? *(Pause)* Do you know him?

INDU

I can't say I know him. Not in any substantial way. It's more like he knows me.

POPS

He was senior to me. Quite close to the top brass. Too close. I'm glad he is nobody close to you.

INDU

Depends on what you mean by close.

POPS

A bloody pain he was for the Sales Division. Regular stick in the mud. God knows how many battles we've fought over how many territories.

INDU

So I understand.

POPS

(Subdued) He ruined my career. He turned so many at the top against me.

INDU

There were others?

POPS

They began ganging up, always after me, always looking for new ways to harass me. And Sudipto Chatterjee was the man behind the whole show. He was the one man responsible for my leaving the company.

INDU

You... left the company? Is that how it was?

POPS

(Firmly) I quit. I couldn't stand it any longer. *(Short pause)* It was a nightmare.

INDU

Does Vic know?

POPS

Know what?

INDU

All that happened... how you happened to leave the Company.

POPS

Of course, he knows I quit the company. The whole family knows. The whole world knows. I quit to show them I have my own two feet. They couldn't push me around. The Sales Division organised a company farewell. You've seen the large rosewood casket in the living room? That was given to me at the farewell. The sales people knew what it was going to be like without me. *(Pause)* Of course Vic knows. Why did you ask?

INDU

I just heard him coming in. I thought if you'd rather not... Should I go out and...

POPS

No, it's all right. Let him come in here... He doesn't know everything. He need not know. *(Indu smiles and moves to clear the tea things.)*

INDU

(Calling out) Vicky! Pick up your mail from the dining table. There's a registered letter for you – a sealed cover.

POPS

(To himself) Bloody pariahs. Gutless stooges – tails between their legs in front of the Company directors. Can't even sell paper clips in the city market without getting buggered on the way – they want to run the company! They'll turn it into a bhoot bangla, the jokers. *(He stops abruptly as Vic enters)*

VIC

Sorry, I got held up.

INDU

Again.

VIC

It's the wretched season.

INDU

Four such seasons in the year...

VIC
No, I was saying...

INDU
Each of three months duration.

VIC
Oh, that again.

POPS
Hah!

INDU
Let me try a fresh start. Hello, Vic. How was the day on the old beat today?

VIC
I know, you're not complaining. It was only an observation!

POPS
Why are you so worked up today?

INDU
He said it!

POPS
You haven't even asked what's for dinner.

VIC
It did occur to me. The kitchen was closed. The table was bare. I didn't see Mama around. Where is Mama?

POPS
Where do you think? In the counting house, counting all her money.

INDU
Pops has been telling me about his new business idea.

VIC
Are we eating out?

INDU
We could. It depends on you. We're okay here.

VIC
What business? The wine making? You can't take that seriously.
(Indu has brought tea for Vic.)

POPS
You can join me, Vicky boy.

VIC
No, thank you. I am happy where I am.

POPS

You can take charge of finance and accounts. You can bring the same penetrating skills to a family business that you now give to your clients.

INDU

(Without looking at Vic) Penetration? Vic does that?

POPS

He is in great demand. That is why I keep telling him that this junior partnership is all bullshit.

VIC

Pops, chartered accountancy is not like...

POPS

They've taken you for a ride. You should be independent. Why can't you get into wine-making?

INDU

You will at least not be buried under somebody else's paperwork.

POPS

That is what I was saying, wasn't I?

INDU

And you won't have to be apologetic about getting home late – that is, if you have come in late.

POPS

You can pull out even now. It is hardly a year, there are no legal obligations.

VIC

Look Pops, Mama gave me the money. Not you. She said I could use it as I wished.

POPS

What does Mama know about business?

VIC

She knows enough not to trust her money in your hare-brained ventures any more.

POPS

Bugger-all she knows about business. Bugger-all she knows about money. She keeps it in a bank – a nationalised bank! Have you heard of anything more insane?

VIC

Pops, I don't think you should be...

POPS

And what about you, you little pisser? Can you piss straight now? Have you found out how business works in that pissing partnership of yours in one whole year of pissing?

INDU

(Laughing) Pops! That's enough! That was funny Pops, but lay off now.

POPS

I'm sorry. You must have been embarrassed. I shouldn't have...

INDU

Me? Not at all. It's all right. You wanted to make a point, and you made it. What do you say, Vic? *(He is silent)*

POPS

What do you think, Vic? You think your old Pops can't run a family business with family money? What do the books say?

VIC

(Slowly) Will you just leave me alone?

POPS

No, really, you've got to tell me. What do you think?

VIC

I think I should have stayed longer at the office. I need not have come back at all. I think I should have... *(He is quiet)*

POPS

Mama's little pisser!

(Pops strides out. Indu is watching Vic from above him.)

INDU

Vic... Vic, dear, it is all right. I understand. You know I understand. *(Pause)* Shall I get some dinner ready?

Vic rises suddenly and rushes out. Indu remains still. Presently, the telephone rings. She crosses to it as the lights close in on the desk.

INDU

Dr Mahesh-Dixit... yes, put him on please... Yes, Dr Sharma, what can I do for you?

Fade out

SCENE 7

Hemant and Lakshmi in their room, Right. She is emaciated, distraught, agitated.

LAKSHMI

I don't care what the neighbours say! Why should I? There is nothing to hide. There is nothing they don't already know.

HEMANT

Still, it doesn't mean we can ignore them.

LAKSHMI

Maybe you have something to hide. You have to prop up the family portrait, don't you? Khandan and izzat and all that – the heavy responsibility on your frail shoulders!

HEMANT

I was just trying to...

LAKSHMI

Nobody need know the truth. Nobody need get even a glimpse of the moving fingers weaving a carpet for the living room wall. Pull out the oil portrait from the attic. Hang it on the front gate. Let the neighbourhood see what a god-fearing, peace-loving, tax-paying, good-neighbourly, palak-paneer family the Prabhu household is.

HEMANT

Calm down!

LAKSHMI

(Climbing on to a chair or stool) The family that blunts the fiercest storm, washes all its undergarments once a week in the privacy of the puja room, teaches its boys that menfolk should be seen and never heard!

HEMANT

You are after me, aren't you? You are after me, because you think I'm behind all that has happened.

LAKSHMI

The family that has steadfastly overcome the menace of halitosis by singing bhajans.

HEMANT

It was Ammaji, I tell you. I had nothing to do with it. You've got to believe me.

LAKSHMI

Did you hear that, out there? He had nothing to do with Mummyji's breaking-in schedule for the bahu recruit.

HEMANT

(Rushing to restrain her) Stop it! You're going too far. Stop it!

LAKSHMI

Ever-patient, ever-loving, Hemant never interferes. Ever understanding, he tugs gently only if she goes too far.

Lakshmi and Hemant speak together, over one another.

HEMANT

If you would only... If you would slow down a bit. Everything would be all right if you... if you didn't feel the need to talk so much.

LAKSHMI

Giving gentle advice – gentle advice – from the side lines – from patient observation for the tired and the weary and the heavy of heart.

LAKSHMI

(Suddenly quieter) Take my right hand, said the rishi to the blushing trickle, for you must river upstream this day. Shame the arrogant mountains, darting up the slopes of peaks yet unnamed. Whittle the chinar of its summer bark under the canopy of echoing fragrances, and the chanting of unschooled tidal waves shall ascend from the village wishing well, lately axiomatic, vermillioned, and anointed with bird calls in festive disguise. The dewdrops waft through the undergrowth and keep at bay the envious. *(Hemant rushes out of the room, frightened. Lakshmi continues.)* The peaks are foaming at the mouth, said the stream, and I fright easily. I hold a prism to the conch shell when the bluebells at my feet drop their petals and turn to horny toads. And the glow-worm whispers to the firefly that all is as should be on the eastern tower, for it has rained vowel and syllable through the weeks to come. Look left, look right, look again, there goes the weasel popping corn between his knuckles, marching to the beat of a leaky tap.

She stops, goes back to the window, and shouts

ELEVEN O'CLOCK AND ALL QUIET ON THE EASTERN TOWER AS SON MEETS MOTHER AT HIGH-LEVEL CONFERENCE.

Enter Ammaji and Baba. Lakshmi stops. Baba goes to the window, pushes Lakshmi aside, and shuts it. Lakshmi tries to reopen it, but Baba holds her tight from behind. Ammaji steps up to her and slaps her across the face three times.

AMMAJI

Sharmaji was right. When the house is on fire you can't use a bathroom mug to throw water. Pills and powders don't work when the blaze calls for drastic treatment.

Crossfade to Indu at the telephone as earlier. Held briefly. Crossfade to Right. Hemant is standing between Lakshmi and Ammaji. Lakshmi is distant, cool, but defiant.

AMMAJI

Did you hear that? The words she used? She called me a pickled shadow of... what? What was that she said?

LAKSHMI

Pickled. Preserved in brine. Brine, as in salt water. The oldest, simplest form of pickling. Allusion, stuck in the past. Associated image, stuck up. Contemporary, hung up. Stale, stale, stale. Bung, rung, dung. Bingo.

AMMAJI

She is possessed. Hemant, she is possessed. My god, this household is bedevilled. There is evil in there.

LAKSHMI

Leather-bound chapter six, gilt-edged verse sixteen. The saviour appears in the entrails of unborn lamb ground on chandan paste and rolled to rudraksh pellets to lace the stainless steel lemon soufflé.

HEMANT

Lakshmi, can't you see you are making matters worse for...

LAKSHMI

Transmission restored from satellite station by booster ground signal. Right in roger left out.

AMMAJI

Look at her. It has taken hold of her. She is not herself. I'll have to beat it out of her. Hold her, Hemant. I'll do it.

HEMANT

Ammaji...

LAKSHMI

(Loud) Eyes down for full house. Lucky for some, two hockey sticks, four and twenty. Friday. *(A short pause. Ammaji steps forward to beat her, stops.)*

LAKSHMI

(Suddenly, to them directly) Hemant! Can't you see what she wants? Do you have to be told everything three times like an imbecile child? Hold me! Hold me so that her aim is perfect – tight in your medicinal bind, true to the arrow's flight. Changed your mind mummy by law? Or would you rather fish out nanima's branding iron? For effects more lasting? *(Short pause)* Dinner will be served at twenty hundred hours. Dress optional.

Lakshmi exits briskly. Crossfade to Indu at the telephone as earlier. Held briefly. Crossfade to Right, Lakshmi in the kitchen. Presently Ammaji enters with a Primus stove. She keeps it next to Lakshmi, who notices but does not react.

AMMAJI

(Slowly, carefully) The gas got over. They said it will take a week. We have to manage with this.

LAKSHMI

We have to manage.

AMMAJI

Be careful how you light it. These things are unpredictable... treacherous if you are not careful with it.

Ammaji exits. Lakshmi turns to the stove. She opens the filler cap. After a moment's thought she begins to pour the kerosene all around the kitchen. She speaks loudly as she goes about it.

LAKSHMI

On your marks, get set, what a way to go. Ammaji, are you ready? Have you lit the arati? Have you picked up the prayer beads? I'm starting. No going back now. (She has picked up a matchbox and has moved to a corner) They will all say, after you have gone, what a noble woman! She died so that her daughter-in-law may live. She was consumed so that Lakshmi of the fiery appetite may be set free. Good bye now. If I hurry, I might still catch the twelve o'clock matinee. (*Ammaji and Baba rush in. They stop to see Lakshmi laughing hysterically at their faces.)*

AMMAJI

Hemant! Hemant!!

Fade out

SCENE 8

Indu in her room, Left. She is seated, relaxed. There are fresh agarbattis at the figurine. Dash appears with wine glasses. They salute silently and sip their drinks. Dash fetches a hassock or cushion and sits at Indu's feet.

DASH

I had never thought about it that way.

INDU

It is the same with most acts of plumage. There is the same balance of forces manifest in them. One part animal, archetypal, an assertion of sexuality that says, 'look out, here I come'. The other part tactical, a cognitive junction switch that evaluates likely outcomes.

DASH

Is there a state of balance that can be called correct? You know, okay, not okay.

INDU

Not in individual, specific acts. But in the aggregate, over the vast repertoire of one's typical behaviours, yes. We can think of a state that is good, healthy, or not so good.

DASH

So, the wildly different kinds of ties that Vic and I wear might have our horoscopes printed on them.

INDU

Or the way you wear them. Vic, for instance, must have a tie pin.

DASH

And I use it as a nada to keep my pants up.

INDU

Do you need to look into the mirror when you are dressing? When you are putting on your pants?

DASH

I don't know. If it's there, I suppose.

INDU

Like, Vic simply must move to the mirror when he is tucking in his shirt.

DASH

It might not be so bad to look at yourself when you are doing that.

INDU

What is the functional value of a frontal glimpse for the simple mechanical act of zipping up? *(Pause)*

DASH

Why do you have a shrine at your table?

INDU

Is it a shrine?

DASH

Well, there is a little figurine there. And you are regular in keeping agarbattis before it.

INDU

Some people rub their feet together before getting into bed.

DASH

I suppose it helps shake the dust off.

INDU

Most rituals do that. *(Short pause)*

DASH

Are you religious?

INDU

Are you?

DASH

I suppose I could be.

INDU

Is it a steady state, like saying you talk a lot, or you don't eat beef? Or is it circumstantial? Here and now? Like, when you are hungry or you feel like a little retreat.

DASH

I don't know. Maybe a little bit of both.

INDU

That's a contradiction in itself. *(Pause)*

DASH

(Rising for refills) What about somebody like Minty? She oscillates. Pious and god-fearing now, rebellious and amoral the next day.

INDU

That's different.

DASH

She is different in many ways, I can tell you that.

INDU

That is different on two counts. One, her personality. Oscillation is her personality. Secondly, she is going through a phase – that tends to aggravate the oscillation.

DASH

I know. She is in love.

INDU

She thinks she is in love.

Dash has returned with refills. From now on, Indu nurses her drink, sipping it delicately, rarely. Dash takes his drink to the desk above Indu. Slowly, gently, he massages her shoulders and neck.

DASH

It's a delightful phase, I'm sure. Euphoric, perhaps, and to be viewed sympathetically.

INDU

It is a violent phase.

(Pause. Through the following passage Indu speaks slowly, without gestures, but not unpleasantly.)

We are not brought up to think of it that way. Words corrupt meaning. Costumed, bedecked by words ceaselessly, meaning itself remains untouched. We have transient truths now and then – through the words we employ. But meaning? *(Pause)* Violence. Aggression. Intimidation. Such awesome beauty in these meanings, if it weren't for the words.

Dash moves to get himself a refill. Slowly, unobtrusively, Indu has slipped off a shoe and stretched a leg gently.

It is nature's design. Violence is the essence of creation itself. (Pause) There was a pair of house lizards on the wall in the kitchen. I hadn't ever heard a cricketing sound so loud from a lizard. When I switched on the light I saw them. They were not in the least disturbed. They were in another chemical state. A foot apart, their bodies curved, they formed an incomplete circle. They might have been figures from a coat-of-arms, equally spaced, one head behind the other's tail in the broken circle. One tail flicked every now and then, without a recognizable beat. Was it a semaphore? An aperiodic countdown? Was that why they were positioned head to tail, to read the instruments? The cricketing ceased suddenly. The tail stopped flicking. In a flash he was upon her, pinning her down masterfully, and keeping her in position with her neck in his jaws.

Pause. Dash has finished his drink. He sits at her feet again, gently removes the other shoe, and begins to stretch and rub her toes and ankles.

INDU

It was a long time ago. I recorded it in my diary. As free of corrupting words as I possibly could.

DASH

You see poetic justice in violence?

INDU

I see justice. There is no injustice in nature. And no room for poetic conjectures.

DASH

There is much poetry in your science.

INDU

Unfortunately, there is not much science in poetry.

Dash kisses her shins one after the other and looks at her. Indu smiles and tucks her legs in gracefully.

DASH

What is the hold you have over me?

Indu smiles faintly. She holds out her glass. Dash rises, takes the glass, and keeps it down. Indu holds out an arm. Dash takes it and raises her. He looks at her briefly, lifts her in his arms, and carries her out.

Fade out

A TRIP

In the dark, three claps. They are followed by other sets of three claps, first one after the other, then tumbling over each other in a continuous clapping. A tight spot picks up Indu Up-centre, standing still, like the figurine on her desk. The rest of the cast is seated cross-legged in an arc facing upstage. They are visible in outline rather than as the characters in the play. The clapping stops.

Indu moves slowly in a choreographed pattern freezing briefly here and there. There are sets of three claps each time she stops. Presently the seated characters are knocked over one by one like wooden figures as she moves, each still cross-legged. After the last figure is knocked over, Indu returns to her original position and freezes.

Blackout

SCENE 9

Indu's desk Left. A case-taking session. Hemant is seated opposite, bent. Indu is on the phone. She keeps it down, turns to Hemant, and makes notes. Hemant only nods or shakes his head.

Crossfade to Down-centre. Ammaji, Baba, Minoo, and Buddhoo are standing in a line facing upstage. Hemant appears and joins them. They move apart to reveal Lakshmi on a seat. She is gagged, her arms are bound. She is struggling. The others move and position themselves above and beside the seat and freeze. Lakshmi continues to struggle, trying to speak to any of them. The lights turn dazzling bright momentarily.

Indu appears with a hypodermic in her hand. She crosses briskly to Lakshmi, gives her an intravenous shot, and wheels the seat away to Right. Lakshmi is limp. Indu removes the gag and binds, and crosses back to Left. As she passes the group, Ammaji follow her in, accompanied by Hemant. Indu takes her seat and resumes the case-taking. Ammaji sits. Pause. She rises and exits with Hemant. Baba enters, sits, rises, and exits. It is Minoo's turn. Indu seems interested in the sheaf and the diary she is carrying. Reluctantly Minoo hands them over and exits. Buddhoo enters. He prefers to stand.

INDU

Are you quite sure?

BUDDHOO

I think so. As far as I can remember.

INDU

All the available information goes in a different direction.

BUDDHOO

But this is not a criminal case. We are not gathering evidence for a conviction.

INDU

It is not, thank goodness. We are not a police station. We do not run errands for the vested interests of big businesses or big politics.

BUDDHOO

Still, the very starting point of a search must make a difference. You begin in the direction you are facing.

INDU

Are you suggesting our diagnostics are in error? Is that your fear?

BUDDHOO

No, I didn't mean to question the competence in diagnostic investigations. I'm sorry, I didn't mean to imply that.

INDU

Would you like to explain?

BUDDHOO

It is something more. How shall I put it? It is like this. The very act of referring a person to a psychiatrist... she becomes a patient then. Is it not something like a First Information Report in a police station?

INDU

In an elementary way, perhaps.

BUDDHOO

What happens then? After the first reference?

INDU

You are not suggesting that the psychiatrist is influenced by the referral, are you?

BUDDHOO

Do you have some parallels to the principles of natural justice? Do we say, for instance, this patient is not sick until proved so?

INDU

But as a healing profession we cannot be led by man-made notions of what is good or evil in health. We must apply an independent, objective set of considerations. The laws of the land must in fact be based on these objective considerations.

BUDDHOO

Can we say, then, that this patient is not guilty of a sickness until proved so?

INDU

That is stretching the analogy a bit, but yes, it is an interesting analogy.

BUDDHOO

Can we say this patient is a person? The person is not a patient until proved so?

INDU

It is always a pleasure talking to an academic. It provides such a refreshing break from the routine interviews. Perhaps we should return to the case now. I believe our real concern – yours as well as mine, I can assure you – is Lakshmi's present condition. More importantly, the correct diagnosis, the correct line of treatment, and effective rehabilitation for her to live a normal, well-adjusted, productive life. *(Pause. Buddhoo does not reply.)* Would you agree?

BUDDHOO

Yes. But in a mental hospital?

INDU

Gautam, we are not in the nineteenth century. We do not treat patients with chains and electric shocks. Modern treatment for mental illnesses is based on good science, greatly concerned about the patient's wellbeing, and humane. The only problem in mental illness is the word mental itself.

The outside world cannot shake off the primitive associations, and still pictures the psychiatric ward as a dog pound.

BUDDHOO

What's to happen to Lakshmi now?

INDU

She will get well. She will be fine.

BUDDHOO

Can you tell me something more? If you are in a position...

INDU

I don't mind telling you. The differential diagnosis has been completed. The picture is quite clear.

BUDDHOO

Are you completely convinced?

INDU

Adequately – to commence treatment. The only small discrepancies arose out of some of your observations. But then there is also the real possibility that as an outsider to the family, and as a literary person, academically inclined, you caught certain glimpses that might not be quite representative of the whole, notwithstanding their peripheral value

BUDDHOO

I am sorry if I haven't been helpful. I didn't mean to...

INDU

Not at all. Different people are helpful in different ways. You care for Lakshmi. That is important. It will be a great help when she gets back.

BUDDHOO

Can you tell me... what does she have?

INDU

Nothing mysterious. It is a well-known condition. There is a long name for it, but you need not be confused by clinical terminology. The signs and symptoms fall into a certain pattern. Flight of ideas. Exaggerated swings of mood and bearing. Heightened verbalisation, with fantasy, vivid imagery, rapid associative chains, rhymes, neologisms – meaning the invention of new words and phrases, flippancy in word and deed, shifting from one idea to another. Gradual loss of control over accepted norms of socialisation and propriety.

BUDDHOO

(Cautiously) You got all the information for this... from the family?

INDU

Not entirely. There were others we met, other kinds of evidence – material – all examined meticulously. They fell into place all right. Of great value was some writing that young Minoo handed over to us – Lakshmi's sister-in-law.

BUDDHOO

Minoo *(He is perplexed, worried)*

INDU

Diary notes, verses, reflections. Very revealing, very valuable. *(Pause)* Yes, Lakshmi and Minoo were very close. Did you know Minoo well?

BUDDHOO

You used the past tense.

INDU

I beg your pardon?

BUDDHOO

Lakshmi and Minoo are very close.

INDU

I am sorry. I didn't mean any... perhaps because you are sensitive, you must have...

BUDDHOO

I think you know that I am like one of the family. As a matter of fact, I will be following up on Lakshmi's treatment with you, because the others – for one reason or the other – find that they cannot.

INDU

I understand.

BUDDHOO

The treatment... what will she...

INDU

The best. She will receive the best attention, the best treatment available.

BUDDHOO

Will she be put on some drugs?

INDU

There will be some medication needed – drugs as you call them – but it will be a facilitating device, to aid the main treatment programme.

BUDDHOO

Which is... ?

INDU

It is called the ICR Programme. You might have heard about it.

BUDDHOO

ICR Programme?

INDU

ICR stands for Intensive Cognitive Restructuring. It was developed by us here, and I can tell you there is much worldwide interest in our work in this field.

BUDDHOO

The treatment – this restructuring... It alters the mental condition?

INDU

Not exactly, not by itself. The ICR Programme works on the countercurrent principle, a rather fundamental principle that applies to many physical and biological states in which there is a process flow. Take the flow of a stream, for instance. *(Using her hands to demonstrate)* Let's say there is some contamination introduced in the stream at point A here. As it flows, the level of contamination gets less and less – points B and C – until it gets quite small at point D here. Now, if you wanted the entire length of the stream to be uniformly free of the contaminant, and you had an antidote for it, how would you go about administering it?

BUDDHOO

I don't know. I suppose there are ways.

INDU

One way is to apply the antidote in a countercurrent, that is to say, it will be strongest at the weakest point of contamination, but will actually give very little of itself to the neutralisation. At the other end, it will be least in content, but will have given the utmost to the cleansing process. It is the way most on-going processes work in nature – our digestive juices, for instance. The same principle is applied in several technologies for chemical treatment.

BUDDHOO

We have, you say, a man-made technology based on a natural principle.

INDU

That's neatly summarised. It's putting nature to work, putting it to effective use. Think of a mental state in a person... any person, not necessarily one who is sick. Think of the mental state as a stream – a stream of consciousness. The contaminants are in the belief systems, in our perceptions, in the way we see the world and choose to deal with it. These must be countered. The ICR Programme does precisely that. It alters the content of the stream. It renovates, replaces, reorders, reorients – in short, restructures the cognitive system.

BUDDHOO

The contamination... the beliefs and perceptions you work on... I suppose you have some way of assessing them. How do you say the stream is contaminated?

INDU

Very simple. There are two touchstone questions. One, is it harmful to the person? Second, is it harmful to others around the person?

BUDDHOO

You have ways to answer the two questions for the patient before you?

INDU

That is what the professional discipline is all about. It is a professional responsibility.

BUDDHOO

And the medication – where does that come in?

INDU

As I said, as a facilitator to the restructuring. It helps suspend the belief systems – so to speak – so that the restructuring may proceed smoothly. *(Pause. Buddhoo is silent.)* Gautamji, the ICR Programme is a major breakthrough in therapy.

BUDDHOO

In re-education technology.

INDU

Do I detect a note of scepticism? Of disbelief, perhaps? Or is it something else that is bothering you?

BUDDHOO

You will pardon the lack of sophistication in my metaphors, but as I listened to you, the first image that appeared before me was that of a gigantic road roller, occupying the entire width of the street, taller than the houses on the two sides.

INDU

That is an interesting association.

BUDDHOO

Is it what you refer to as the way one chooses to see the world?

INDU

I would accept the association without hesitation. Why not a road roller indeed? The road roller serves an invaluable function. You could even think of it as indispensible for smooth motoring.

Blackout.

Spot on Lakshmi, Right. For each of the three passages below, Indu crosses to Lakshmi, leads her to the clinic Left, where she speaks. After the passage Lakshmi returns alone to her place, Right. This sequence is repeated. Lakshmi is quiet when she returns the third time. The paragraphing below is for the three sequences, with Lakshmi getting progressively subdued through them.

LAKSHMI–1

Blazing hell! I am going to recant! They got away dragging Galileo through the streets. Bloody coward, chicken livered, knobbykneed weakling! None of that is going to work with me. I have scream on my side. I'll hang by the TV antenna on this house of sin and scream. And scream!

And scream!! Scream is my birthright. Right at birth I screamed till the midwife turned blue. I was a scream baby. I had a blue midwife. I'll bring down pox and pestilence on this house of sin. Line them up there, against the wall. Let me look at them, let me spit on their faces. Their eyes like lizard droppings – look at them squirm when they are reminded of their births. They've kept it a secret, they think. *(Striding back Right)* The whole world will learn about the ghosts in the family tree! The whole world will see. They will see deformed foetuses dangling all over the family tree!!

LAKSHMI–2

Honorificab down the road. Billynitatibus said the flying machine to greying spiders. Three score and twenty, hard black, well uncorked to match the diseased Hodgkin nine days older than springtime. If he wasn't a gunner she wouldn't be fired, butterfly fingers on lip marks ending paraphrases, evening shadows tightening the noose on tailor-made editors. *(Walking back Right)* Alack, verily, and topsoil eroded to plus or minus.

LAKSHMI – 3

Pasty – twentysiz – gusty hole – some – Pressilip fortifip – in Oxpuss keychain – freck lib guava – pos – trem – nin ban nokky – tuss – arbicharge lockspurn – hepaps – prrril – *(Limping back Right)* Linnso – oht – loht – lope – ochre – loh – locus...

She sits and remains very still, calm, relaxed. Indu crosses to Right once more. She regards Lakshmi for a moment and then speaks.

INDU

Good morning, Lakshmi.

LAKSHMI

Good morning.

INDU

And how do you feel today?

LAKSHMI

I feel well. Thank you.

INDU

Did you sleep well?

LAKSHMI

Yes.

INDU

How is your appetite?

LAKSHMI

I am eating well, thank you.

INDU

You are writing too, I see. *(Lakshmi smiles)* How nice. Will you show me? No hurry. Whenever you feel like it.

LAKSHMI

It is nothing... nothing, just...

INDU

You must be thinking of all that you'll be doing when you get back. *(Pause)* It will be very soon, you know. I'm going to recommend that it should be as soon as possible. There are just a few small formalities.

Crossfade with Indu moving to her desk, Left. She picks up the telephone.

P443... Prabhu, Lakshmi... Reference Dr PK Sharma... Remission satisfactory... Discharge Monday 10:00 am.

Crossfade to Lakshmi seated in her room, Right. She opens her diary, tears out the pages slowly and tears them up further into bits, carefully, systematically.

Crossfade to Indu at the telephone again.

Dr Simpson? Put him on please... yes, I'm holding the line... Yes, Dr Mahesh-Dixit here... Dr Simpson? Ah, Ray, Indu here. I believe I have a lovely case for presentation at the London conference... yes, I'll work on it right away. I'll write in detail... Bye.

She keeps the receiver down, turns in her seat and poses. The lights turn dazzling bright for a few moments.

Blackout

Close of play

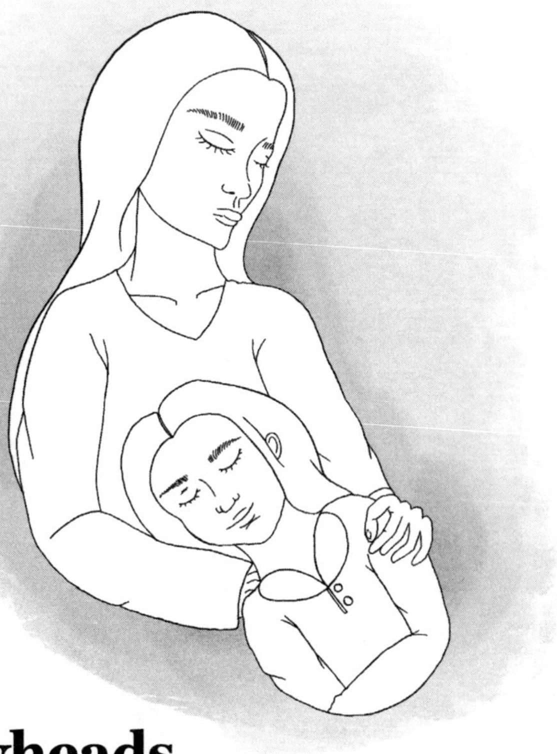

Arrowheads

The paths not taken

Vijay Padaki

FOR
SHEKHAR SESHADRI

CHARACTERS IN THE PLAY

UMA	*A counsellor*
VANI	*A single parent*
LATA	*Vani's daughter*
VIVEK, BUZZ, DILIP, CHIPS, RENU, POLLY	*Lata's friends*
BINA	*Polly's sister*
PRADIP	*Lata's brother*
SHEKHAR	*The father*

Scene 1: At a centre for personal growth. Some time in the past.
Scenes 2 to 4: In Vani's flat. The present.

INTRODUCTION

Arrowheads is an early play. It began as notes from a discussion (in a theatre group exercise) on the increasing rate of divorce in urban India, and then developed into a play. Scene 1 is in the nature of a prologue. Vani finds a point of view and takes a position. A group wishing to avoid a statement in its performance may omit the prologue, and find the rest of the play compact and complete in itself. On the other hand Scene 1 may be seen as a useful springboard for the storyline to follow. It is also a capsule in itself, and offers scope for fresh explorations in rendition.The time gap between the prologue and the rest of the play is not indicated, and is left to the imagination of the performers.

Language Notes

Shastropakar: In deference to the Shastras, in accordance with custom
Didi: Older sister, often the pet name for one
Haan: Yes
Thana: Station, police station
Hukum: Command
Rekha: Line – allusion to Lakshman Rekha in the Ramayana, the line/ boundary drawn by Lakshmana, beyond which Sita was not to stir

FIRST PERFORMED

By Bangalore Little Theatre as part of SPOT 1992 Festival.

Uma .... POORNIMA VYASULU
Vani .... VANI KRISHNASWAMY
Lata .... MALLIKA PRASAD OR MEGHANA NAYAK
Vivek, Buzz, Dilip, Chips, Renu, Polly .... ABHAY TOSHNIWAL, SEAN MATHEIKEN, AJITH SAMUEL, MALLIKA PRASAD, ADITYA SUBRAMANIAM, NIRMALA GOVINDRAJ, LEENA PISHE, MEGHANA NAYAK
Bina .... JONNA VYASULU OR NIRMALA GOVINDRAJ
Pat .... ADITYA SENGUPTA OR ARUN
Shekhar .... SHIVAKUMAR BELAWADI
Backstage .... VIDYA
Assisted by .... LATHA, ANEESH, JOEL, PAYAL, NISHA, CHRISTOPHER, DEEPAK
Production support .... KN JAYANTH, POORNIMA VYASULU, VIJAY PADAKI
Directed by .... PREETAM KOILPILLAI

SCENE 1

A circle of chairs. Vani is seated on one of them. The rest have just been vacated. Uma is seeing off the last of the group.

UMA

Same time next Friday. Don't forget a big Hi to Pintoo. He's very sweet. Always asks about a Guinness record on the phone. Bye then... Take care. *(She returns to the circle)* Give me just half a minute, Vani. I'll put these papers away...

VANI

Take your time, Doctor.

UMA

Uh-huh... I thought we'd left that behind. It was Uma till a few minutes ago. What's this Doctor business?

VANI

I'm sorry. It just comes... I didn't mean to...

UMA

Maybe I should say Mrs Narasimhan then.

VANI

Oh, no, please! There is no need for any such... I'll remember.

UMA

You'll remember, what?

VANI

I'll remember, Uma.

UMA

See? It's as easy as that. It's not meant to be some sort of cult ritual. What is our whole approach all about? Freedom of the spirit, freedom from dogma, freedom from fear. Many, many facets to that.

VANI

Standing up is an important one, I'm sure.

UMA

It is. It helps a lot. Addressing somebody by a title does not. Right, I'm ready now.

VANI

You don't mind, I hope... this extra time beyond the session...

UMA

Not at all. A lot of people do that, especially newcomers. You've been with us – what, two months now?

VANI

Just about. And seven sessions, today included.

UMA

Yes, so it is quite natural to have things to talk about outside the sessions. How is it coming? How do you feel?

VANI

Well, I must say I enjoy the company very much. It is a nice group. I've made a couple of new friends. I felt good. New friendships are useful when you... I can see other friendships here that seem to have come out of the sessions.

UMA

That's right. It is as it should be.

VANI

Yes, it is nice.

UMA

Yes.

VANI

But it's... I don't know, there's something...

UMA

You've had some problem with... ?

VANI

No, no problem. I told you. The group is fine. They are all nice – nice people.

UMA

Some difficulty then... you've had some difficulty.

VANI

You could call it that. But it's more a difficulty with myself, I suppose. Within myself.

UMA

Yes...

VANI

You must believe me when I say, it is not... you know... it's not like a complaint or anything. I mean, it is not as if you or Dr Saxena or the programme in any way...

UMA

Come on Vani, you know you can speak to me with complete frankness. *(Pause)*

VANI

I feel it is somehow incomplete.

UMA

What is?

VANI

What happens here. What we do here.

UMA

In the sessions?

VANI

I'm sorry. I should have said what happens to me here, what I do here.

UMA

No, no need to feel sorry. If that is what's bothering you – if that's the difficulty you feel – then you should talk about it.

VANI

It feels okay when we are here. We are working on something, it is seriously done. Of course, there is fun too. But we know there is some purpose to whatever we are doing. *(Pause)* But, when we step out of this room – when I reach the flat, turn the latch key, and enter – I feel so shaky. No, that's not the word. I don't think I feel shaky. I feel spent.

UMA

Uh... huh... in what way?

VANI

Betrayed. Lifted high and dropped. Like an unexplained rude end to the bumps you are being given on your birthday. *(Pause)* The scene that keeps coming back to my mind is the walk my daughter and I used to take in the evenings. The southern end of the beach. It was very soon after the split. She needed me close to her, I thought, and I had to give her that at any cost. No diversions. The evenings were booked... exclusively hers. Of course, I realised soon enough that I needed her too. Why fight that? As soon as I'd accepted that, our companionship grew more firm. It had more truth. We used to stop at the bandstand, overlooking the bend, where the waves kept lashing the rocks on the shore. It was a wide belt of rocks, hugging the bend below, like a choker of exquisite tribal design around a lovely neck. I remember watching a V-shaped driftwood being tossed in the waves just beyond the rocks. V for victory, Lata said. He's celebrating his victory, isn't he, I said. Yes, yes, his Victory, she said. Look how happy he is, carried on the shoulders of his people, the sea of admirers, I said. She asked, 'How do you know he is happy?' I replied, 'How do you know I don't know?' and pulled her pigtails. Intrigue. A first introduction to philosophical puzzlement. She was so impressed. Nothing original, of course. It was as old as Confucius. After a few moments of deep reflection she burst into a giggle and hugged me tightly. *(Pause)*

We stood there, the two of us in pure unison, watching the sea, watching the driftwood riding the waves.

UMA

It must have been a beautiful moment, Vani.

VANI

But the multitude there was a democracy, you see, and they had a right to a change of opinion, a right to express a change of opinion. They'd had enough of the driftwood hero. He had to go now. The tallest wave coming in from the north was given the job. Thumbs down – and the driftwood was dashed against a faceless grey-brown crag of uncertain descent. He lay there, broken, limp, confused... let down. Lata, too, shared the despair of the poor V-for-victory driftwood. Her arm around my waist tightened, but in a moment it relaxed again. She understood. A second lesson, built so neatly upon the first. *(Pause. She stares at Uma.)*

UMA

Vani, are you upset about something?

VANI

Is it something you can spot easily? A colour code or something?

UMA

You are upset, aren't you? Why not try and...

VANI

Upset? Cheerful? Furious, frightened, lovey-dovey? How does anyone know? What's the colour code? How do you know these states of mind are really what you believe them to be? Haven't you ever been blissfully frightened? I have. Or violently in love, ready to tear down buildings or at least smash the telephone that does not ring? Or stung to delirious laughter? They are all there, and lots and lots more. Waiting to be released from their colour-coded slots, and whirl and mingle, revealing infinite patterns in never before colours, never before melodies.

UMA

Vani, do you see that you are trying to say something to me, but are not actually getting down to it?

VANI

Am I? Am I not, that is? I am sorry. That is part of the difficulty, I suppose, the difficulty in making ourselves understood.

UMA

And we have been seeing how that is quite acceptable. The difficulties in making oneself understood... to others... to oneself...

VANI

Thank you, Uma. It is nice to know you understand.

UMA

Of course I do. And we owe it to each other to make the effort if we don't.

VANI

Then you do?

UMA

Do what? Make the effort?

VANI

No, I am sure you make the effort, that's hardly in doubt. But you do understand, don't you?

(Pause. Uma does not reply.) You do understand what I feel? That I am not upset? You mustn't think that. Because everything you hear me say will then get slotted in one corner of one rack. No, I am not upset at all. I am as happy as a giant ice cream sundae, with so many delightful flavours brought together all at once.

UMA

Then you must tell me more about it.

VANI

Will you listen?

UMA

We will give it a try. Let's start from where you left it just now.

VANI

No, we need to start at the beginning.

UMA

At the beginning, then. We'll close the view of the sea from the bandstand for a while.

VANI

Are you... upset?

UMA

About what? I am sorry if I sounded as if it was not...

VANI

No, no, no... it's nothing you said. I just thought you might have... you know... all this must be so... all this rambling, taking so much of your time.

UMA

Listen Vani, every job must be given the attention it deserves, the time it deserves. We are now doing something, you and I, for which we've kept aside this time. So there's no need to feel apologetic about it. *(Pause)* Shall we go ahead?

VANI

It just happened again.

UMA

What happened?

VANI

I felt like... I felt like a patient again. I was getting somewhere. I found the way, I was pedalling away quite freely, picking up speed. Suddenly, the spill. Is there something wrong with the bike, with the handlebar, the pedals, or is there something the matter with me?

UMA

You know what they say about riding a bike. You can never forget. It's always there in you.

VANI

Uma, I don't think I want to continue. No, it's not the group or you or Dr Saxena, or any of these things. You must believe me when I say that.

UMA

You want to...

VANI

Drop out, yes. It sounds odd, put that way, dropping out. But I don't think I can continue with the sessions. I'm sorry.

UMA

You feel you are not getting anywhere? It is not helpful?

VANI

I wouldn't say that. I did honestly learn a lot here.

UMA

Let's start at the beginning, then – once again – exactly where you wished. *(Pause)* Did you say you felt spent? Let down?

VANI

Don't close the view from the bandstand, Uma. The sea is where all life began on this earth. It has an infinite memory, and has kept alive the connections with all its children and children's children over the four billion years of its life. How do we dare disconnect? *(Pause)* Uma, all things living, all things healthy, vibrant, and throbbing with joyous life have one thing in common – only one thing. They breathe. I don't mean just the 'in-2-3 oxygen, out-2-3 CO2' stuff. That – yes, but that as one little part of something bigger. Building up things, breaking down things, putting them together again, taking them apart again, over and over and over, tirelessly, uncomplaining, all part of a beautiful, magnificent, spectacular rangoli that isn't even seen in its whole in one lifetime. Have you ever wondered what happens when this pattern is disturbed? You don't need to be an Einstein to know the answer. Poof – death! You can't keep breathing out, out, out, and just forget to breathe in. You can't have a high tide that goes on and on as high tide for two thousand years – or even two weeks! Or water going up in evaporation and never coming down as rain again. Is it any different with laughter and tears? What do we do here? We analyse things so well. I mean, really, we are so good at it, analysing problems, analysing situations, analysing persons, personal equations. But building up things from there... ? We become experts in analysing problems in life, not in dealing with them. We know nothing about living life. And when it is one-sided like that, what we see of the world out there gets one-sided too. We see problems! We see problems everywhere. We seek them out in our own lives, in the lives of every neighbour, friend, fruit vendor, and post office clerk, and every stock figure in the bus stop queue. Raw material for our analysis engines – we need more and more of it day by day.

UMA

You are saying you haven't benefitted from the group sessions... ?

VANI

I didn't say that – not exactly that.

UMA

Not exactly that – but that! You are hesitating to say that the explorations in the group – analysis, you called it, although we have hardly ever used the word – you are saying that finding out more about what bothers us is... well... that it's a waste of time. *(A beat)*

VANI

And possibly injurious too. *(Short laugh)*

'Warning. Exploring bees-in-bonnets may be injurious to health.'

UMA

Oh?

Long pause, in which Uma begins to put chairs away and Vani collects her own things. Finally only Vani's chair remains, with her seated on it. Uma reverts to her.

UMA

When did you first feel this way? About the group?

VANI

Last Friday.

UMA

I see. Was there anything particular... did something happen in the group?

VANI

I knew you would ask. No, nothing happened in the group. As a matter of fact, that was one thing bothering me – somewhere in one corner of my mind – that nothing happened in the group. I was returning home drawing a peculiarly unfamiliar train of thoughts – unfamiliar terrain, uncertain directions. I stopped to pick up onions and potatoes from the roadside shop, I had known for years, but there was still an expanding hollow in my tummy. The girl next to me must have been there well ahead of me. She had two huge plastic baskets full of supplies. For the week, I supposed. Or maybe she was entertaining people over the weekend. She was a green and red blur when I stopped next to her, my mind still wandering restlessly. It was her bindi that first came into focus – like a five-pointed leaf from some

Himalayan pine. And then the face itself – chiselled marble in form, but with the softest, most unhindered smile etched lightly under her brows. I stepped back a bit to take her in fully, now returned to my everyday surroundings. She collected her change and, rising, gently enquired of the old woman selling the vegetables if her husband's drinking changed in proportion with the price of onions. The old woman laughed. I laughed too. 'All things that go up must come down, but somewhere in Dubai,' she said with a sideward glance. I found myself helping her with the plastic bags. Thanks – not at all – awfully sweet of you – love to help – a pit-pat exchange merged into a friendly chatter. She lived just the other side of the main road, she said. I helped her across the road. With six kilos of veggies and god knows how many packs of grocery between us, I can't say who was really helping whom cross the road. We laughed like schoolgirls on a picnic when we dodged an auto rickshaw and had him shaking his fist at us.

UMA

You reached her home?

VANI

Of course I did. I had time. I helped her unload the baskets and put things in their places – in the pantry – in the fridge. When I left her place after a cup of tea, it was like we'd known each other for years... since childhood... maybe even from an earlier birth. Does this make any sense, Uma?

UMA

I think so. You thought you were lonely, that you wouldn't ever have another friend, and then you ran into someone buying vegetables, and now you have a new friend.

VANI

I'm sorry Uma, but Rita is not a 'friend', as you put it. That's right, her name is Rita, but she is not listed under R in any diary of mine – friends, enemies, debtors, creditors. And I hope to god she never does get reduced to that. It will be an ugly end to the most beautifully honest companionship I have felt in a very long time.

UMA

You have a friendship, but not a friend...

VANI

Now, that is something to analyse! Our joys, our good vibes, our exhilarating moments of love and kindness and compassion – why don't we analyse them too, with the same systematic attacks, to decode messages, to find out where they hide and how they may be brought back into our everyday lives again? Rita helped me do that. No, she doesn't know anything about my life, I haven't blabbered it all out to her. We just held hands to cross the road and we laughed, and we had tea together. And then, as I walked back to my own flat, I knew I had stumbled upon something vital –

something I had been looking for with increasing desperation without knowing what it was and what it looked like.

Pause. Vani extends her hand. Uma shakes it politely. Vani turns to go, pauses, keeps her things down, and embraces Uma warmly. She picks up her things again, noticeably cheerful.

I am all right, Uma. Take my word for it. I'll be quite all right. And I'll keep in touch, of course. You will explain to Dr Saxena, won't you? Please do give him my regards. Bye now.

She leaves. Uma watches her leave, puts away her chair, picks up the phone, and dials a number.

UMA

Dr Saxena's office? Could you connect him please?... Is that Mohan? Doc, this is Uma... Fine, thank you. And how about you? Uh... huh... Oh, the usual, Okay on the whole... Mohan, would you care to join me for a nice cup of tea in my room? Oh, just like that... Lovely.

SCENE 2

Vani's flat. There are two acting spaces – a kitchen-dining area and a living area that is sparsely but neatly outfitted, mostly for floor seating. When the scene opens, Vani and her daughter, Lata, are at the compact dining table getting things ready. It is Lata's birthday. She is an attractive girl, smartly but simply dressed, and fully nineteen in her carriage which makes her an inch or two taller than Vani.

VANI

How many phone calls?

LATA

Oh, the usual. I didn't keep count.

VANI

That's the nice thing about a birthday. Each time the phone rings, you wonder, 'Who could it be this time?' It's nice being remembered on your birthday.

LATA

It's nice hearing from some, at least once a year!

VANI

Like Vasan uncle in Madras.

LATA

Like Vasan uncle... and Lakshmi aunty... and your classmate Rima and Ashok in Los Angeles. They send me a birthday card, bang on time, every year.

VANI

They've always been very fond of you.

LATA

So sweet of them. They must have seen me last when I was four or something.

VANI

And how does it feel to be nineteen today?

LATA

Great! I mean, eighteen was really something, it was the best birthday I'd ever had, but nineteen is nineteen. I'm older by a year and all. I feel good. I feel great.

VANI

And you know what! I feel so good too! It's lovely watching you grow like this.

LATA

Well, make the most of the time you have with me! Who knows when I'll sprout my wings and fly off into a world of my own? Isn't that what Granny says every time a birthday comes around?

VANI

Well, I was the first to take off from her nest. So, she must feel there is something being passed on down the line – like some hereditary thing.

LATA

She's sweet! Even when she nags, she's sweet.

VANI

That's it. You got it quite right, I think. She has this knack. She has a way of steadily prodding you not to do something, until you can't help actually doing it, and she looks at you as if to say, 'Oho, there you've gone and done it.' And you can't help feeling it was somehow preordained, and that if we all appear properly foolish and repentful about what has happened, it will go through okay. We will all end up really quite happy.

LATA

God's own plan, on schedule.

VANI

With just the right touch of ceremonial remorse. Shastropakar two-minute silence.

LATA

There just might be a genetic basis to it, you know.

VANI

Lata, you are not suggesting...

LATA

No, I didn't mean you or Granny or anybody. I meant things like that in nature. Do you remember that wild life movie we saw on my twelfth birthday – about a family of foxes. It's like that with all animals. Well, with all mammals anyway, I think. At some point the parents actually drive the young out of the nest. They have to go. They've got to get out and fend for themselves in the big bad world out there.

VANI

I suppose that is the greatest act of kindness from the parents.

LATA

And I suppose there is a natural gender difference. The father bares his fangs and stages a mock attack, and the mother nuzzles the little one gently, firmly, but out! *(Pause)*

VANI

And when it's time for you to go... how will I know? What will I find myself doing?

LATA

Oh mama, you will know, because I will nuzzle you myself to help me with the packing. And I'll give you a tight hug every ten minutes to tell you that you're the best mama a girl could have.

VANI

At least I don't have fangs to bare. Five years of braces took care of that.

LATA

Mama, all the world's a nest – school, college, workshop, office – every job, every gathering. When you outgrow something you must move on. And if we get complacent about it, there must be other ways to get our backsides moving. Fangs maybe. Banishment maybe. We can call it different things, but it's all the same.

VANI

Do people leave nests on their own? No nuzzling, nothing... on their own?

LATA

Isn't that the best thing to happen? The least this species can do with its God-given intelligence. *(Sounds of Lata's friends coming into the living area)* Oh... oh, they've come.

VANI

It's okay. We have almost everything done here.

FRIENDS

Nineteen, nineteen. Where's that girl of nineteen? Nineteen, nineteen. We want that girl of nineteen!

The friends are Vivek, Buzz, Polly, her sister Bina, Chips, Renu, and Dilip. The following scene is best improvised by the actors themselves, adding words, horseplay, rhymes, and so on. As felt apt, but maintaining the following sequence:–

Rushing into the kitchen area, carrying Lata out.

Putting Lata on to a sheet or durry and tossing her for her birthday 'bumps' – one... two... up to nineteen.

Vani joining in just a bit later and lending a hand in the bumps.

About half way through, Lata's father Shekhar enters with her younger brother, Pradip (called Pat).

The revelry continues briefly after the last bump, with impromptu songs, gifts, hugs, etc.

Vani moves over to Shekhar and Pradip to receive them.

Finally, Lata notices them and joins the trio, receives gift, etc.

LATA

Daddy! Pat! Hi! So nice you could come. I thought daddy was still on tour.

SHEKHAR

No, not really. It was just...

LATA

(To Pradip) Guess what? Mama has done it again. My birthday – and your favourite cake!

PRADIP

(Giving her a gift) This is for you.

LATA

Thank you, thank you. So sweet of you.

Shekhar and Vani move to the kitchen area as the lights fade slowly in the living area. The friends settle down in twos and threes on the floor. Lata is with Vivek. Polly introduces Pradip to Bina and leaves the two of them together. They sit awkwardly on two hassocks or modhas.

SCENE 3

Shekhar is stirring his coffee as he stares in the direction of the living area. Vani is putting away the last few things in their places. Presently, she joins Shekhar at the table getting her own coffee. They sit silently for a while, Shekhar continuing his on-and-off stirring.

VANI

Ninety-five, ninety-six, ninety-seven, ninety-eight, ninety-nine, one hundred! Ready or not, here I come, one brown coffee pot, two tots of rum! *(No response from Shekhar. Pause. She tries again)* 9,995, 9,996, 9,997, 9,998, 9,999... and... here it comes... nine thousand nine hundred and ninety-ten... and that's ten thousand! A new Guinness record by Mr Chandrashekhar Narasimhan of Bangalore, India, as he stirs his coffee in ten thousand anticlockwise movements, without a rest, pause. *(Pause. Shekhar stops stirring. Quieter now).* Some things really don't change, huh! *(Pause)*

SHEKHAR
Mm...

VANI
Like a good clinkety-clinkety-clink for a good cup of coffee.

SHEKHAR
Like good flippant yak-yak.

VANI
Oh?

SHEKHAR
Here we are, meeting after... what, how many months... I can't even remember. We haven't said hello, how are things with you, or anything like that – and you go yak-yak-yak about something or the other!

VANI
Hello, how are things with you?

SHEKHAR
I don't believe this!

VANI
Did I ever, in all the time we were married, did I ever crack a joke about your stirring your coffee? No. It's only when you are properly distanced that you get to see the divine comedy in things.

SHEKHAR
God, you make a pair, the two of you.

VANI
No, I'm not going to say it.

SHEKHAR
Say what?

VANI
So do you, the two of you. But I didn't say it!

SHEKHAR
We are not flippant. And we don't go yak-yak all the time, thank you.

VANI
Lata and I do yak-yak a lot, and we should say we quite like it. Thank you for noticing. But flippant? We have to think about that. Like, I could say Pat is a quiet young man, can't I? But would it be right for someone to say he is unsocial?

SHEKHAR
Pat is growing up fine! He is growing into a sensible young man. *(Vani smiles. She strokes Shekhar's cheek lightly and looks at him intently, with a genuine warmth. Shekhar looks away.)*

VANI

I forgot to ask. Was the sugar all right?

SHEKHAR

The trouble is I think you actually mean it. *(Pause)*

The sugar was fine, thanks. Just right, in fact.

VANI

You have new glasses. Has the power changed?

SHEKHAR

No, it's the same – just a new frame. *(Pause)*

How is Lata doing in her studies?

Crossfade to living area. The group is dancing to lively music. The song ends and lap dissolves to a slow number. To sighs of recognition, the group breaks into distinct twos, dancing close. Lata and Vivek move to an upstage corner position. Pradip and Bina are left downstage.

PRADIP

You want to dance more? *(Bina shrugs)* If you want to... why not sit down for a while? I could get a coke... *(Bina shrugs)* Actually, I don't... I don't like slow dances... Are you very keen? *(Bina shrugs)* Like, I never bothered to learn the steps and all... You know, I don't think I know this song... I don't think I can dance to this at all.

Bina bursts into a giggle. Pradip is startled momentarily. As the understanding occurs, both of them sit down, just a little closer. Crossfade to kitchen area.

VANI

That's what split custody of children is all about, I think. Pitted against each other, the parents will do their damndest to prove themselves right. And to prove the other wrong. Food, clothes, books, movies – even friends and pastimes – what we choose for the little one handed to us by the toss of the judge's coin must obviously be righter than right. Because we are right. Ergo, what the other one is doing with the other child must be suspect.

SHEKHAR

Did I say anything about you bringing up Lata badly?

VANI

(Cheerful, unprovoked) Not in so many words, no. I don't think you could say such things directly. It's not like you.

SHEKHAR

But I did things that said things...

VANI

And your parents, and your sister, who practically wrote your script for you for all of those Saturday meetings with the children.

SHEKHAR

Vani, there is no need to bring the family into this. What happened was strictly a matter of...

VANI

Don't you see how hopelessly incomplete it is without that? How can you not bring your mother into this? Especially if we are not shouting senselessly at each other, but looking at things with a sort of mellow cool fifteen years later?

SHEKHAR

My mother was concerned first and last with the happiness of the kids.

VANI

Weren't you? Wasn't I? Was this concern so specially your mother's? And to ensure that happiness to the kids, did she have to invent so many facts and figures about my life, to be dropped discreetly in conversation here and there? *(Pause)*

SHEKHAR

I suppose Amma was a bit like that, but you shouldn't...

VANI

Did you ever feel, at any point, that you should interrupt the goings on and say, 'I'm sorry, you are wrong, that's not true about Vani?' *(Pause)* Wait a minute! Why am I forgetting what we are talking about? I was thinking how terribly important it is to have things around you that can help change the way we see things – the way we want to see things.

SHEKHAR

You mean you were not after my mother!

VANI

I am sorry if I sounded like that. I'm really sorry. That wasn't it at all. I was trying to tell you how distancing helps. How important it is. It took some time, but I realised how natural it was to look for faults on the other side. I could see it happening to me too. It was something I couldn't possibly have intended. It was all wrong – abnormal. And what made it really terrible was the feeling of helplessness, knowing it was there eating up your insides, and watching yourself actually feed it every day.

SHEKHAR

(Looking at her directly at last) The daily dosage. It was like some tonic... You felt that way too? *(Pause)*

VANI

It takes a long, long time to realise that sometimes it is perfectly normal to be behaving abnormally. And that others too have the right to...

SHEKHAR

To their insanities?

VANI

No, to their search for sanity.

SHEKHAR

And pain... the right to pain.

VANI

To feel pain, to give pain. *(Shekhar turns away)* The pains we take to keep up the pain.

SHEKHAR

(Abruptly) How long will the party be? Can I come back later?

VANI

I don't know. It's up to the kids. They might all go out or something.

SHEKHAR

You mean Lata will just...

Pradip enters and looks around for something.

VANI

What's up Pat? You want something?

PRADIP

Uh... yah, do you have a coke here somewhere?

VANI

Here, let me get you one. *(She fetches a bottle of cola.)*

SHEKHAR

A coke? I thought you hated the stuff.

PRADIP

Uh... yeah, I just thought...

VANI

Here you are. Chilled enough, I hope.

SHEKHAR

Comes in here, just like that, and asks for a coke!

PRADIP

This is... Bina wanted a coke... I'm taking it for her.

Pradip takes the bottle over to Bina. Crossfade to living area. The group is sprawled on the floor again, concentrating on a game in progress. Bina and Pradip move away upstage.

POLLY

Bittu, is that a Thums Up in your hand?

BINA

Haan, didi, I just got it.

POLLY

But I thought you hated the stuff.

BINA

Yeah, but... Pradip here got it for me. I never said, I hate Thums Up!

The group ad libs teasing Bina a bit. They concentrate on the game again.

POLLY

Bittu, are you sure you don't want to join?

LATA

Pat, why don't you ask Bina if she'd like...

BINA

No, didi, it's okay. You all carry on.

VIVEK

What do you mean, join the game? Those two get together, and we've had it. Pat is really deadly on this.

BUZZ

Hey, enough of board games. Let's play something else.

ALL

Yeah, yeah... Good idea... Let's do something else... etc.

CHIPS

I know, I know. Let's play that – what was it called – that thing we saw in the movie last week – you know, they all get into this girl's apartment – her name was Stella wasn't it?

DILIP

Good idea. The Jodie Foster movie. She works in that shop next to...

RENU

You're mixing it up. It wasn't Jodie Foster. That was another movie. Stella was the part-time help in the record shop.

LATA

That's right. You're always getting your girls mixed up!

CHIPS

Disaster! It was called Disaster, right?

DILIP

Okay, that's what it was called, if that's what you say. Now, how do we begin?

RENU

You need an empty bottle of scotch to start.

BUZZ

Well, Thums Up zindabad! Bittu sweetie, do you think we could get the empty coke bottle here when you're through? Please?

POLLY

And would you hurry – please?

LATA

Come and join us, both of you. Did you get to see the movie?

VIVEK
Lata, Pat and Bina – they might not have been allowed to see the movie.

LATA
Nonsense, it wasn't that kind of cassette. It was a fun movie, that's all.

PRADIP
Here. *(Gives them the bottle)*
You carry on. We'll watch. *(Bina and Pradip draw near)*

CHIPS
Right! We put this bottle on the floor... and we spin it like this... and it stops... pointing at... Buzz!

BUZZ
So what do I do?

POLLY
You get shot!

VIVEK
Okay, we begin with the person on your right, which is me!

POLLY
Vivek will ask the first question.

CHIPS
No, Vivek will set the scene. Then the questions get fired.

VIVEK
Okay – fasten seat belts – here's the scene. Buzz is cycling down MG Road... and he finds the bottom seam of his pants have gone r-r-rip! *(Reactions, sounds, from all, throughout the game, now on)*

BUZZ
I duck into the first side street on the left.

VIVEK
We go in this direction. Next on my right – Lata.

LATA
It's a one-way street. The cop stops you, he asks you to get off.

BUZZ
I ask him to hold the bike for a minute and run towards an auto rick.

LATA
Dips.

DILIP
You slip on a banana peel and land thud on your back. You can't get up by yourself.

BUZZ
I whisper into my wrist watch radio transmitter and call for help from headquarters.

RENU

And help arrives... in the persons of Asha and Usha of Second Year Botany.

BUZZ

Groan! Double groan! I say... oh god, what do you say to these two? I tell them Girish Karnad is auditioning young carnivorous botany types for his next movie, Love in Lakshadweep, and they go scurrying off. Happy dereliction of duty!

CHIPS

Okay Buzz, I've got you now. They find out you're lying down in a no parking zone and a crane truck comes to tow you away – by your feet of course.

BUZZ

Hah! Easy-peasy! They realise when they reach the thana that they've got only my boots.

DILIP

Your turn Polly. Give it to him.

POLLY

BUT... you were helpless when you slipped on the banana peel and fell down, so you are stuck there with your legs up! *(General celebration of Buzz's plight)*

BUZZ

BUT... The Times of India reporter offers me a hundred bucks for his candid camera shot which he wants to title, Banana Split! *(They all laugh, exchange cracks.)* Do I spin the bottle now? My turn, right? Okay, here goes... aaaand... it's Lata!

LATA

You've got to start, Dips.

DILIP

I fix you?

ALL

Yeah... fix her right... birthday special... etc.

DILIP

You are alone on a desert island with nothing else but this empty bottle of coke.

BUZZ

Nothing else or nothing else on?

ALL

Shut up Buzz... wait for your turn... okay, okay... That's supposed to be a joke... corny joke... etc.

LATA

As I roll the bottle between my hands, a grinning genie comes out and says, 'Salaam madam, your hukum!'

DILIP

Clever, clever, but you can't get away so easily. The genie says, 'Ho ho ho, I have tracked you down at last. I was your husband in your previous birth. Don't you remember?'

LATA

I despatch him back to the future to track down my husband in my next birth.

RENU

But before leaving, he draws a genie-rekha straight across the island in front of you, and says that if you cross it to reach the rescue boat your... what should we give you... you will... yeah, he says your coke bottle figure will turn as thin and as straight as the line.

LATA

Mercy! Mercy! Come on Buzz, give us the sound effects.

BUZZ

Groan! Double groan!

LATA

I will not cross the line! Not from above, that is. I will start digging a tunnel to cross it below.

CHIPS

Down there you find a room full of ghosts – all survivors of stale desert island jokes and stories. They shout in a tinny chorus, 'Welcome home, dearie!'

LATA

You are there too? All you guys would be there, I'm sure. Anyway, I will... let's see... I huff and I puff and I bring the house down.

ALL

Great... clever... you brought the house down... good one... etc.

POLLY

Okay, so a part of the debris falls on your head and you lose your memory. So when the rescue boat guys arrive, all you can say is goo-ga-go goo-ga-go.

BUZZ

Rescue boat guys, you see. Sailor types. Hungrr-rr-y!

CHIPS

Sweet, helpless Lata. Memory loss too. Perfect!

VIVEK

(To Chips) You've had your turn. *(To Buzz)* And you have to wait.

DILIP

Vivek, the one-man rescue team! Look who's getting upset...

VIVEK

You guys are always overdoing things.

BUZZ

But it's disaster time – and Lata's in a jam. The sailor guys are drooling. Let's peep into their heads through our mind scanner monitors. What do we see? Oh... oh... cut by the censors!

VIVEK

I told you, you are going too far.

LATA

It's okay, Vivek. It's only a game. *(General cheer returning)* Let's see now – goo-ga-go, round I go, if I miss, I take this! Simple – divide and rule. I insist on being carried out by only one of them. As they start killing each other off, I swim to the rescue boat. Polly!

POLLY

Well, there are sharks in the water. Snap-snap. You escape, of course, but the sharks have torn your clothes off.

LATA

But the rescue boat is an inflatable one, you see, made of some plastic. Polka-dotted actually. So, before I step on to the mother ship, I fashion a gorgeous lounging gown out of it.

BUZZ

Inflatable lounging gown! More like a maternity gown that would be.

DILIP

Okay, you are a celebrity – the baby doll survivor of a desert island ordeal. The TV crew is catching the crowd-filled reception, waiting to interview you, when two little kids run up to you shouting Mom-ee, Mom-ee, Mom-ee.

LATA

God, sounds like a police car in the European movies – mom-ee mom-ee. Okay, so I shout back, 'Where's your Dad-ee, Dad-ee, Dad-ee?!' *(All laugh, catching Lata's spirit)* Foo – made it! No, there's Vivek still. *(Short pause)*

VIVEK

You are hounded by bloodthirsty movie moghuls who want to film the whole story with you in it.

ALL

Oh no... that's too easy... he's letting her off... that's no disaster... etc.

LATA

(With a wink) I turn to Swami Vivek, the dispenser of Ananda, and start on a new life altogether!

There is general cheer, backslapping, and preparation for a third round. Pradip and Bina join the circle, enlarged. As the bottle is placed in the middle for its spin, there is a fade out.

SCENE 4

The kitchen area. The crowded table suggests that the eats part of the party is over. Vani has just started to clear up. Shekhar is half way through a drink. On second thoughts, Vani decides to put off the clearing up, and sits down.

VANI

Oh, this can wait. *(She joins Shekhar)*

Nice party, wasn't it? Nice bunch of kids. *(No response)* I like Lata's friends. Full of fun, always up to something... nice bunch. Sometimes I feel I am one of them... that's foolish, of course. It's always somebody else's birthday that tells you how old you really are. Especially when you're exhausted by 8:00 pm. *(Pause. No response.)* I am wondering – I can't decide if I should light a cigarette or join you with a drink.

SHEKHAR

Are you smoking now?

VANI

Oh, regularly – twice a year. If the lines on your brow are saying, 'thank you for not smoking', the choice is made. I'll have a drink. *(She rises)* How about your glass? *(He signals he is doing Fine)* Well, you will help yourself, won't you? (*Lata enters. She is followed by Pradip who stays at a distance, Lata moves to help clear up.)*

LATA

You want to clear up now, Mama? We can all help.

VANI

No, no – don't bother. There's no hurry at all. *(Noticing Pat)* You want something more from here?

LATA

No, mama, we don't need anything. Actually, they are all so stuffed they don't even want to dance any more.

VANI

So, you all want to go out for a drive.

LATA

Right. Are you sure about not clearing up now?

VANI

Which means you'll return sort of latish.

LATA

Not really. It is a working day tomorrow.

VANI

All of you packed into Vivek's Maruti?

LATA

Oh, Dips and Renu have another car. And we were wondering... can Pat come along too?

VANI

Sure... that is, it seems to me... Shekhar?

SHEKHAR

Well, it's getting to be 8:30 – and I don't think I'll have more than one small one after this one. What time do you think... ?

LATA

Oh, Pat can be dropped off, Daddy. He'll come directly home. And I promise it won't be late.

SHEKHAR

All right. It is your birthday after all.

LATA

Lovely! Go on Pat. Get into the first car. And tell them to go ahead. We'll follow in a couple of minutes. *(Pradip looks at Shekhar again and hurries out)* Thanks, daddy. You really should drop in here more often with Pat. Mama, I thought I'd at least clear the dishes from the table. It's so messy. *(She has already brought a tub. She piles plates, bowls, dishes, and cutlery into the tub, puts it away, wipes her hand, gives Vani a warm hug and starts to leave. She stops, gives Shekhar a peck on his forehead)* Thank you again, Daddy. It was sweet of you to come with Pat. Bye. *(She leaves, and calls from offstage)* We'll drop Pat home. Bye!

A long pause. Vani picks up a remaining spoon from the table, moves to the tub, drops it in with ceremony, returns to the table, waits.

VANI

Well, she won't make a great scriptwriter, that's clear.

SHEKHAR

(Looks up) Umm?

VANI

I mean, if she had left everything on the table, I would at least have something to do – while I am inventing time-pass conversation.

SHEKHAR

You haven't got yourself a drink.

VANI

Oh, the drink, the drink. *(She moves to get herself one)*

SHEKHAR
Does she go out like that always?

VANI
Like what?

SHEKHAR
You know what I mean...

VANI
Do I know what you mean? Yes, I think I know what you mean. No, she does not...

SHEKHAR
Hmm.

VANI
Only when she is sure she wants to. Nobody can push her into something she doesn't want herself.

SHEKHAR
Not even you?

VANI
Not even I – happy to report.

SHEKHAR
Not even Mr Vivek S Ganapathy?

VANI
Oh?

SHEKHAR
He takes more than an ordinary interest in Lata, does he not?

A pause. Vani smiles. She strokes Shekhar's cheek with a finger once again.

VANI
Just as a certain gentleman took an interest in a certain young lady twenty years ago... Well, the first question first. No, I don't think Vivek can make Lata do something she does not herself want to. But that is not a satisfactory answer, is it? What if Lata wants to do something that Vivek wants her to do? What if poor Lata doesn't know what she should or should not want? In other words, what if poor, innocent, helpless Lata doesn't know what is good for her?

SHEKHAR
Well, I can't interfere in your... in the way you run your family...

VANI
But you can't help noticing things.

SHEKHAR
You just allowed Lata to go out with Vivek. Just like that.

VANI

Just like what? And how come you did not notice that there were others going out – Polly and that madcap Buzz, and young Chiplunkar, Renu and Dips. And Bina, Polly's little sister.

SHEKHAR

Sure, sure, a whole jolly group.

VANI

And Pat.

SHEKHAR

And Pat dragged along too.

VANI

Really Shekhar, are you saying Pat didn't want to go out with the group?

SHEKHAR

I don't know what that is supposed to mean, but I just thought I should tell you, that's all.

VANI

Well, then, tell me.

SHEKHAR

You're trying to be funny.

VANI

It is not intended. I am only trying to tell you that this is so typical of you – working yourself up, beating about the bush, not coming to the point. *(Pause)* What do you know about Vivek?

SHEKHAR

Not much. He has a fine Iyer nose.

VANI

As good a point as any to start, I suppose. What else?

SHEKHAR

That his father is part of a firm of lawyers. And that he has an older brother who went to Stanford, but has not returned. That's all.

VANI

That's all?

SHEKHAR

That's all. Yes, that the mother is, well...

VANI

You see, you know quite a lot. So do I, actually, but the difference is that everything I know about him is from Lata, and Vivek himself, in more recent times.

SHEKHAR

Are they... ?

VANI

Almost to the point at last! The correct answer is, maybe. Are you satisfied?

SHEKHAR

Humph! Maybe!

VANI

Okay Health Ministry Warning – one mischief question coming up... now! How much do you know about Bina?

SHEKHAR

Vani, I can't help getting worried about you.

VANI

Worried?

SHEKHAR

About you and Lata. It's like you are giving up, allowing yourself to be pulled away, in any odd direction, by anybody.

VANI

Not anybody. Not any odd direction. I had only to stop whipping myself on to be in control of everything in my life, to stop pretending that it was even possible. Suddenly the north side stone wall had an opening in it – a little skylight that soon grew into a bay window with a magnificent view of the mountains. And I could see Lata there, at the halfway mark already, waving to me in triumph, and calling out – no, urging me – to join her.

SHEKHAR

And you joined her. And then came Vivek. And then this one and that one, until you had a nice big party, and life was a nice big picnic.

VANI

Yes! Just like the one last year – on Lata's eighteenth birthday. It was a great big treasure hunt, masterminded by Polly – that's right, Bina's sister – and we were out the whole day from seven in the morning. There must have been over thirty of us, but only five of us parents. It felt so good to be included. When we got home I was in a sort of trance, so completely exhausted, but so completely refreshed. I must have dreamed a hundred dreams that night, each no longer than a few seconds maybe, and all of them strung together like teaser clips before the main show. They kept hurtling further and further back in time until I was just a three-year-old, watching a wedding procession in front of our Civil Lines house – in my trademark frilly knickers and twin ponytails. *(She stops, notices that Shekhar is staring at her)* I woke up to find myself huddled in Lata's arms. Lata's arms – so long, so lovely, so strong. I hadn't noticed. *(Pause)* I suppose all this girl talk...

SHEKHAR

No, it's all right. Boys dream too. Only they don't talk about it.

VANI

Shekhar, Lata and her friends are all right. I'm not romanticising things. It's not for Readers Digest. They are like kids anywhere else, I suppose. But I have learned many things from them. They are the arrowheads in a very special Himalayan treasure hunt – each new day presenting a delightful new clue, teasing you on to wonderful new gifts. And to get there I have only to learn the code. I have only to keep my eyes open, and learn to trust them.

SHEKHAR

And you feel safe?

VANI

I feel the danger now and then. The clues are perplexing at times. But I feel safe. I look again, and I see the reassuring sign – pointing ahead always.

SHEKHAR

Lata was always like that. On the fast track always. You are lucky.

VANI

You don't think...

SHEKHAR

Got it from my cousin Prema, they always said.

VANI

Yes, Prema. She is... well?

SHEKHAR

Oh, she is going as strong as ever. They've just got a new farmhouse about an hour's drive beyond the TV tower.

VANI

And Pat? He has grown well too, I can see.

SHEKHAR

Yes, he is doing well. He tops the class in half the subjects – always in the top three in the totals.

VANI

Good for him! Good old Pat-a-cake-baker's-man Pat.

SHEKHAR

Now and then he talks about becoming a photographer, but he will settle down soon, I'm sure.

VANI

I noticed something else... he doesn't call me Mama any more. *(Pause)* Is it in preparation... ?

SHEKHAR

Not really. There's nothing... nothing definite. You have heard things?

VANI

My god – why are you looking so glum? Yes, I have heard. It is good news, isn't it?

SHEKHAR

I told you – there is nothing definite. Do you want to be the first to be informed?

VANI

Only if you want to do it. You and her, that is. Hey, that is really good! *(She extends her hand. He takes it.)* Congratulations! *(Pause. She withdraws her hand.)*

Okay, we'll stop there. Anything more will displease the authorities. But you will let me know!

SHEKHAR

Of course, I'll let you know.

VANI

And then Pat will call me – what – Vani aunty?

SHEKHAR

Pat is... I didn't want to talk about it... Pat is going through some sort of... I don't know... he is behaving funny.

VANI

They call it a phase, I think.

SHEKHAR

That's what you called it every two months or so, from the time he sucked his thumb.

VANI

Well, I haven't given any opinion the last few years.

SHEKHAR

You didn't have the burden.

VANI

I didn't have the privilege.

SHEKHAR

Vani, I can't help showing it, but I think you know I am worried.

VANI

I think I see it. But worried about what?

SHEKHAR

I wish I knew. About Pat, about the second round coming up, about all of us.

VANI

You know something? It's the clothes you wear.

SHEKHAR

Oh, come on. This is no time for...

VANI

No, really, if you had a little more colour in your shirt and pants, a lighter shade of blue here, nice T-shirts on Sundays, you wouldn't have a steel grey view of the world all the time.

SHEKHAR

Okay, the next time I come...

VANI

And shake off that question mark slouch, and get back to the old exclamation mark again!

SHEKHAR

That, I suppose, is the great difference between you and me!

VANI

I am sorry – I had no intention of making you feel...

SHEKHAR

How self-satisfied can you get? Can't you see – whatever clothes you wear, whatever you do on Sundays – you will always be a member of that exclusive club? Ammamma used to say – you remember – you may decide to give up your caste mark, but your caste will never give you up. The exclusive club of splits – the badge is worn all your life.

VANI

Then wear it as a veteran, Shekhar, and not with guilt or shame. The world hardly ever looks at a badge closely, but it always remembers the wearer.

SHEKHAR

It is so easy to say that. But we are first generation members – the founder members of the club.

VANI

And so we carry an even weightier responsibility.

SHEKHAR

I've been meeting people – single parents, present and past. I've been reading.

VANI

Shekhar, I have to tell you something.

SHEKHAR

Will I listen carefully?

VANI

Will you?

SHEKHAR

Go on.

VANI

Do you remember the brochure you sent me on the smart new housing colony in Shastri Park? It was two years after the split. Contemporary styling, modern interiors, designed with the independent small family in mind. You were so sweet in arranging it for me, and chipping in with the instalments. But I left suddenly, and didn't so much as drop you a note to say what had happened, you must have thought...

SHEKHAR

Oh, that chapter – yes, I was puzzled, to say the least. I was also mad.

VANI

When I did get in touch six months later, it was after some aimless wandering to clear my head. But I gave you a cock and bull story about an unbearable allergy from some unknown corner of the designer flats.

SHEKHAR

Yes, I remember.

VANI

Ready for the truth, eleven years later?

SHEKHAR

Maybe. If it's not to rake up things.

VANI

No, only to clear up things. Here's what really happened. In the first month we were all excited over the split-level architecture. For two months we were ecstatic about the stylish plumbing. But in the third month I had to come to grips with the neighbours who peopled the colony – who, as you surely know, at least by now, were mostly single mothers like me – all settled comfortably in the smart interiors by well-meaning real estate developers in collaboration with conscientious ex-husbands. I ran away. Lata had to be saved, I told myself. I had to save myself too. Lata and me, both of us had to be saved. And so I ran – gutless, reckless, with nothing in my grasp except Lata's podgy little hand. Sweet, innocent Lata, with her illustrated Panchatantra tales. *(Pause)*

Well, I've got that out at last!

(Shekhar rises, moves to keep his glass away, returns to the table.)

Are you still mad? It was a long time ago.

SHEKHAR

I must go now.

VANI

Must you?

SHEKHAR

Yes, it is quite late.

VANI

When do we see you next?

SHEKHAR

Oh, by and by.

VANI

With news? Will we be the first?

SHEKHAR

Good night.

Shekhar leaves quickly. Vani looks after him a while, begins to clear up the remaining things, changes her mind, and decides to pour herself another drink. She then takes out a cigarette from anywhere but a cigarette pack, lights it, picks up her drink and walks over to the living area with a crossfade. She selects a cassette, puts it on, volume low, and settles down. After a while, Lata enters, notices Vani.

LATA

Hi, Mama. You are up still.

VANI

Yes, relaxing.

LATA

(Recognising the music) Ah, nice! You haven't played that in a long time.

Vani smiles. Lata takes her shoes to their place, takes down her hair, goes to Vani, and sits by her. They are close, warm.

VANI

Good birthday?

LATA

Mmm! Super. You were great, as always. You didn't have to wait up for me, Mama.

VANI

I didn't. It was just... I just wanted to sit down for a while. How come you are back so early?

LATA

Oh, everybody was tired. We didn't even go anywhere. Just parked next to the lake, sat on the stone steps for a while, chatting, and then suddenly Buzz says, 'What is this? If we are going to sit on our haunches all night, we might as well go home and do it in front of the TV.' So we all wound up. I guess we are getting old. *(She giggles)* Also, we had to drop Pat. *(Pause)* When did Daddy leave?

VANI

Oh, some time ago.

LATA

Mama, he was looking... is everything all right there?

VANI

How was he looking?

LATA

I don't know... he was different. I thought I'd hear him say, 'And how are we this birthday?'

VANI

You are right. He was different.

LATA

Is there something... ?

VANI

No, nothing to get worried. *(She smiles at Lata)* It is a phase you go through, I suppose. *(Lata is quiet.)* Daddy has been reading.

LATA

Reading what?

VANI

Daddy reads a lot. Too much, sometimes.

LATA

I know what you mean. He went through that when there was some small increase in his blood cholesterol.

VANI

He is now into divorce statistics, I think. Successes, failures, the social strata of those afflicted, problems in second marriages, splits down the line, and so on.

LATA

Down the line?

VANI

(Looking at her) You know, the probability of people with divorced parents having splits in their own marriage – that sort of thing.

LATA

He is worried about... *(Pause)*

VANI

He is worried about running out of things to worry about one day.

LATA

Mama...

VANI

I'm sorry. That was not nice. I don't know why I said it.

LATA

But you needed to say it. Isn't that so? *(Vani does not reply)*
Anyway, I know one thing about statistics and probabilities.

VANI

Oh?

LATA

All of it is quite true. That is, if things are run by nature, and nature alone. People forget that in most things happening in their lives, they have done some things themselves.

VANI

You mean increasing the chances of something happening.

LATA

Chance is not some mystery force. What they are looking at is not the creation of chance, but something in which they have had a hand too.

VANI

Like, if it's raining outside, that's nature I suppose. But getting wet and catching a flu cannot be nature's design.

LATA

It can't be. These things are in our control.

VANI

It's amazing how many things are actually in our control – little things, big things.

LATA

We must never stop being in control, taking control.

VANI

And it's possible to do that without being arrogant?

LATA

(Smiles) It should be. I know what you mean, Mama.

VANI

(Looks at her warmly) You are right, Lata. Maybe it is nature's design that we have control over events in our lives.

LATA

(Curling up on Vani's lap) And it is a great responsibility in control. We must control wisely. Mama, I'm going to lie down for a while.

VANI

(Strokes her) Good birthday?

LATA

Of course, Mama!

VANI

Goodbye eighteen.

LATA

Hello twenty.

VANI

What about tomorrow? Early breakfast?

LATA

No class first hour. *(Pause)* Mama, I want to tell you something.

VANI

Mmm?

LATA

It's about Vivek.

VANI

Uh... huh... tell me.

LATA

No, it's okay. I'll tell you tomorrow. *(She turns over, making herself comfortable on Vani's lap. Vani strokes her again.)*

You have such cute little hands.

VANI

(Picking up Lata's hand) You have long hands.

LATA

You have soft hands.

VANI

You have strong hands. *(They play lovingly with their hands)*

LATA

Rose petal hands.

VANI

Sunflower hands.

LATA

Labrador ear hands.

VANI

Umm... Cocker spaniel ear hands! *(They giggle)*

No, let me think... they are... no, they are one-of-a-kind hands – Lata hands.

Lata curls up more snugly. The hands continue to play for a while. Vani keeps Lata's hand down gently, takes a sip, and continues to stroke Lata softly to a slow fade out.

Close of play

Credit Titles

The Draft Blowing In
Vijay Padaki

From a storyline by ***Vinod Vyasulu***
The Hindu award for Best Contemporary Play Script, 1993

FOR
PEARL PADAMSEE

CHARACTERS IN THE PLAY

LEELA AND LALEE .... *Narrators*
PRABHAT KUMAR, RATNA KUMAR,
DR RAM KAPUR, MIRA AURORA .... *Four friends*
SWAMI ANANTANAND
VIJENDRA KUMAR
THE JUDGE

It will be evident that the narrators, Leela and Lalee, also play some of the supporting parts. All the Judges are best played by the same actor.

INTRODUCTION

Background

In the early nineties, India opened up its economy and joined the world economic order as a player, thus becoming a participant in the globalisation of trade. This meant conforming to global practices in Intellectual Property Rights. It also meant joining the World Trade Organization. Arthur Dunkel was the Director-General of *General Agreement on Tariffs and Trade* between 1980 and 1993. He compiled an international agreement about the scope of intellectual property rights and its procedures. It came to be called the 'Dunkel Draft'. The Draft was accepted and became the foundation of the World Trade Organization. The early nineties saw a great deal of debate on several issues arising from the Dunkel Draft. An important one was the ethical-legal question of patenting life forms. In other words, 'Who does life belong to?'

Professor Vinod Vyasulu and I were colleagues at the Indian Institute of Management (Bangalore) during its formative years. We have published work together combining development economics and the behavioural sciences. The play *Credit Titles* came out of a conversation around the Dunkel Draft. The conversation was part serious and part light-hearted. It was clear that a lot of the heated debate was driven by anger at having a rule book thrust on a nation. Most people had not actually read the Dunkel Draft. (Why does that sound familiar?) Professor Vyasulu suggested that since 'dunkel' in German meant 'darkness', it might well be that the poor countries in the world were dealing with a 'darkness draft'. They did not know what they were getting into and were perhaps being prevented from knowing what they were getting into! Very soon Professor Vyasulu had written it all up as a short story. He then asked me if I would like to make a play out of it, which I did. I shared the play script with a few close friends, including two in Chennai. One of them wrote back immediately and suggested that I should submit it to *The Hindu*, which had just then announced the (first) awards for contemporary play scripts. The friend even offered to submit the play script on my behalf. Months later, when all was forgotten, I received a phone call informing me that *Credit Titles* had won the award. Three scripts were given the award of Best Contemporary Play Scripts. The extraordinarily talented dramatist, Pearl Padamsee, was chairperson of the award jury. Later, in a meeting in Mumbai, she congratulated me for turning out a play that was ahead of its time in form and construction.

Performing the play

Credit Titles is, first and last, a play. It is a drama script. It is not a discourse, treatise, or academic statement on the subject of intellectual property rights or the Dunkel Draft. It is the conviction of the author that the power of a script to agitate minds lies only partly in its didactic content and largely in the playing of the script.

Following from the above, it would help if the performing group is sensitive to the dramatic elements of the script. Adherence to the given script is a necessity. It might be understandable if a word here or a phrase there was substituted because it proved difficult, but it would be unhelpful, even counterproductive, to attempt changes that amount to alterations in syntax, idiom, rhythm, structure, and so on.

There may, of course, be some change in the rhythm of the script if translated and performed in another language. However, an appreciation of the basic construction in the English language script should help.

In this version of the script, the vernacular interspersing the English language dialogue is Hindustani. Needless to say, this may be substituted by any other regional language.

The author and BLT would welcome feedback on *Credit Titles* whether or not it is actually performed. Likewise, the group in Bangalore would be happy to provide any additional information on the script or production suggestions if sought.

The running time of the play is about a hundred minutes. A straight run without any intermission is recommended. If there is to be an intermission, it is best taken at the end of Scene 5.

The play script suggests a minimalist set made up predominantly with stepladders of different heights. A round table serves multiple purposes in the Prabhat and Ratna home. An open-frame cubicle with a desk is the doctor's lab and office. Other scenes are created by movable props. The wicker basket for the baby is central to the design for the play. It is useful to have a large area of floor space for the rest of the action. The performing group may wish to explore other forms of minimalist design. The Bangalore production used a set of cubes very effectively to create different heights.

The play is a string of ten scenes. It is best performed, without interruptions for scene changes, as a seamless succession of scenes.

Language Notes

Taal: Beat, rhythmic pattern.
Paan: Betel leaf
Trichy: Tiruchirapally, South Indian city, famous for its cigars.
Teen paisa: Three-penny
Sutradhar: Narrator, stage manager in traditional drama.
Chup: Quiet
Peda, laddu: Sweets for festive occasions – traditionally peda was distributed on the birth of a baby boy.
Baaja: Loud music, instrument.
Achchi baat: Literally, good word – to mean okay, of course.
Bhijwa deejiye: Have it sent.
Tangri kabab: Kabab of tender leg (chicken kebab).
Farmaiyye aur Suniye: Request/ask and listen – from radio programme of listeners' requests.
Khansama: Master cook – from Raj establishments.
Kadamb: Tree under which Lord Krishna appears in legends.
Bhajan: Spiritual song.
Kaliyug: 'Age of Kali' is the last of the four ages (or eons) that the world goes through as described in the scriptures.
Lo – yeh bhi koi kehne ki baat hai: There! Is that an answer now?!
Ratnabehn: Behn – meaning sister, a suffix added to a name to suggest respect. (In case of male it is bhai, meaning brother)
Ji: Suffix or prefix added to a name to give respect. As in Swamiji, Ji haan (Yes sir/ma'am)
Raag durbari: A classical raga
SPICMACAY: A panIndia youth/student movement to promote the performing arts, active in many campuses.
Aram: Rest, leisure. Connotation – goofing off.
Haram: Illegitimacy. Connotation – sinful gain/product. Popular saying 'Aram haram hai' to mean laziness is illegitimate/sinful. Opposite of 'Work is Worship'
Buddhu: Fool, dope
Bhoosa: Hay (in the head)
Pooja: Ritual worship
Arati: Ritual with an oil lamp, followed by offering of flame to others. Refers both to the ritual and to the lamp.
Panchanga: Almanac
Prasad: Offering (sweet, fruit) to worshippers after the ritual

Passage in which Judge and Ram break into Hindustani

Farmaiye doctor Saheb ... aap ki seva mein?: Do tell, Doctor Saheb, how may I be of service?
Ghar mein sabki tabiyat... ?: The health of folks at home... ?
Bilkul theek thaak!: Everything is tickety-boo!
Sab log raah dekh rahey the... : Everyone was waiting for you...
Suna, bahut saare log aaye the. No taash session... : Heard a lot of people had come. No cards...
Haan haan, dekh letey hain: Yes-yes, we'll look into it, of course
Buss!: That's all!
Yeh DTT hota hai kya?: What is this DTT?
Haan Haan, zaroor ayenge ek din: Yes-yes, we'll certainly come one day
To yeh chamatkar hai aapki technology mein... : So, this is the miracle of your technology...
Aap toh jaantey hi hain... : You know of course...
Jalebi: Popular sweetmeat
Athreyesh Gotra, meena rashi: Referring to genealogical/astrological identification signs
Pranaam: To bow with folded hands in a gesture of deep respect
Doon School: Elite public school in Dehradun
Bonda: Fried snack made of lentils
Panchayat: Village council
Faltoo: Counterfeit, fraud – useless
Natak: Drama

FIRST PERFORMED

First performed at **The Hindu & Madras Players Theatre Festival**, Madras, October 1993

Leela .... NEHA SHARMA
Lalee .... DEEPAK THIMAYA
Prabhat .... VIJAY MUNDKUR
Ratna .... PRIYA GANAPATHY
Dr Ram Kapur .... SHIVAKUMAR BELAWADI
Mira Aurora .... MOHENA SINGH
Swami Anantanand .... AJITH SAMUEL
Judges .... PETER ISAAC
Vijendra .... PATHY AIYAR
Lighting design .... PRADEEP BELAWADI
Make up .... NANI
Costumes .... SUSHMA VEERAPPA
Property .... ABHAY RAO
Sets and stage .... MUSHTAQ, MITHRAN DEVANESEN
MADRAS PLAYERS

Designed and directed by .... PRAKASH BELAWADI

Performed at the **VP@80 Festival in Bangalore**, July 2019

Leela .... RASHMI VADAVI
Lalee .... GURUPRERANA SHABADI
Prabhat .... SANJEEV GADRE
Ratna .... BRINDA NAIR
Dr Ram Kapur .... NAVEEN TATER
Mira Aurora .... DIVYA KRISHNA
Swami Anantanand .... ANISH ABRAHAM
Judges .... SHAILESH RUDRA
Vijendra .... JAYADITYA PARAKH
Lighting .... MURTUZA KHETTY, S ABHISHEK
Make up .... MINTI JAIN
Sound .... MURTUZA KHETTY
Sets and stage .... ADITYE NAIR, S VENKATESH
Designed and directed by .... ARCHANA KARIAPPA & MURTUZA KHETTY

SCENE 1

When the play opens, the stage has an assortment of stepladders and stools of different sizes standing in a seemingly haphazard formation. At the top of the tallest stepladder is seated the Judge. Seated or standing midway, facing the Judge – at different levels, on the other stepladders – are the other principal characters in the play, Ram Kapur, Prabhat Kumar, Ratna Kumar, Mira Aurora, and Swamiji.

Downstage, corner, is a wicker basket or a baby's carry cot. Above it, seated on the floor, is Leela.

Silence. The Judge raises his gavel slowly, cautiously, and strikes once. All the characters on the stepladders come to life, speaking all together, to each other, to the Judge, building up to a noisy peak. The Judge strikes three times. Silence. The Judge clears his throat. So does Leela, coming out of a reverie.

LEELA

That's my cue. Stand by. We begin any second now.

The Judge raises his gavel slowly, cautiously again, and strikes once. All the characters resume their talking and arguing at full volume. The Judge strikes three times. Silence. He clears his throat twice. So does Leela.

LEELA

Second bell. Just a little patience. All good things come to those who count three – a very auspicious number – very neat. Like the story of the king with three daughters... or the three sparrows, or the three pigs, or the three Brahmins in the forest, or whatever. Put three lines on your forehead and see for yourself how much holier you feel. Why, until you stick three wooden rods into the ground it is not cricket. If you ask me...

The Judge clears his throat three times, loud, with a hint of a sideward glance at Leela. She stops abruptly, clears her throat three times in response, but manages an aside quickly.

LEELA

If you ask me, they make super rolling pins. Each one of those cricket stumps can give you three rolling pins.

The Judge raises his gavel once more and strikes. The characters burst into noisy jabber, louder than before. The Judge raps the gavel down several times. Silence.

LEELA

Nine. Three times three. That's a nice taal. Didida, didida, didiDAA! That's the way to do it. *(The Judge rises. So do the others, including Leela.)*

JUDGE

Court adjourned!

He steps down slowly, looking spent. The others remain in their places as he makes a circuitous exit, passing Leela. He stops at the baby basket, peers in, straightens, and speaks to the baby.

JUDGE

Court adjourned. Until further notice! Indefinitely!! *(He leaves quickly. So do all the others.)*

LEELA

End of epilogue. Epilogue. It used to be done – whenever done, which was not very often, I don't know why, when you think how elegant it looks in a programme, a nice firm statement after a lot of humdrum dialogue, coming just before the national anthem – it used to be done at the end of the play. We've changed all that. First, the epilogue. We can now get on with the play.

She leans back and claps three times. Lalee hurries in with a basket of props, stops before Leela, and bows in anticipation.

LEELA

Paan!

LALEE

Yes, dear. *(He produces an ornate casket, places it on a tray.)*

LEELA

Spittoon!

LALEE

Yes, dear. *(He produces one)*

LEELA

Hookah!

LALEE

Yes, dear. *(He fumbles, produces a box of cigars instead.)*

Uh... no hookah in any of the shops on Central Street. These will do, I hope. Fine Trichy make... *(She glares. He returns the box into the basket.)*

LEELA

Number three again. Did you get that? Every teen-paisa scriptwriter has got it too. Third time going, and bang! We'll try again. Coke!

LALEE

Yes, dear. *(He produces a silver snuff box. Leela takes a pinch into her nostrils and brightens up.)*

LEELA

Now... hookah!

LALEE

Yes, dear. *(He fumbles, produces the box of cigars.)* Uh... no hookah in any of the shops on Central Street. These will do, I hope. Fine Trichy make, packed in Havana, imported by Harrington India Ltd. through their principals in New York, Harrington Parks, Inc.

LEELA

Harrington Parks who?

LALEE

Knocking at the doors of Fortune 500.

LEELA

Is that enough?

LALEE

420.

LEELA

Much better. You have what it takes to make a good understudy Assistant Stage Manager one day. Pack up!

LALEE

Yes, dear. Thanks, dear. *(He begins to clear up)*

LEELA

(Rising) You know who this is, don't you? The simple and innocent, but witty and pretty, tag-along to the narrator.

The narrator, stage manager, sutradhar, commentator, chorus, interpreter, animator, facilitator, initiator, guide, philosopher, friend, whatever. A nice part, the sutradhar. Always played by a male. A severe looking male, with a simple-innocent-witty-pretty tag-along female. We've changed all that, of course. For generations upon generations, since god knows how long, we were looking at things standing on our heads, it seems.

(She snaps instructions to Lalee) Strike scene 1! Set 2!

LALEE

The epilogue is over?

LEELA

How sweet! The epilogue is over? How can we get to the last scene unless the epilogue is over? And how can the epilogue get over unless we change the scenery and set it for the last scene?

LALEE

The baby – it is not in my checklist. Do you... do you think I should...

LEELA

Don't!

LALEE

Yes, dear. Then... will you... will you just...

LEELA

I won't! Abandon the baby, that is, if that is the thought entering the hollow expanse of your mind. If it is – the thought entering your mind, that is – then put it right out. *(He stares at her in awe)* Out!

LALEE

Yes, dear. Right away. It's out, dear.

LEELA

Abandon a baby! *(Peering into the crib)* Look at him, look at the shweetie-pootie smile curling on his pinky-winky lips. Oh, you shweetie-pootie darling baby. How can anybody abandon this sweet, innocent, helpless little babe just like that?

LALEE

He is eighteen years old.

LEELA

He is not!

LALEE

He has hair on his upper lip.

LEELA

He has not! Oh, you dumbo! You've got it all mixed up again. That comes only in Act III.

LALEE

But the judge... he was just...

LEELA

Yes?

LALEE

He was just...

LEELA

Playing his part. When in doubt, put it off! Or close shop for vacation. That's the first law they are taught in law school, you know. It says, 'Never put off till tomorrow what you can put off till the day after tomorrow.'

LALEE

Yes, yes, but the baby – what do we do with the baby? It is not on my checklist!

LEELA

We are left holding it.

LALEE

Precisely!

LEELA

The classic plot. High-and-mighty folks. High-and-mighty complex lives. Enter baby. High-and-mighty troubled by troublesome baby. High-and-mighty solution. Exit baby. Wicker basket to the woodcutter, wicker basket into the river, etcetera, etcetera, etcetera.

LALEE

Baby saved by low and humble woodcutter, shepherd, wandering minstrel...

LEELA

Low and humble sutradhar.

LALEE

Etcetera.

LEELA

And the tag-along assistant who does not have a baby in a wicker basket on the checklist.

LALEE

Definitely not on this checklist.

LEELA

We are left holding it. *(Pause. They look at each other.)*

LALEE

(Breaking into song) Why keep the audience waiting? Why keep their dentures grating?

LEELA

(Joining) The lights were dimmed so long ago

LALEE

The latecomers are waddling in... Elbowing in and trampling in

LEELA

We still have such a long way to go

BOTH

We still have a long way to go!

LEELA

Right! Have you got the rest of the stage all set? Well, get on with it!

LALEE

Yes, dear. Same as yesterday?

LEELA

The same as yesterday.

LALEE

No changes?

LEELA

No changes.

LALEE

No changes at all? Are you sure? Eternally fixed, day after day, night after night?

LEELA

Till the sun rises in the west.

LALEE

You think that might happen sometime soon? This week? *(No response)* Before you and I... ?

LEELA

There is a slight chance.

LALEE

I knew it, I knew it!

LEELA

Of course, you did! You've heard it before. Night after night.

LALEE

But it's marvellous to hear you saying it – the way you say it. It is like a new daybreak. Every night a new daybreak, with no two daybreaks the same.

LEELA

(From the song, a reminder) But we still have a long way to go!

LALEE

Yes, dear. I understand, dear.

By now Lalee has rearranged the stepladders and props on stage to form the different acting areas for the play.

LEELA

(The storyteller now) It was the age of dazzling white darkness. When the sun rose on the eastern horizon – as had been his custom since his birth countless years ago – he saw all the peoples of the earth turned west.

Puzzled and angered, the sun heaved himself across the sky to the other side to catch their attention. For if he had not their attention, how could he counsel them, as he had counselled their forefathers and their forefathers' forefathers? But no, they had turned eastward again. They had turned their backs on him. He was there, and yet not there. His was the everlasting gift of warm cheer, but the cold around him seemed impregnable.

LALEE

Etcetera, etcetera, it's all been said before. Night after night, play after play. But the best line comes now.

LEELA

(Continuing) Worst of all, from any position he took in the sky, through the day, the sun could see all around him only a vast expanse of darkness. But when his day was done, and it was night again, the peoples of the earth were enveloped, horizon to horizon, by an immense shroud of pure white light.

LALEE

Dazzling white.

LEELA

Blinding white light.

LALEE

(Singing) It was the new age dawning
The night turned into morning

LEELA

(Joining) The stars declared an indefinite go slow
The rainshowers going upwards
The beanstalks boring inwards

LEELA

We still have such a long way to go

BOTH

We still have a long way to go!

LALEE

(Trying to impress) The darkness of noon!

LEELA

(Not approving) Uh-huh.

LALEE

(Trying again) The dark is white enough...

LEELA

(Stronger) Uh-huh.

LALEE

(Feebly) The candle at the end of the tunnel?

LEELA

Third time lucky. Something original at last!

LALEE

Thanks dear. Will that do for the curtain raiser?

LEELA

It had better. We still have a long way to go...

LALEE

What about the improvisations? The impromptu spoofs on political goings on?

LEELA

You mean the comic philosophy to preface the philosophic comedy?

LALEE

You put it so well, as always.

LEELA

You know we've changed all that! No improvisations, no spoofs. No ad-libbing, no goofs. Is that clear now?

LALEE

Clear as candlelight, dear.

LEELA

The subject is... darkness. From Old English deorcnys.

LALEE

Latin root, tenebrae. Old High German, tarnjan.

LEELA

In Sanskrit, tamas.

LALEE

Obscurite' in French.

LEELA

Esperanto, Mallumo

LALEE

Dunkel in German.

LEELA

Pronounced Doonkel.

LALEE

In German, yes, Doonkel – but popularly called Dunkel, as in Dunkin' Donuts.

LEELA

The subject is darkness, and the play is titled...

LALEE

Why don't we call it 'The Black Box?' *(Leela glares)* or 'The Dark Pandora?' *(Leela is not pleased)* I'll tell you what – we could call it 'The Darkness Package'.

LEELA

I told you – no politics for us! The writer of the play has chosen to title it 'Credit Titles' and 'Credit Titles' it shall be. Now, get on with your own job.

LALEE

(Aside) It is quite an ordinary script really.

LEELA

That is not for us to worry our heads about.

LALEE

Not a patch on what we have put on in the past. On these very boards.

LEELA

To every froggy his own little well. We simply get on with the job given us.

LALEE

And the cleverness with which they pad up the hollowness. Did you look into the programme? It says the playwright drew inspiration from conversations with the renowned economist, Professor Vinod Vyasulu.

LEELA

Halt! *(He does)* Now, get your wobbly wheel back on the rails. Right! No more diversions now. Ready? Set? Steady now – go!

LALEE

CREDIT TITLES. When the play opens, the stage has on it an assortment of stepladders and stools in apparent disarray. We discover soon that the stage comprises several action areas cleverly arranged by the stage hand in the opener epilogue – the home of Mr and Mrs Prabhat Kumar, the clinic of Dr Ram Kapur, the workplace of Ms Mira Aurora, the counselling and prayer centre of Swami Anantanand, the public places for smaller private meetings, not forgetting the public meetings in the courtrooms of several Justices of Law, small and great.

LEELA

It is the year 1993. That is as good as today. India, that is Bharat, that is Hindustan, the land which gave us the poetic tale of the elephant's form...

LALEE

And many more tales of many more beasts in many jungles.

LEELA

This ancient land, in its quest for a modern state, has after much debate and discussion within its populace agreed to be a participant in a new international order, and has thus agreed to be party to a new international treaty.

LALEE

A new treaty on...

LEELA

A new treaty on... how does it matter? It was an international treaty!

LALEE

But while the heads of state of hundreds of nations might have gathered in New York or Geneva or on the silvery beaches of Mauritius to pore over the fine print of countless drafts before the grand signature ceremony on the final document, what did it all mean to the tinkers and tailors dotting the countryside?

LEELA

Or the doctors, salesmen, housewives, and office secretaries going about their everyday routines?

Prabhat Kumar, his wife Ratna, Dr Ram Kapur, and Mira Aurora have appeared on stage. They are led by Lalee and Leela and seated at a round table.

LALEE

I think they can take it from here. So I'll slip out to look into a few things myself.

(He leaves)

SCENE 2

Prabhat Kumar, his wife, Ratna, Mira Aurora, and Dr Ram Kapur are a foursome at a card table. Leela, now the maid, wheels in a service trolley with tea for all, positions it above Ratna and waits. The game is proceeding slowly, silently, with the players completely absorbed in their own hands. They drop or pick up cards, one by one, without talking. After a while, Leela speaks.

LEELA

End of scene! That will be all. Thank you, ladies and gentlemen.

The three of them pack up and exit. Ratna remains.

Lovely little scene, what? No noise, no fuss, no speechifying. They don't speak, you see, because they don't know what to say. All that could be said has been said so many times over the years. And yet, they can't stop thinking about it, can they? That's the noble, indestructible quality of the human spirit. The thought must go on.

So, when the four friends meet nowadays, and they find themselves gravitating to the card table, it is a good sign that the undercurrent is active. It continues even after the guests depart. Scene change!

Ratna is alone at the card table playing solitaire. Leela stands above her at the service trolley. Presently Prabhat enters and joins Ratna at the table.

PRABHAT

The good doctor has agreed. He thinks it should be possible.

RATNA

That will be all, Leelamma.

LEELA

Sir, having tea?

PRABHAT

Yes, Leelamma. Is there enough?

LEELA

Yes, Sir, plenty. I make?

RATNA

I'll do that. You can go now, Leelamma. There's nothing more for you here.

LEELA

No problem, Amma. All work over. I wait Sir finishing tea.

PRABHAT

Amma and I want to discuss something, Leelamma.

LEELA

Oh, no disturb! I stand chup here, you and Amma talk. No problem.

RATNA

Leelamma!

LEELA

Right, right, Amma. I go. *(She moves reluctantly)*
You call when you finish discuss. *(Exit)*

PRABHAT

(As he gathers cards, shuffles, and deals) He said he wondered why we hadn't thought about it before – why we did not bring it up with him. After all, we are not the only childless couple in this...

RATNA

We are not childless! Did you tell him we were childless?

PRABHAT

Well, I don't remember the exact words I used, but he did see we have no children.

RATNA

But it's different.

PRABHAT

What's different? There is no child in this house. No pit-pat footsteps, no line of nappies on the clothes line, no crayon artwork on the walls. That's what Ram Kapur knows.

RATNA

But, for that you don't say we are childless.

PRABHAT

You don't like the word...

RATNA

It somehow... it sounds too final somehow.

PRABHAT

Maybe you're right. There is no evidence for either of us that we cannot produce a baby.

RATNA

It might have remained hidden somewhere.

PRABHAT

(Kisses her to restore cheer) You and I might actually have produced several babies, huh? Without each other's knowledge?

RATNA

Oh, you men! Anyway, tell me more about what Ram said.

PRABHAT

First, he said congratulations!

RATNA

As if the good news...

PRABHAT

Yes, he said it was as good as done.

RATNA

Just like that?

PRABHAT

Just like that. This is not the nineteenth century, you know, he said, when people thought babies came only from boy meeting girl.

RATNA

And he had a dozen test tubes in his fridge, I suppose, to show what he was talking about.

PRABHAT

He actually showed me a so-called test tube as part of the lecture.

RATNA

I wish I hadn't stayed back. I wish I had come along.

PRABHAT

Yes, you could have gazed into the bubble and sighed, 'you've come a long way, baby'.

RATNA

What else? What else did he say?

PRABHAT

He asked if we want to distribute pedas or laddus?

RATNA

You mean... ?

PRABHAT

Yes. You can choose right at the start. Boy or girl, what'll it be?

RATNA

Why, I suppose... but go on with what he had to say. What about...

PRABHAT

No, tell me what you have in mind first. Boy or girl?

RATNA

Well, a boy I suppose. What about you?

PRABHAT

Just one?

RATNA

One will do, thank you. And you?

PRABHAT

If it's two for one, it must be one for two.

RATNA

A boy?

PRABHAT

'A boy for you and a... boy for me! Can't you see, how happy... '

RATNA

Fine. The band-baaja can wait for a while. What about – you know – the procedure?

PRABHAT

Procedure!

RATNA

Will it be some kind of operation? Hospitalisation?

PRABHAT

No idea. We'll get to know soon enough. *(They are gradually slipping into a card game.)*

RATNA

We are not forgetting something, are we?

PRABHAT

Like?

RATNA

The cost. How much will all this cost?

PRABHAT

Oh, the cost...

RATNA

Whatever happens we are not giving up the flat that daddy has booked in my name.

PRABHAT

It shouldn't be necessary.

RATNA

Don't these operations cost the earth?

PRABHAT

Ram is no ordinary garage-wallah doctor. He is a big name. And he is our friend. He has a huge research grant for this kind of work. He says he will take care of everything.

RATNA

That's awfully sweet of him, but it is not...

PRABHAT

It is not everybody who has the chance of producing a made-to-order baby.

RATNA

A-la-carte?

PRABHAT

More than that. You can order anything you like outside the standard menu.

RATNA

A test-tube special, I suppose.

PRABHAT

A designer test-tube special.

(They are now both absorbed in their cards. They speak over their hands.)

RATNA

Sex

PRABHAT

Check

RATNA

Date

PRABHAT

Check

RATNA

Colour

PRABHAT

Check

RATNA

Zodiac

PRABHAT

Check

RATNA

Kindergarten

PRABHAT

Check

RATNA

School

PRABHAT

Public

RATNA

College

PRABHAT

Private.

SCENE 3

The clinic of Dr Ram Kapur. Lalee, in a white duty coat, is seated at Ram's desk, talking into the phone.

LALEE

Yes ma'am... yes ma'am... no ma'am... not at all, ma'am... you can take it confirmed, ma'am... he knows, ma'am. It is in his diary. 1994 January 15, 3:00 pm... What? You want to cancel... Fresh date, ma'am? Well... no ma'am, not possible. Next two months fully booked. No Sunday, no holiday, no lunch break... Amsterdam, ma'am... No, no, no. Zurich before Amsterdam ma'am. Bangkok after Amsterdam. After that, full time in research project ma'am...

Why I am talking like this? *(Change of tone)*

Because I have to introduce the scene in Dr Ram Kapur's clinic. And this is what I have been told to do. Opener – thirty seconds chatter on telephone by Lalluram! *(He hangs up, rises, and begins to address the audience)*

Actually, this was the only way... *(The phone rings. He picks it up.)*

DTT Foundation, Dr Kapur's office... Yes sir, no sir, 1994, sir... From the North Pole, sir. *(Hangs up)*

One little chance is all we stage hands... *(The phone rings. He picks it up.)* DTT Foundation, Dr baby corn soup what?... Lunch appointment... Please hold on.

(Opens diary) 1994, January... Club sandwich what? Today 1:30 pm? Impossible! Sorry, tender chicken, wender chicken, no go. Earliest appointment is... ohh, Kamal Katering? Okay, okay... Hello, how are you sir?... Today? Achchi baat, fine. Bhijwa deejiye.

He hangs up, watches the phone for a few seconds, and clears his throat to address the audience. The voices of Ram, Ratna, and Prabhat are heard off-stage. Lalee curses under his breath, hurriedly takes off the duty coat, drapes it on a hanger, fetches his own apron and cap, puts them on, and takes his place. The group enters.

RAM

That's all there is to it, really.

RATNA

Interesting. Very interesting.

PRABHAT

So, the fact that we have not succeeded so far does not mean...

RAM

That will be all, Lalluram.

LALEE

Thank you, Sir. *(He does not move)*

RAM

Lalluram...

LALEE

Sir!

RAM

Go now. Carry your filing work out there. Wait there. *(Lalee begins to leave reluctantly)* Oh, yes, I've ordered some lunch for us here from Kamal Katering...

LALEE

Yes, Sir. Baby corn soup, tender chicken tangri kabab, club sandwich, cold coffee. 1:30 pm sharp.

RAM

Thank you. *(He waits. Lalee leaves. To the others)*

Like a mule in the army – stubborn but indispensable. Sorry, we were talking about...

PRABHAT

Our past attempts... does it mean... ?

RAM

What I said earlier. A couple can be childless... *(looking at Ratna)* I know it is an unfriendly sort of word – a couple might not have had a child for a dozen different reasons.

PRABHAT

Well, we put it off in the beginning because of... you know...

RAM

And then when you thought you were ready for it...

RATNA

We thought we were ready for it. How were we to know... ?

PRABHAT

How little we knew!

RAM

Actually, it is a good thing you did not have your child early. Even after you decided that you were ready for it.

PRABHAT

You mean...

RAM

Look at what you would have missed – the options you have now that were unknown even five years ago.

RATNA

Are you sure we can actually...

RAM

Of course!

PRABHAT

Ratna, you saw the test results yourself.

RAM

I don't mean just the basics. The tests merely confirmed your production capacity, so to speak... the basic raw material availability, from both parties, the plant, the machinery, the process control facilities, and so on.

PRABHAT

We did think earlier it was a machinery snag.

RAM

A snag once upon a time. It's the easiest thing today to pull out a dot from here, a dash from there, put them together in a drop of pea soup, you know, get them going – one-two-four-eight-sixteen, zoom! Then at the right time, just tuck it snugly in place in mama's secret little hiding place. Do not disturb. Open after 270 days.

RATNA

Is there nothing for us to do here? The parents?

RAM

Well, you are the promoters of the enterprise. You are the ones who get it going.

RATNA

Commission the plant, sit back, and watch the profits rolling in!

PRABHAT

(To Ratna) Depends on the product.

RAM

It depends on the product-mix. And that's the big difference between the run-of-the-mill test-tube baby of last year's design and what is possible today.

PRABHAT

Like choosing the sex of the baby.

RAM

More than that.

PRABHAT

Height? Weight?

RAM

More than that.

RATNA

You mean, like colour complexion.

RAM

More, much more. *(Pause. Ratna and Prabhat look at each other.)* Go ahead, try us. *(Opens a scribble pad, pen at the ready.)*

PRABHAT

You mean...

RAM

Go ahead.

PRABHAT

Intelligence...

RAM

Check.

PRABHAT

Aptitude for...

RAM

Check.

RATNA

Voice.

RAM

Check.

PRABHAT

Wah! That's a true designer baby.

RAM

We'll even give it a logo birthmark – pigmentation jugglery is among the simpler tricks.

RATNA

Ram...

RAM

Wait. Let me show you the computer programme we have developed for optimising the product-mix decision. *(He takes out, very carefully, a small disc from a pack within a pack within a pack, and places it on a specially produced plate on the table, covering it immediately with a glass bowl-like cover.)*

Do you see this?

RATNA

It looks like...

PRABHAT

It looks like a carrom board striker.

RAM

And what a striker! This little disc contains – well, to put it in simple English – it contains the mathematical translation of instructions to mix and match hundreds of options from each of dozens of bio-manifest variables – you know, morphology, neurochemistry, hormonal imprints, and so on and so forth – giving you about twelve and a half million permutated variants.

PRABHAT

It's all there, in that?

RAM

In the outer half. At the core is the real masala of the system! When connected to the DNA accelerator unit via the GPlasma interceptor, it automatically takes over the processing of all the chosen critical variables in the starting zygotic substance.

RATNA

How... how far have you come in your project with this... baby designer?

RAM

The first pilot project had a target of six prototypes. They were all – you might have guessed – Bingo! Perfect models. Zero error.

RATNA

And they are all...

RAM

Alive and kicking. Perfectly normal, and growing beautifully. But Phase I, if you remember, was the simple programme, producing perfect prototypes, but with quite ordinary characteristics. That's why it was code named Project TDH – for Tom, Dick, and Harry.

PRABHAT

Has the advanced programme been tried out after that?

RAM

That was Phase II. Concluded last November. Six more prototypes, with random combinatorial patterns from the full range of variables in the programme.

RATNA

You mean...

PRABHAT

There are actually six babies somewhere with fully programmed features?

RAM

(Smiling) Well, yes and no. *(Now the scientific mystique at full)*

Six perfect specimens, as per design specifications to the nth detail. But... specimens programmed to switch off, the moment they reached full-term stature and were delivered, so that we may subject them to the strictest analytical tests for total process control. *(Pause. Ratna and Prabhat look at each other.)*

No, they were not stillborn... because they did not die in the conventional sense – certainly not in the mother's womb. You see, the creation of optimal uterine conditions was already perfected in Phase I. In the second phase, we were concentrating on the prediction and control of person specific characteristics in the mix and match programme. So, the entire experiment was carried out in volunteer mothers, carefully selected for the project – that is, having a willingness to serve the cause of scientific progress, but without any interest in having the end product for themselves. Their identities will be kept strictly confidential forever.

PRABHAT

And you are now perfectly ready? *(Ram smiles)* This technique – method – whatever it's called... is it perfect?

RAM

Definitely state of the art. You will be surprised how far ahead we are in this field. And how many envious labs there are all over the world! *(Pause.)*

PRABHAT

Where do we begin?

RAM

Ask and ye shall be given.

PRABHAT

(Looks at Ratna) What do you say? You had something in mind, didn't you?

RATNA

(Beginning cautiously) Well, we could begin with intelligence, I suppose.

RAM

Of course! As good a point as any to begin. Wait. I'll put it down straightaway... I-F – 12 – Crossover 21-D... What sort of level have you thought of?

RATNA

Do you think an IQ of...

PRABHAT

Is 160 in order?

RATNA

Prabhat's mother and grandmother were both...

RAM

Why not? One-six-zero – variance factor 3 – two generations pater-maternal – additive factor A-T 36. Next.

RATNA

He must be musical, Ram. I can't think of a tone-deaf son in my house.

RAM

Shoot! Farmaiyye aur suniye.

PRABHAT

(Producing a sheet of paper) Actually, we've had a discussion about this, and... here, we have tried to put down some things as they...

RAM

Give me that sheet! Let's see now *(He busies himself)* Father... violin... Paganini. *(Business of entries)* What's this about cricket?

PRABHAT

All-rounder, but basically a pace bowler.

RAM

Say... 95 mph... Imran Khan...

PRABHAT

Blossoming in high school, you know, like Tendulkar, no problem about college studies, admissions, job hunting... *(Ratna has withdrawn.)*

RAM

Counter-current measures – P-L 240 throughput – P-Q 110 – diabetes in mater-fraternal quadrant ... premature greying zero-point-three -four-two...

PRABHAT

Actually, Ratna was thinking of dark brown – dark reddish brown hair.

RAM

Like prefab henna...

PRABHAT

What do you say, Ratna?

RATNA

Excuse me.

PRABHAT

Yes, darling. You were going to...

RATNA

Excuse me. I was thinking... I just remembered I have to attend to something. You two carry on, just go ahead.

She leaves hurriedly. Prabhat looks after her. Ram is completely absorbed in the programming.

PRABHAT

(To Ram) Do you want to continue now? Or shall we...

RAM

Next, next!

PRABHAT

(Looking into the paper) How far have we come? Ah, here, something more on sporting qualities.

RAM

Legs long – supple – endurance factor...

Lalee bursts into the room pushing the service trolley.

LALEE

Tangri kabab – tender legs of chicken, marinated in rare herbal sauce kept secret by only surviving branch of a vanishing North-West Frontier khansama family. Baby corn chicken soup – aperitif of the season, with the personal compliments of the chef. Club sandwich Oxbridge – from the recipe book of Alistair Peabody, esquire, grandfather of Jonathan Alistair Peabody, first caretaker of the Royal Bengal Cricket Club in Calcutta. East-West Salad bazaar, courtesy...

SCENE 4

The outer chamber of Swami Anantanand. The inner chamber, unseen, is behind a simple cloth partition. When the scene opens, a woman (Leela) is seated with her back to the audience, facing the Swamiji.

SWAMIJI

And what do you hope to derive from conceiving a son of your own, my child?

WOMAN

The joy of motherhood!

SWAMIJI

And... ?

WOMAN

And all the joys that follow the first joy of motherhood.

SWAMIJI

But these joys are momentary – a minute, an hour, a whole year – still momentary. They come abruptly, they disappear as abruptly. Are you sure that is the state of joy you desire – on, off, on, off, so like the electric lights in your home in Bangalore city?

WOMAN

Yes, I do. I would be an incomplete woman otherwise.

SWAMIJI

What if you were to be shown the way to a more enduring joy, transcending the baser gratifications from mere motherhood?

WOMAN

Is it possible? Is there such a state of joy?

SWAMIJI

Motherhood is but a small corner in the expansive sky that is womanhood. The joy of womanhood is infinite, eternal. It is the most precious, sublime gift to a woman – a truly divine gift. Foolish man, absorbed in selfish pursuits in his fleeting passage on this earth, is blind to the divine gift conferred on his mate. He suppresses her capacity for infinite and unending joy for his own selfish ends – his short-sighted ends.

WOMAN

Yes, yes. It is like that! You are truly the all-knowing swami, the saviour of lost souls... my saviour... *(Pause.)*

SWAMIJI

Are you a seeker?

WOMAN

(Slipping into a trance) Yes.

SWAMIJI

Are you a believer?

WOMAN

Yes.

SWAMIJI

A believing seeker?

WOMAN

Yes.

SWAMIJI

A seeking traveller? *(She nods)* A traveller in search of the divine truth? Divine joy? Then rise... *(She does, slowly)* Stretch out your arms. Open your heart... open your mind... open yourself completely to receive that which you have sought with such resolution... Let the knowledge of eternal joy come to you from all directions... *(He starts to lead her inside. There is an agitated voice outside.)*

RATNA

(Off) Swamiji! Swamiji! My lord, Swami Paramanand Mokshanand Anantanandji!

SWAMIJI

(Restrained annoyance) Who dares to disturb me in my hour of meditation?

RATNA

It is me, your holiness. It is I, Ratna, your ever-indebted disciple.

SWAMIJI

You wish an audience? It is a Tuesday. Your time is on Thursdays.

RATNA

I must see you, Swamiji.

SWAMIJI

Hmm. Commence your invocation immediately, at the very spot at which you stand. You will receive my call presently. *(He conducts the woman into the inner chamber, draws the partition to close again.)*

It never rains, but pours. Enter, my child.

RATNA

(Entering) Swamiji, a miracle! I am going to have a baby! *(She prostrates herself before him.)*

SWAMIJI

(Unable to conceal surprise) A baby – it can't be! Rise woman... *(Controlling himself)* ... woman of celestial design, model of womanhood sent to earth... rise my child. *(She does.)*

Now, tell me about the events surrounding your mortal incarnation in the five days since we last... since your last holy communion.

RATNA

It is true. I am going to have a baby.

SWAMIJI

You are... are you certain?

RATNA

As certain as the sun rising in the east.

SWAMIJI

Is that certain, my child?

RATNA

As certain as the flight of the shiny brown striker on the carrom board.

SWAMIJI

That does merit serious consideration. Yet...

RATNA

As certain as the aching anticipation in my breasts to suckle the infant god descending upon my household.

SWAMIJI

Certainty appears in our lives diversely manifest.

RATNA

It is as you predicted, my lord. To close one's mortal eyes is to open one's mind. To drive out the fears of earthly motherhood is to take in the joys of divine womanhood. It is proved right. It has been proved in my life.

SWAMIJI

So... you are with child.

RATNA

(Slipping into a trance) He comes! At first, I thought it was a shadow, the stretching lines at dusk playing tricks on my senses. Then I saw him clearly. The backyard tamarind tree, withered and barren, transformed into a luxuriant canopy of kadamb. There was a rainbow of fluttering wings as hundreds of birds chorused a welcome song. And the cows, the calves, and the music in their bells. Over them, the purest notes of a cowherd's flute, full-bodied in tone in the humid air after an evening shower. He

stood still at first, shining grey blue figure that I had always pictured him to be. And then...

SWAMIJI

Ratna, my child, my gem, you must...

RATNA

(Continuing) And then he broke into his dance. The lord of the dance had chosen to appear before me. It was exquisite. The sweet call of the bamboo reed flitted all around me – here a moment, there the next instant. And whichever direction I turned, in ecstatic wonder, I would see the flute first, dangling mischievously in midair, and then there would appear the figure behind the flute – first the smile, then the face, and then the rest of his form.

SWAMIJI

My child, you must get a hold on yourself. What has happened? Ratna, my gem...

RATNA

(Continuing) Through the dance he changed – he became younger, smaller, more radiantly beautiful... there was a long concluding note, held for a count of ten or so. And there, before me, was the infant god, the dark god in infant form, the most serenely peaceful smile on his face that seemed to be saying...

SWAMIJI

You have been hallucinating! Ratna, my child, listen...

RATNA

Ratna, my gem, you said. Nothing less than a gem for Ratna, you said. Patience – faith, submission and patience – oh, how grateful I am for your instruction in patient submission. It is now confirmed. He shall be the gem I have waited for.

SWAMIJI

You believe it will be a boy child?

RATNA

Of course! Dr Kapur has it all down to the last detail.

SWAMIJI

Dr Kapur?

RATNA

Down to the dimple on the belly button.

SWAMIJI

You are not, by any chance, on some drugs?

RATNA

Swamiji! You know me...

SWAMIJI

Not, by any chance, been persuaded into – what do they call it – a second opinion?

RATNA

A second... ?

SWAMIJI

For instance, that despicable quack, the self-proclaimed yogi, the so-called Atmanand in Kailashnagar?

RATNA

(Prostrating again) Swamiji!

SWAMIJI

(Regarding her seriously) Then it must be true. You are indeed possessed. Two whole years of effort wasted! The purification of your fluid life force was making such good progress – all upset now. Soiled, contaminated.

RATNA

(Rising, puzzled) Swamiji, my lord Swamiji, Dr Ram Kapur is a renowned medical professional. He is currently...

SWAMIJI

Dr Kapur! Dr Kapur!!

RATNA

You must know about him.

SWAMIJI

And he has confirmed your pregnancy?

RATNA

(Only slightly embarrassed) Not quite. Not quite yet.

SWAMIJI

Not quite... ?

RATNA

Well, the tests are all done, and everything is – what do they call it – all systems go. He will now perform the actual insertion.

SWAMIJI

When the world is stood on its head, it is indeed the Kaliyug as prophesied!

RATNA

It comes at last. I am fully prepared. Dr Kapur will not fail us.

SWAMIJI

Woman, you know not what you utter in your state of possession. You say this doctor of a certain reputation is now going to give you a child?

RATNA

From a shiny little disk this small, that holds twelve-and-a-half-million bits of heads and tails.

SWAMIJI

And you are telling me, here, to my face, that you have permitted this good doctor with that sort of reputation to take you away from home and hearth and...

RATNA

Oh, Prabhat is all for it! In fact, he was the one who quietly fixed it all up.

SWAMIJI

All in five days! It is all over in the cosmic sigh of five sunsets. A culmination of two years of patient searching.

RATNA

Exactly, Swamiji. Your wisdom is boundless. You taught me patience. You taught me perseverance. Without your steadying hand, I might never have found my way to Dr Ram Kapur.

SWAMIJI

This Dr Ram Kapur, how does he – if you will pardon the curiosity of a spiritual seeker – what manner – what method does he choose to employ for the professed goal of presenting you – you and Prabhatji – with an heir?

RATNA

(Girlish excitement now) It is the most fascinating technique ever. It is frightfully sophisticated, but oh so beautifully simplified. You can't imagine the array of gadgets and instruments involved. Very complex functions, very, very complex manoeuvres. Yet, the whole thing is designed to go like a shot, almost effortless to the onlooker. And do you know why I simply had to see you today, Swamiji?

SWAMIJI

Enlighten me some more.

RATNA

To take your blessings back with me for the great occasion – the greatest moment in my life. I am going to mother Dr Ram Kapur's first Designer Test-Tube baby. It is a historic moment for all of us.

SWAMIJI

Psychopath! Sociopath!! Allopath!!! It shall not be. Do not delude yourself, woman. Do not destroy yourself. It is desecration of the temple. An unholy intrusion. A designer baby goes against the grain of mother nature. It is against the will of god. It is a defilement of the most sacred gift of god to woman. You invite damnation and ruination upon yourself and your family. The curse of the mother of the universe will strike five generations of your descendants – if you have any progeny at all – with the harm you inflict upon yourself.

A pair of bhajan cymbals begins a rhythmic beat in the inner chamber. Swamiji, red-faced, glares at Ratna. She is confused, controlling her tears. The woman's voice behind the curtain begins a bhajan, 'I wait in patience, oh Lord. How long do you keep me in this wretched state?'

RATNA

Swamiji, my lord swami, please tell me... your blessings, I beg you... I wish only to hear it from your lips that it is...

SWAMIJI

It is against the will of god! No man or woman on earth can tread long on the path that goes against his will! *(Ratna rushes out)*

Rapid fade out

The sound of the cymbals and bhajan continues through a stanza in the dark. It is cut abruptly by Swamiji's roar.

SWAMIJI

And you! Will Dr Ram Kapur have a cure for your weekly migraine?!

SCENE 5

The lights are held low to reveal the foursome at the card table in the Prabhat Kumar home. Leela stands above Ratna as in Scene 2. The players pick up or drop cards one by one without talking. After a while, Leela steps down to speak to the audience.

LEELA

Back to the drawing board, as they say. It was not half as traumatic as the playwright had expected it to be. Ratna went home, fixed Prabhat's dinner, popped a Calmpose into her mouth, scribbled a note for Prabhat on the dining table, and went up to bed. Prabhat, returning just a little later than usual, at a quarter past eight, read the note, 'Man proposes, God disposes'. He shrugged, and then proceeded to serve himself his instant dinner from the kitchen platform. Dr Ram Kapur, when he heard about the couple's second thoughts the next day – yes, they expressed their reservations to him – Dr Kapur merely changed the topic and enquired of them if they had seen the latest film on the video circuit on the goings on in an all-woman prison in a breakaway East European republic. Their dearest friend, Mira Aurora, brought over a picnic hamper, helped clear the dishes, and took them out to spend the afternoon in the crafts bazaar. Swamiji enquired discreetly over the telephone if Ratna's Thursday engagements were to be held or terminated. Of course, they would continue, she said. Nothing had changed. Life went on as always, she said.

Leela steps aside to allow the scene to proceed. The lights brighten. The scene continues with the desultory but silent picking and dropping of cards. Leela shrugs. She begins to wheel the service trolley out.

LEELA

It might be best if I left the group to themselves for a while.

She leaves. The scene picks up gradually.

MIRA

So?

RATNA

No.

PRABHAT

No?

RATNA

No go.

RAM

Lo – yeh bhi koi kehne ki baat hai? *(Pause)*

PRABHAT

So?

RATNA

I told you long ago.

MIRA

Ratna, Sweetie...

RATNA

No go. *(Pause)*

PRABHAT

You know...

MIRA

We must not give up, you know.

PRABHAT

After all...

RATNA

Life goes on.

MIRA

Ratna, sweetie...

PRABHAT

Ratna, darling, you must at least listen...

RAM

Ratna, my dear, you must at least think about consequences of a more down-to-earth kind.

RATNA

Oh?

PRABHAT

Yes, the setback to the cause of science.

RAM

The cause of science will manage to plod on, thank you.

RATNA

It is nice to know that. Nice to know that life in the lab will go on.

RAM

Aren't you both forgetting something else for which you own some little responsibility?

RATNA

I know. We've put you to a lot of trouble.

PRABHAT

You must not hesitate to tell us how much it has cost so far. Since Ratna – Ratna and me – since we are dropping out, we cannot presume your research grant will cover all the...

RATNA

We'll work it out. Some insurance policy or medical claim or something. We'll work it out.

RAM

It is not money. I have never brought that up in the past. It is not a problem now.

PRABHAT

We are really sorry, Ram. I know your project targets are all upset because of our...

RAM

How nice of you all to be concerned about my project targets. That's what friends are for. Thank you for your kindness.

MIRA

They mean it, Ram. The friendship in this room is real. We have always been sincere to each other.

RAM

Thank you once again for the reminder. Now, let us turn our sincerity to what should concern us all. We have already got something going in the lab, you know. It is a human life, already formed – and a magnificent specimen of a human at that. What do we do with him?

PRABHAT

Oh... him!

MIRA

Oh, the poor boy! To be abandoned even before arrival.

PRABHAT
Well, in a way, even before that – before he has the capacity to know.

MIRA
A mere bubble – a tiny bubble flushed down the lavatory.

RAM
Rhymes with laboratory.

PRABHAT
Better than a full-grown baby in a wicker basket let off down the river. *(Pause)*

RAM
Ratna?

RATNA
Can't we...

RAM
No, we cannot!

RATNA
My god...

RAM
Mine too.

PRABHAT
Can it not be stopped – recalled – something like that?

RAM
As Ratna-behn Kumar might say, 'no go'. Once it is switched on, the programme takes full control. It must go through as programmed.

RATNA
But the switch – that is in your hands.

RAM
It is against the will of god! My god, too, makes some demands. *(Long pause)*

RATNA AND PRABHAT
(Together)
What happens now... ?
You mean you will just go on...
I don't understand how...
The baby is supposed to...
Etc. Leela has appeared with a dinner gong. She strikes the gong once. The four friends freeze. She steps downstage and talks to the audience.

LEELA
First bell before the break. Yes, there will be two more. Three bells – can't get out of that. Now, let us see how we can help our friends get out of the jam they find themselves in here. The playwright has a definite view on

this. His social scientist friends have one too – not quite the same one, I'm afraid. All of them with their intellectual analyses! All quite wishy-washy, if you ask me. The stage is no public toilet – for people to inflict their pet graffiti on a tax-paying public. So, it is really up to us – we who live and work and suffer and die on the stage – it is for us to show the way. And the way is simple. Give all the characters a chance. Why let only a pair of them get all the attention?

She steps aside, regards the tableau on stage affectionately, and rings the bell twice. Ratna and Prabhat repeat their lines after Ram's last line.

RATNA AND PRABHAT

(Together)
What happens now... ?
You mean you will just go on...
I don't understand how...
The baby is supposed to...
Etc.

MIRA

(Over their voices) Wait! *(They stop. All three turn their attention on Mira.)* Ram, do you think I can...

RAM

Yes, you can!

MIRA

Will it make any... ?

RAM

No, it won't make any difference.

RATNA AND PRABHAT

(Together) Mira!

MIRA

The name's Aurora. The dawning was a bit late, but it is here.

RATNA

Are you sure...

MIRA

For a little bit of sunshine in your lives. And a little bit in my own life.

PRABHAT

Mira, you can't imagine what...

MIRA

You are my best friends. This is the best gift I can think of for your tenth anniversary, coming up soon.

RATNA

Mira, darling...

MIRA

The least I can do.

The two women embrace and sob on each other's shoulders. Prabhat walks up to Ram, who takes out his digital dairy.

PRABHAT

Everything on schedule?

RAM

Right on. I'll take Mira in for her tests first thing in the morning tomorrow.

PRABHAT

Rather short notice.

RAM

We can't wait till January 15, 1994, can we?

PRABHAT

No, I suppose we can't.

RAM

So – we go on. As per plan, on schedule.

PRABHAT

Except...

RAM

Except for a small change of address for the production unit!

Leela rings the dinner gong thrice and calls.

LEELA

Dinner is served!

The four friends regain their composure and move out chatting. Leela watches them leave.

LEELA

It is not an easy part to play – Mira Aurora, long time close friend of Ratna and Prabhat Kumar. There's more to it than mouthing the lines.

Swami Anantanand enters stealthily and waits behind Leela. She notices his presence and moves to welcome him.

SWAMIJI

Shhh!

The following passage by Leela anticipates Swamiji's questions and reactions, and is rendered with full control of the situation. The Swamiji manages only to gesture in between her lines, beginning with controlled curiosity and ending quite dumbstruck.

LEELA

Swamiji! Pranaam Swamiji... Yes Swamiji, she is in. May I call... Ji Swamiji, I will not disturb her... Ji haan Swamiji, she is going ahead with it... No, no, no, Swamiji, it is not Dr Ram Kapur. It is Prabhatji... Well, it is Dr Ram Kapur's baby, yes, but it is Prabhatji's child – Prabhatji and Ratnaji.

No Swamiji, she is not – she won't... You see, Miraji has insisted that she will have the baby... Yes, the child... Yes, yes, Swamiji, Dr Ram Kapur's baby, Prabhatji's child, which is Ratnaji's child too... Miraji? They are all going to be so happy... *(Swamiji rushes out)*

Swamiji? Swamiji, are you there... ? *(She shrugs and rings the gong once, loud). Rapid fade out*

Intermission here if desired

SCENE 6

The time is now eighteen years later. In the dark, a lullaby is heard. A rough, untrained male voice, but gentle and sincere in song. A light comes on to reveal Lalee, on his knees, gazing into the wicker basket in wonder as he sings.

LALEE

(Singing)

Close your eyes, little one, close your eyes.
There's a white cloud of a chariot in the skies.
When you conquer distant lands,
Will you let me hold your hand.
Little one, close your eyes.
When you smile, little one, as you smile
The hurricanes in our hearts rest awhile.
A dance of dragonflies
greets the bulbul's cries,
Little one, when you smile
The lines on your brow
Were hymns to your birth
Embracing the stars
Encircling the earth.
Close your eyes, little one, and you'll see
All the wonders of the world that can be
Wrapped in morning dew
Lilies white for you
Little one, you will see.

Lalee remains with the basket. A crossfade to Ram's office reveals the good doctor examining various records and making notes or entries into the computer. The crossfade returns to Lalee who repeats the refrain and the last verse.

The lines on your brow
Were hymns to your birth
Embracing the stars
Encircling the earth.

Close your eyes, little one, and you'll see
All the wonders of the world that can be
Wrapped in morning dew
Lilies white for you
Little one, you will see.

The crossfade returns to Ram's office. He is examining some more records with obvious satisfaction. He punches the data in, looks up to heaven in gratitude and joy, and then slumps on the desktop in ecstatic exhaustion. The crossfade returns to Lalee. He speaks into the wicker basket.

LALEE

(Repeating Leela's lines from the first scene) Abandon a baby! Look at him – look at the shweetie-pootie smile curling on his pinky-winky lips – oh, you shweetie-pootie darling baby. How can anybody abandon this sweet, innocent, helpless little babe just like that? *(He can't go on. He takes out his checklist to consult. Leela appears and stands next to him, tapping her foot. Lalee repeats the last line.)*

How can anybody abandon this sweet, innocent, helpless little babe just like that?

LEELA

He is eighteen years old.

LALEE

Is he?

LEELA

He has hair on his upper lip.

LALEE

Has he?

LEELA

And he is a gorgeous specimen of young humankind. *(Lalee examines his checklist and looks up)*

Not on your checklist? No? Here, give that to me. *(She takes the notes from Lalee's hands, tears it up methodically into small bits, and thrusts the lot into one of his pockets.)*

Now, just position yourself for the start of this scene and things will turn out fine – just fine. *(Lalee positions himself at the entrance to Ram's office. Leela moves to a corner and calls out)*

Gorgeous specimen of young humankind!

Vijendra, a handsome young man with a picture-book physique steps onto the stage, notices Leela, and bows lightly in politeness. Leela returns the bow, leads him to the entrance of Ram's clinic, and then exits. Lalee springs to life.

VIJENDRA

Is this...

LALEE
Dr Ram Kapur's laboratory and DTT research centre.

VIJENDRA
Dr Kapur is...

LALEE
In.

VIJENDRA
Ah, good. I have an...

LALEE
Appointment. At zero-nine-zero-zero.

VIJENDRA
Yes, at nine. My name is...

LALEE
Vijendra Kumar. Dr Kapur will see you at zero-nine-zero-zero, Mr Kumar. *(Looks at his watch)* It is now...

RAM
Lalluram! I'm expecting Mr Vijendra Kumar at nine o'clock. Please send him in as soon as he arrives.

LALEE
Sir! He's here, dot to dot sir. *(He motions Vijendra in.)*

RAM
Ah, Vijendra, Vijendra! So nice you could drop by.

VIJENDRA
So nice to be here!

RAM
I was afraid with all your commitments...

VIJENDRA
Oh, no, Ram uncle! How could anything come in the way of a visit to your place? As soon as I got your message...

LALEE
He was to start on the South African tour yesterday, Sir. But they simply had to go ahead without him. His appointment with you came first.

RAM
Thank you, Lalluram. *(Pause)*

LALEE
That will be all!

RAM
Yes, for now. Oh yes, take these papers with you for filing.

LALEE

Yes, sir. Straightaway, sir.

Lalee moves to another downstage position and begins to examine the papers in his hands, even as he speaks to the audience. Through the following passage, the scene in Ram's office runs in parallel.

LALEE

It started as a slim scrapbook – a loose collection in a folder. The lime and spoon race here, the sack race there. At age three, when his classmates were lisping singa-songa-sisspense in the kindergarten concert. Then came the elocution contests and the junior chess championships. Age seven. We needed an index file. By age twelve, we had a line of box files.

RAM

First things first. Happy birthday!

VIJENDRA

Thank you, uncle.

RAM

And many happy returns. Not just more birthdays, you know, but many more happy returns from each birthday!

VIJENDRA

(Modest) Well, I can only keep trying, I suppose.

LALEE

A whole line of box files, in alphabetical order, from run-of-the-mill athletics in A, through numismatics in N, to Vedic Maths in V, to zugzwang victories in chess, zither compositions in raag durbari, zen applications in endurance, zapateado, and such like. You see, I happen to know what zapateado is – a traditional Spanish dance.

RAM

How does it feel to be eighteen?

VIJENDRA

Great! I mean, sixteen was okay, when you put me on to the summer course in Uppsala University, but eighteen is eighteen!

RAM

Yes, eighteen is eighteen. The laws of the land haven't changed much, have they? You still have to wait to be eighteen to do so many things.

VIJENDRA

Like getting my driving licence.

RAM

Your parents were strict on that, I know.

VIJENDRA

Yes, they were. But I didn't mind, really.

RAM

Although, you did the souping-up job on your dad's car yourself.

LALEE

Look at these. IQ at 185 with the most stringent measures. Violin concerts in the SPICMACAY circuit. Rank 1 in all the three all-India entrance exams – the IITs, the National Institute of Design, and the National Law School of India. A test cap in the Indian Eleven with tours to Sri Lanka and the West Indies in the same year. Six wickets for nineteen runs in his maiden appearance. That does sound out of place, maiden appearance! A tally of eighteen wickets in the first three tests. And he swung a mean long handle in plucky defiance when the established order was skittled out – which was, alas, more than once in both the domestic and overseas circuits. Here's the best caption of the year past, 'The future hope of Indian cricket.'

RAM

And now – you can vote. You are part of the great eunuchracy in democracy that is India.

VIJENDRA

(A soft laugh) Uncle Ram! Always in fine spirits.

RAM

Lovely to see you, young man, lovely to see you.

VIJENDRA

The same with you, uncle.

RAM

With your busy, busy schedule...

VIJENDRA

And when I am home, you have to be out of town! The last three weeks...

RAM

Yes, the last couple of months have been rather extraordinary.

VIJENDRA

Anyway, it was so nice I could see you today.

RAM

I am very happy too. It is an important day.

VIJENDRA

Not just the birthday.

RAM

No, not just the birthday. It is an important day.

VIJENDRA

The South African tour – I am sure my visit here will bring me good luck.

RAM

Luck? It's the South Africans who must be buying up all the talismans and good luck charms.

VIJENDRA

Oh, uncle Ram! Anyway, you will wish me for the trip, won't you?

RAM

On this very important day of the year, may all things nice happen to all nice people in all nice ways!

VIJENDRA

Thank you, uncle. Is there anything else... ?

RAM

No, that's it. That's it for now.

VIJENDRA

Bye, uncle. I'll get in touch when...

RAM

Off you go then!

(Ram watches Vijendra leave, smiles to himself, punches one last entry into the console, and sits) Lalluram!

LALEE

(Entering) Sir!

RAM

Lalluram, Malluram, come in, come in. How are things in the front office today?

LALEE

No aram, no haram.

RAM

Do you want a vacation?

LALEE

Sir?

RAM

A holiday – a week off in Kodaikanal or on the beach in Goa...

LALEE

Something good happened, sir? Celebration?

RAM

What day is it today, Lalluram?

LALEE

Sir?

RAM

What day is it?

LALEE

Friday, sir.

RAM

And... ?

LALEE

Thirteenth, sir. Ah – you want to close for bad luck day, sir?

RAM

Oh, you buddhuram, bhoosaram! Try again *(Pause. Lalee looks blank.)* I'll give you a hint. People wanting to look properly civilised, light candles and cut cakes on a day like this.

LALEE

A birthday... Sir is celebrating... no, it is Vijendrababa's birthday!

RAM

And, he is... ?

LALEE AND RAM

(Together) He is eighteen today!

LALEE

Yes, sir, I follow now, sir. Yes, sir.

RAM

It is an important day today, Lalluram.

LALEE

Sir!

RAM

A very important day.

LALEE

Sir!

RAM

Ah, good, you haven't finished filing those papers yet. Here's one more. Put it in the right place. 'VICE CAPTAINCY FOR VIJ, THE WIZ, IN SOUTH AFRICAN TOUR. From our special correspondent in the Bangalore training camp. All eyes are on Vijendra Kumar, the darling of cricketing fans the world over as he prepares... '

LALEE

I will make copies, sir. I'll put one each in A, C, and S. *(He leaves)*

RAM

We will open a separate box file in P. P for prize moneys.

(He dials a number on the phone.)

Hello, is this 22244468? The firm of Sunder, Sunder, and Sunder? Please connect me to Mr Pratap Sunder... Hello, Pat? Hi, this is Ram here... The patent registration business – I'm ready for it now... No, not just Indian.

We'll make it international... Yes, every goddam country in the world that still produces babies...

Rapid fade out

SCENE 7

Festive music. Dimly lit stage. Leela enters with a dance in her steps. She has flowers in her hair, on her wrists, and ankles. On her head, she carries an earthen pot, jet black, kept in an ornate tray and surrounded with flowers and pooja paraphernalia, including a small camphor or oil lamp. She places the tray on the floor and begins a ritual pooja before it. Lalee enters, cartwheeling, and bursts into a vigorous dance in time to the music which has an intoxicating beat by now. The music – and the dance – ends on a crashing high note. Leela motions Lalee to sit by her side. He does. She lights the lamp, rises, and begins to walk around the pot, Lalee following – once, twice...

LALEE

If this goes on, she might suddenly announce that we are married!

LEELA

Shhh!

LALEE

(Aside) Not that I mind, not really.

Leela stops, performs a short arati to the pot with the lamp, and offers the arati to Lalee who accepts it. She keeps the lamp down, prostrates before the pot, 'takes' the arati herself, and then carries it downstage to offer it to the audience. She returns and places the lamp once again before the pot. Lalee and Leela kneel on either side of the lamp.

LEELA

Ready?

LALEE

I suppose so.

They take deep breaths and together blow out the flame in the lamp. The lights on stage turn bright. Leela speaks to the audience.

LEELA

The annual festival of The Flame of Eternal Darkness. Just one of the myriad cultural traditions that makes this land of ours truly fascinating.

LALEE

The Lonely Planet included it only in 1995, and in just the last six years it has become one of the top three Indian festivals in the international tourist schedule.

LEELA

The symbolism in the festival ritual is truly sublime. The lamp represents a level of illumination that is limited by human intelligence, the limits to human understanding. True wisdom remains elusive, out of reach. And yet it is always available to us, from powers beyond the perimeters of our lives, if we only recognise its presence. *(She refers to the pot.)*

It is a brilliant white light that is all encompassing, all knowing, all powerful. For precisely those qualities, man, humble humankind, can never gaze upon it directly. To do that would be to turn ourselves to ash. And so we must learn to submit ourselves before the great white light and, in doing so, rediscover the beauty and dignity of mortal surrender. On this day, at this hour, there must be two hundred million homes on this subcontinent who are rededicating themselves to their spiritual roots by this simple but elegant symbolic act of... extinguishing false pride in our illusory assets so that... the Flame of Eternal Darkness may be perpetuated in our lives. *(She bows.)*

LALEE

The festival was included in the National Panchanga and declared a Public Holiday by a special ordinance of the Government of India on the 26th day of January, Nineteen hundred and ninety four, to commemorate the dawn of a new republic, a renewed tryst with destiny.

LEELA

The twenty-sixth day of January, two thousand twelve. In a mere eighteen years, less than a cosmic eye-blink, the light we have gathered and stored in our land is truly wondrous.

LALEE

While for centuries upon centuries we wandered helpless in barren forests for twigs and dried shrubs that grew lighter and lighter with each head-load.

LEELA

The light let into our lives is truly wondrous.

LALEE

After knocking out the first five batsmen for twenty-five runs, Vijendra Kumar has belted the South African bowling for a double century!

Festival music again. Leela and Lalee feed each other bits of prasad and apply vermillion on the foreheads. They hold hands and spin in glee.

Slow fade out

SCENE 8

A tight spot picks up the Judge standing still, perhaps at the same place where the black earthen pot was in the previous scene. He takes out a piece of chalk from his pocket, draws a circle around the spot, and then walks around it as if to test the circle. He then picks a short stepladder from those arranged on stage, places it above the circle, and seats himself on it. The spot expands.

JUDGE

December 31, Nineteen hundred and ninety three. The Chief Executives of one hundred and fifty-two nation-states affixed their signatures on an International treaty that activated a new International Law on Intellectual Property and Patents. India was one of them, appearing thirty-eighth in the list, arranged alphabetically. Automatically, the archaic and impotent Indian Patents Act of a bygone era was rendered null and void.

Lalee enters, pushing a wheelbarrow with a heap of sealed envelopes. He wears the headgear and sash of a court orderly. He stops it inside the circle, bows to the Judge, and steps aside.

LALEE

Incoming, sir.

JUDGE

The usual?

LALEE

Usual, sir.

JUDGE

Anything out of the ordinary?

LALEE

One suspicious one, sir. *(Picks up a cover and hands it to the Judge.)* Foreign stationery, sir.

JUDGE

Directly.

LALEE

Directly, sir. (*He leaves, pushing the wheelbarrow out. The Judge opens the envelope in his hand and puts on a pair of reading glasses.)*

JUDGE

(Reading) In the matter of the patent registered under the title Designer Test-Tube Baby Vijendra, designated thereinafter as DTT, it is hereby brought to the notice inter alia... *(He puts the papers aside and takes out a gavel.)* Posting for hearing!

LALEE

(Off) Sir! *(He enters, leading Dr Ram Kapur, stands him in the middle of the circle and steps aside.)*

Dr Ram Lakhan Kapur, father's name Lakhanrai Kishanrai Kapur, age forty-five, residing in door number A5 Belvedere Park, Jawahar Nagar, present in court!

JUDGE

(Strikes once with the gavel) That will be all. *(He glares. Lalee leaves.)* Pharmaiye doctor sahib – hamari taraf se aapki kya seva ho sakti hai?

RAM

Ghar me sabki tabiyat...

JUDGE

Bilkul theek thaak!

RAM

Haan, we missed you at Rastogi's dinner last Friday.

JUDGE

Oh, last Friday. We just couldn't make it. Savitha's sister had come down from Raipur...

RAM

Sab log raah dekh rahey the... We waited till ten-thirty and then went in for dinner.

JUDGE

Suna bahut saare log aaye the. No taash session with such a large crowd, I suppose.

RAM

Arrey, half the crowd was just the courtesy callers. They were gone even before dessert was served. We moved to the cards table around half past eleven.

JUDGE

How can there be a get-together at Rastogi's without taash!

RAM

How can there be! Achcha – after we're through with the business here, just remind me, I have to give you some papers that Rastogi asked me to pass on to you. They are in connection with Munna's admission into...

JUDGE

Haan haan, dekh letey hain.

RAM

Right – what is the agenda now? What is required of me?

JUDGE

Nothing much. Nothing at all. You make this deposition before me – which can be taken as done – and you answer questions that the Judge deems fit to raise. And then you sign these papers in my presence. Buss!

RAM

Okay. Right, your honour. Let us begin.

JUDGE

Achcha, tell me something, for my own education, yeh DTT hota kya hai?

RAM

Judge sahib, what can I tell you! The best thing is for you to come and visit our Centre one day. You will see everything for yourself.

JUDGE

Haan, haan, zaroor aayenge ek din. Why not?

RAM

It will be an honour.

JUDGE

And what do you get by registering this patent?

RAM

(Sharp, business-like) Oh, about 80-85 lakhs this year – for starters. It can only keep increasing over the years as Vijendra's multifold talents bring in more and more royalty from higher and higher conquests.

JUDGE

(Understanding) Ohh... to yeh chamatkar hai aapki technology mein...

RAM

Of course the takes are not mine alone.

JUDGE

Of course not.

RAM

There is the whole establishment. There are so many people behind the success.

JUDGE

So many people to make your success possible. *(A beat.)*

RAM

You are coming this Friday, aren't you?

JUDGE

This Friday – yes, we'll be there.

RAM

Good, we haven't seen you at the table in a long time.

JUDGE

Yes, it has been a long time. *(A beat.)*

RAM

Is Savitha's spondylitis under control? That was a bad patch she went through last month.

JUDGE

Yes, it was a bad patch. *(A beat.)*

RAM

Right. Is there anything more? Any more questions? *(An understanding nod.)* Jayantilalji, aap toh jaantey hi hain – you can come back to me with any questions, any time later. It is a fairly straightforward case, right?

JUDGE

Yes, it is straightforward.

RAM

What happens now?

JUDGE

You can sign the papers here. On the strength of this document, the patent already registered under your ownership will come into effect for the purpose of all commercial transactions – in the case of the product Vijendra Kumar as well as all other products in future from all like processes.

RAM

The invoice, I suppose, can be sent directly to Vijendra, as he is a major now.

JUDGE

Precisely.

RAM

Shriman Vijendra Kumar, His Royalty Highness!

JUDGE

The 30-day notice is already posted to record objections, if any. Two weeks ago that was. So you can go ahead on the first of next month.

RAM

Vijendra is away on an overseas tour.

JUDGE

That does not matter. You have done your job.

RAM

Thank you. *(He takes out his pen and prepares to sign.)*

LALEE

(Entering) Objection, your honour.

Lalee wheels in the barrow, stops, and hands the Judge a sealed envelope. The Judge opens it.

JUDGE

Stay order from the higher court!

RAM

But Jayantilalji...

JUDGE

Dismissed!

Lalee wheels the barrow out, Ram following. The Judge steps down, puts the stepladder away, places a taller stepladder in its place, and in the process partly strikes the set for Dr Kapur's clinic. He seats himself on the stepladder. He reads.

JUDGE

On my left, weighing in at 152 pounds, twice champion of the company annual picnic jalebi race, Prabhat Jayakrishna Kumar, father's name Jayakrishnadas Harivallabhdas Kumar, age forty-six years – red! On my right, weighing in at 149 pounds, current titleholder of the District Rotary 'Passing the Parcel' championship, Ram Lakhan Kapur, father's name Lakhanrai Kishanrai Kapur, age forty-five years – green! *(The two men approach from either side and wait outside the circle. The Judge raises the gavel.)* Seconds out of the ring...

(The Judge strikes. The two men enter the ring, stalk each other cautiously for a few seconds, and burst into verbal attacks simultaneously. The words clearly heard in the din are figures – thousands, lakhs, millions...)

JUDGE

Break! Break it up! *(The two men separate.)* Mix it!

PRABHAT

I AM THE FATHER!

RAM

I made him. I made the baby.

PRABHAT

It was my idea. The sanction for a designer baby came from me.

RAM

The entire project was conceived, planned, designed, executed...

PRABHAT

He was merely the carpenter. I was the architect and promoter...

They fall into a shouting match once again. The Judge raps the gavel and interrupts.

JUDGE

Break it! Break it up! *(They do.)* Mix it!

PRABHAT

The raw material – it was my spunk!

SCENE 9

The Prabhat Kumar home. Ratna is at the table, lost. Leela is pouring her a cup of tea, which she does with some ceremony. She places the saucer and cup before Ratna, and stands in her place. A beat.

RATNA

But it's my egg! *(A long burst)* How on earth can he claim ownership of the baby – all by himself – just because he has a fancy carrom board? What does he know about life and birth – about motherhood, womanhood, the joy of womanhood? He calls himself a doctor scientist – doctor, scientist, atheist. Has he ever – watered a plant in a garden – watched a flower bloom – raised a fruit tree? Does he know his birds and bees? He thinks babies are made of glass and stainless steel... Ohhh...

She puts her head down in her arms on the table. Leela remains motionless. Prabhat enters, waits at the edge. Leela moves to him.

LEELA

Fifth day today. No appetite, no mood.

PRABHAT

Does she talk? Anything about... ?

LEELA

About nothing else!

PRABHAT

I see.

LEELA

That will be all?

PRABHAT

Yes, Leelamma. That will be all. *(Leela leaves. Prabhat goes up to Ratna.)* We have won. *(Ratna looks up.)* Yes, darling, we have won.

RATNA

Did Ram... ? Has he withdrawn his claims?

PRABHAT

Not exactly.

RATNA

Then?

PRABHAT

Nobody expected him to withdraw, I suppose. It was a true and proper deadlock. The Judge gave us two hours to talk things over. We could use his anteroom, without his presence, he said, to work out something. An out-of-court settlement.

RATNA
A compromise.

PRABHAT
Well, a compromise, if you wish. So we thrashed things out, we looked at dozens of little details...

RATNA
You settled.

PRABHAT
More or less. The lawyers will work out the final details.

RATNA
But he can't have it!

PRABHAT
Ratna, darling, let's not start...

RATNA
No, he won't have it! He must not have it!

PRABHAT
Must not have what? He has been stopped effectively from running away with the loot, has he not? He has admitted the legitimacy – yes, the legitimacy – of our parenthood. We have sat down and discussed things across the table in a civilized manner.

RATNA
How much?

PRABHAT
Fifty-fifty. More or less. It's difficult to be exact on some counts like TV ads and guest appearances.

RATNA
No go!

PRABHAT
What do you mean... ?

RATNA
No way! Ram Kapur is not getting away with this fifty-fifty deal.

PRABHAT
Ratna, Ram has been...

RATNA
He's not getting away. I'll cook his goose for him. What does he think? I am the mother who laid the golden egg.

PRABHAT
But it is quite fair, Ratna. After all, he has put in a helluva lot himself into the venture. And when two parties find themselves in a dispute, the right thing to do...

RATNA

Two parties?

PRABHAT

Well, there's Ram Kapur and...

RATNA

You and I might use the same tube of toothpaste, but our towels are marked His and Hers.

PRABHAT

Come on, Ratna, you can't mean...

RATNA

Of course I can. I do. I am not part of the deal you have struck with Ram.

PRABHAT

But there's enough for all, and more. An escalation clause has been put in too. All we can ever ask for in this lifetime – and two more – will be met from this agreement.

RATNA

I am not a party to the agreement.

PRABHAT

Ratna, you and I...

RATNA

Are not one party.

PRABHAT

The deed has already been drawn up.

RATNA

No go!

PRABHAT

Listen, Ratna, this is a Hindu family. Vijendra is a son in a Hindu family.

RATNA

And this is the year 2012. I brought you into this Hindu household, I set up home, and I produced the son.

PRABHAT

He is my son!

RATNA

Prove it! *(She strides out, leaving Prabhat gaping.)*

PRABHAT

Leelamma! *(Leela enters and waits at the edge.)* Take Amma's tea to her room.

LEELA

Yes, sir. I take now?

PRABHAT

She'll have her dinner there too, I think.

LEELA

Yes, sir. I serve dinner in room.

PRABHAT

You can take the whole bloody house into her room!

He strides out too. Leela watches, puts back the tea service on the table, and wheels the table out. Crossfade to the Judge. He steps down, puts the stepladder away, places a taller stepladder in its place, striking a part of the set for the Prabhat Kumar home in the process. He takes out a pocket book and walks along the circle slowly, reading to himself. He climbs up the stepladder. He opens another page and reads.

JUDGE

(Reading)

O, that this too, too solid flesh would melt,
Thaw, and resolve itself into a dew
Or that the everlasting had not fix'd
His canon 'gainst self-slaughter!
O God! O God!
How weary, stale, flat, and unprofitable
Seem To Me All The Uses Of This World!

LALEE

(Entering with the wheelbarrow) Incoming! Winter session specials: Four nurses in old folks home confess despatching fourteen inmates to heavenly pastures with overdoses of barbiturates. Stud farm owner dies leaving the entire estate in his will, including the 22-carat four-poster double bed, to his champion Arab mare Noorjehan. Cabinet Secretary seeks ratification of funds from Public Sector enterprises for election campaign to fulfil social objectives.

JUDGE

Thoughts black, hands apt, drugs fit, and time agreeing,
Confederate season, else no creature seeing,
Thou mixture rank, of midnight weeds, collected
With Hecate's ban, thrice blasted, thrice infected,
Thy natural magic and dire property
On wholesome life usurp immediately.

LALEE

Oh, winter theatre season! *(To audience)* Life member of Bangalore Little Theatre, better recognised locally as BLT.

Founder and patron member of Foundation for Artistes in Retirement Theatre, recognised the world over as ART... with an F. *(To Judge, picking up a sealed envelope.)*

Mother of egg seeks stay order on claims by father of sperm.

JUDGE

(Looking up) Here's metal more attractive. Bid the good woman enter.

(Lalee begins to wheel out. The Judge calls after him.)

This envelope has been opened.

LALEE

(As he exits) Fingers on our lips!

JUDGE

All the world's a waiting room, a crowd of plebeian upstarts, ears cocked for a break on the stage.

LALEE

(Off) Ratna Prabhat Kumar – nee Mangaldas – dadadadadadadadada – present in court!

Ratna enters and reaches the edge of the circle. She is subdued, even tranquil, as she stands before the Judge, the edge of her sari covering her head.

JUDGE

Ratna Prabhat Kumar, your petition before the highest court of justice in the State is being accorded a priority hearing on account of the profundity of its implications to the very core of social organization, and for the possible path-breaking directions it may provide in every sphere of human endeavour. The case, Madam, is at the cutting edge of jurisprudence.

RATNA

Your honour, I am honoured.

JUDGE

Speak, then, and let your words come tripplingly on the tongue, crisp to the count of fingers.

RATNA

One, he is my son. Two, his earnings are as clearly mine as his. Three, the earnings from the patent by other sons from other mothers are as clearly mine as Dr Ram Kapur's.

JUDGE

And... ?

RATNA

Four, my share of the earnings shall be in the service of humanity. They shall fund a Public Trust dedicated to humanitarian deeds – in the service of God and humanity.

JUDGE

And... ?

RATNA

The rest is silence.

Ratna leaves.

JUDGE

Go to, I'll no more on't, it hath made me mad.
I say, we will have no more marriages:
Those that are married already, all but one, shall live,
The rest shall keep as they are.
To a nunnery, go.

Blackout.

In the dark, a pair of bhajan cymbals begins a beat. A woman's voice is heard singing the bhajan in Scene 4. The light comes on to reveal Mira swaying as she sings the bhajan in Swamiji's ashram, before the drawn curtain. Presently, the voice of the Swamiji is heard from within, booming.

SWAMIJI

Who dares to disturb me in my hour of meditation?!

MIRA

It is me, your holiness. It is I.

SWAMIJI

And by what name is this attachment to the self-proclaimed?

MIRA

It is Mira, my lord. Mira, the devoted. Mira Aurora, at the dawn of awakening.

SWAMIJI

Your business, woman – do you come in idle curiosity or as a seeker?

MIRA

I come... to find out.

SWAMIJI

Very well. You shall receive me presently. Resume your chanting, immediately, at the very spot at which you stand.

Mira resumes the beat on the cymbals. As she gets into the bhajan, a woman (Leela) steps out from behind the curtain, her head and face covered by her sari. Mira stops.

WOMAN

(Woman to woman) New here?

MIRA

Yes, I thought today...

WOMAN

Motherhood?

MIRA

Well, yes, in a way...

WOMAN

There is but one way.

MIRA

I don't know.

WOMAN

All in good time. Know your way around here?

MIRA

I have just arrived.

WOMAN

The rest room is down that corridor, on the left. Self-service coffee/tea in the pantry – nine to two, two to five, and again seven to eleven. There is a dispensary in the annex to the reading room, where you can, you know... The reading room-cum-lounge has... Well, make yourself at home. *(She begins to leave, stops.)* Tuesdays! Why must it be on a Tuesday?!

She leaves. Swamiji enters, regards Mira carefully.

SWAMIJI

Why, Mira Aurora, BCom, ICWA, age forty-four, Executive Assistant to the President and Chief Executive of Sheffield Finance & Leasing Company, Athreyesh gotra, meena rashi, educated in St Agnes High School and Junior College before shifting to Vidyasagar Evening College for Working Women, father last seen in 1988 before posting in Muscat construction company, dependent mother with increasing medical bills, not including gin and tonic, first job as receptionist-cum-secretary in Trident Tours & Travels, gentleman caller abruptly disengaged after outstation tour in the summer of...

MIRA

Swamiji! Nothing is concealed from you! *(She bows in pranaam.)*

SWAMIJI

(Continuing) Guide, companion, and reliable friend-in-need to the Kumar family. *(Mira is startled.)* Ratna and Prabhat Kumar, and their illustrious son, Vijendra Kumar.

MIRA

Swamiji...

SWAMIJI

Or is there an error in my reckoning?

MIRA

Yes, there is – no, not in what you said, Swamiji, not in your vision, but – oh, how shall I put it – you see...

SWAMIJI

Vijendra is, perhaps, your son.

MIRA

Yes. That is the point!

SWAMIJI

And is it not an illusion? One among the countless illusions crammed into our consciousness?

MIRA

But I had him. I bore him for a full term of nine months and ten days.

SWAMIJI

As you bore your swollen tonsils when you were nine, and the appendicitis when you were nineteen. Where are those bits of flesh now?

MIRA

They were useless bits of flesh.

SWAMIJI

They were, would you say, unreal?

MIRA

Yes, unreal, when you think of it, but unreal because they were useless.

SWAMIJI

Vijendra is real.

MIRA

He is real. He is all there. The whole world knows, there is a Vijendra Kumar there.

SWAMIJI

Because... he is not useless.

MIRA

Swamiji, you don't know Vijendra. My Viju is no Doon School plastic toy soldier.

SWAMIJI

He is worth... how much?

MIRA

Nobody knows. Crores–billions maybe. It's impossible to estimate what it will be in the future, even five or six years from now.

SWAMIJI

And you claim... you made the baby?

MIRA

Didn't I?

SWAMIJI

Did you?

MIRA

Swamiji, it's all in the records. It was my womb that nurtured the seed into a baby of human form. For full six months after his birth he was nursed by me. Mine was the mother's milk that raised him.

SWAMIJI
As guide, companion, and reliable friend-in-need to the Kumars.

MIRA
The actual process was mine. *(Emphatic)* Besides, I took all the risks...

SWAMIJI
What do you think you should be claiming?

MIRA
Fifty per cent of all royalties from the patent.

SWAMIJI
And from Vijendra... your son?

MIRA
I will then renounce all claims of parenthood on him.

SWAMIJI
I see...

MIRA
Swamiji, is all this sensible? Is it irrational?

SWAMIJI
It is not unreasonable.

MIRA
Is it right? Will I be doing something wrong?

SWAMIJI
Mira, my child, to harness reason in one's conduct is to acknowledge the presence of the Almighty in one's being.

MIRA
Oh, Swamiji – I knew I would solve the riddles in my life by coming to you.

SWAMIJI
This ashram is open to all genuine seekers.

MIRA
May I come again?

SWAMIJI
Whenever you wish. Later, earlier – do you wish to be initiated?

MIRA
Oh, Swamiji, will you take me?

SWAMIJI
The question is not of the ashram taking you. But will you take the ashram?

MIRA
Yes, Swamiji, yes. When should I start?

SWAMIJI

Since you have taken the trouble to come all the way, perhaps a small beginning now...

MIRA

As you command, Swamiji.

SWAMIJI

Sit here... sit erect facing me... your spine straight, but without undue strain at the small of the back... Shoulders square, but relaxed. That's nice... Now, close your eyes... very nice... Breath deep, but slow... slow and easy. Relax... does it feel relaxed? *(She nods)* That's the way, my child... The first lesson in the journey to unburden the self... leave the cares of your city existence. Relax... you will soon open yourself to new knowledge, a world of new knowledge... A new awakening...

Fade out

SCENE 10

Lalee, still the court attendant, is seen tiptoeing to the partition curtain in Swamiji's chambers. He zips it off, to reveal... Leela, standing arms akimbo, glaring.

LEELA

So, you got your big break, did you?

LALEE

Shhh! The Judge will be here any moment.

LEELA

He won't! I've fixed a bonda-chutney snack for him in his chamber. There's hot coffee following.

LALEE

Well, help me set his courtroom, then. If we finish early, we might also get a coffee break before the action.

LEELA

Right! You work the stage. I'll do the props.

(They talk as they rearrange the set, extending the acting area, placing a taller stepladder for the Judge) It's not every day that you get to do a scene in the highest court of justice in the land.

LALEE

You mean this is... ?

LEELA
Of course it is! This is no panchayat scene by a faltoo natak company under the peepal tree.

LALEE
Wah! The Supreme Court of India!

LEELA
That is why it is so important to get things absolutely right. Now... *(She sits downstage as at the start of the play)* Where is that checklist of yours?

LALEE
Right here, dear.

LEELA
Let's go through it once. Paan.

LALEE
Check.

LEELA
Spittoon.

LALEE
Check.

LEELA
Hookah.

LALEE
Check – that is to say, cigars, paraphernalia.

LEELA
Good. And what about the baby? Have you got that into your checklist at least now?

LALEE
Yes, dear. *(He rushes out.)*

LEELA
(To audience) You've got to keep them in check, always. One small gesture and they think they have everything. God knows what kinds of demands they'll come up with next – equal rights, equal pay – that sort of language. But wait... *(She raises her arms)* I hear footsteps. It is the Prince! The Little Prince arrives!

Lalee enters, cradling the wicker basket lovingly and crooning the refrain and last verse of the lullaby. He sways in slow waltz-like steps through the end, placing the basket next to Leela. He then moves quickly to take his position below the stepladder.

The Judge enters briskly, stops before the circle, eyes it carefully, takes out a fresh chalk stick from his pocket, and gives it to Lalee.

Lalee enters the circle, gauges it, and marks the four cardinal points of the compass at four points of the circle, stands the chalk in the centre, and steps out.

The Judge climbs up the stepladder to take his place.

Leela, matter-of-fact, claps once. Ram, Prabhat, Ratna, and Mira rush on and position themselves at the four points of the circle. Leela claps twice. The four speak up.

RAM
The cause of science

PRABHAT
Must be made to serve

RATNA
The cause of human life

MIRA
The means to match the ends.

RAM
The noblest service to god and all things sacred to man is drawn

PRABHAT
From just and fair transactions among fellowmen, levelling inequalities

RATNA
That cloud the true distinction of man from beast

MIRA
Of mother's milk from synthetic white goo in tetra pack.

RAM
One small equation

PRABHAT
In social geometry

RATNA
Kaleidoscope crystals

MIRA
Fragile, this side up, with care.

PRABHAT
Speaking out of turn
The playpen wet bottom
With piglets pink in sailor suits
Served in fractured tea sets
Dons a lab coat.

RAM
Mix and match
That is the first and last law
In all things living.
Unlettered unguided
The blind lead the one eyed

On the backs of the lame
Chasing mischief trails of rainbow droppings.

RATNA
What manner of man

MIRA
Is there

RATNA
That walks

MIRA
On earth

RATNA
Chest out

MIRA
A strutting rooster

RATNA
But bent in shame

MIRA
The head rolling steps behind.

RAM
Infant youth and full grown

PRABHAT
Man from bondage free

RATNA
Mine!

PRABHAT
Wealth from common weal

RAM
To each according to and from

MIRA
Mine!!

Leela claps three times. They stop. The Judge leans over and speaks.

JUDGE
Thank you. While the depositions in the case present an apparent focus on the legitimacy of registration of the patent on DTT, it is nevertheless amply evident that the locus rationale is really the DTT-derived specimen offspring, that is, the person of Mr Vijendra Kumar. The disputed offspring may now be summoned into the courtroom.

LALEE
Mr Vijendra Kumar is not readily available for summoning, your honour.

PRABHAT

He is far away.

RAM

In Zimbabwe

RATNA AND MIRA

(Together) The concert tour in Europe was on the way.

JUDGE

A Habeas Corpus then!

Lalee steps downstage, picks up the wicker basket, and brings it before the Judge, who peers into the basket, smiles with satisfaction, and straightens up again.

JUDGE

Proceed!

Lalee steps into the circle, removes the chalk stick, places the basket in the centre, and steps out. The four claimants each grip one part of the basket and wait.

JUDGE

Truth will prevail. Let the claims begin!

The four tug at the basket with full force and ample conviction. Leela rises and rushes to the circle.

LEELA

Stop! Stop this murderous game! Take your hands off him, you pretenders!

She snatches the cradle from the group, returns to her corner, sets the basket down lovingly, and sits down.

JUDGE

What a masterstroke! Well, ladies and gentlemen, you have seen for yourselves how truth does prevail, how you can't fool all people all the time, and how justice in time is reason with rhyme. We may now regard the verdict of this court.

LALEE

(Interrupting) Objection, my lord! There is a stay order from the International Court of Trades and Tariffs.

(He produces a sealed envelope and hands it to the Judge.)

JUDGE

(Opening the envelope and reading) Objection to the hearing in the Supreme Court of India... moved by three parties... separately represented but considered together by the International Court – Messrs Thornbush Combines of the Republic of Texas, part-time affiliate-territory of the Unlimited States of America, Messrs October Blue of the People 's Republic of Moscow, erstwhile Russia, and one on the stationery of The Great Wall Corporation of Greater China, for and on behalf of the Eastern hemisphere. *(There is a general hubbub in the group from the announcement. The Judge restores order with a neat rap of the gavel.)*

Well, ladies and gentlemen, due process is the hallmark of justice.

LALEE

Your honour, my Lord. A late submission, just received.

Lalee produces another envelope, from under his headgear, and hands it to the Judge.

JUDGE

(Reading) In the matter of... Designer Test Tube... Vijendra, hereinafter... I, Swami Anantanand, do hereby proclaim...

Swamiji enters, moves to the centre of the circle and squats cross-legged facing the Judge, who acts quickly to instruct Lalee.

JUDGE

Put them all together. Well, ladies and gentlemen, time to move on in due process. Court dismissed!

The Judge climbs down and with Lalee's help, does the last bit of rearrangement to set the stage back to its layout at the start of the play. The five others on stage move their stepladders (or stools) to their places and position themselves. Lalee stands by the Judge's stepladder (the tallest) as he climbs up to take his place. Freeze. The Judge raises his gavel slowly, cautiously, and strikes once. All the characters come to life, speaking all together, to each other, to the Judge, building up to a noisy peak. The Judge strikes three times. Silence. The Judge clears his throat. So does Leela, coming out of a reverie.

LEELA

That's my cue. Stand by. We begin any second now.

The Judge raises his gavel, slowly, cautiously again, and strikes once. The characters resume their chatter, but drop gradually to silence with a fade out. Leela remains in her downstage position. She leans back and claps three times. Lalee hurries on with the paan casket on the tray, stops before Leela, and bows in anticipation.

LEELA

Paan! *(Lalee hands it to her affectionately.)*

Hmmm... you are getting better with every show.

LALEE

What happens now?

LEELA

Oh, they will go on. They have their jobs to do, and we have ours.

Vijendra Kumar enters. He is dressed in a natty three-piece suit and carries a smart leather-bound briefcase. He stops before Leela and Lalee.

VIJENDRA

Good evening. Is this the court for depositions in the matter of Intellectual Property Rights and Patents?

LALEE

Yes, it is. The court is in session just now.

VIJENDRA
Oh, I will have to wait then, I suppose.

LALEE
Yes, I suppose so. May we help you? *(Vijendra hesitates.)*

LEELA
We would be delighted to help.

LALEE
We are very good at helping people who are kept waiting.

LEELA
And you look so much like you could do with some help.

VIJENDRA
You see, I hold an international copyright on a Designer Test-Tube Baby Process, designated for short as DTT, and I am afraid there have been some attempted violations of the copyright without the due royalty transactions.

LALEE AND LEELA
(Together) You hold... the DTT patent?

VIJENDRA
Why, yes. The Mark II patent, that is. DTT Mark II.

LEELA
Mark II. What does that do?

LALEE
There is a DTT case on right now in there.

VIJENDRA
Ah, that's old stuff. And obsolete. Quite useless in modern use, for present-day applications.

LALEE
It doesn't interest you... ?

LEELA
What's going on in there?

VIJENDRA
Oh, they can keep it. We are not the least bit interested in those babies.

LEELA
You're not...

VIJENDRA
Not one bit. I'm afraid it's a faulty concept. *(Lalee and Leela wait to be enlightened.)* You see, the simpler the truth, the more intelligent you have to be to get it. It needs extraordinary natural talent to spot the most elementary laws of nature.

LEELA
And DTT Mark I gave you the ability to see that truth!

VIJENDRA

I shall be ever grateful to the inventors for that. It's what led me to develop Mark II.

LALEE

As industry grows, so must its methods grow.

LEELA

And as the methods grow, so must the human intellect grow with it. *(Vijendra smiles.)*

LALEE

Human intelligence, human competence – wah!

VIJENDRA

What I saw clearly was that the human intellectual material available in the world was a total mismatch for the actual requirements... especially the way industry has been developing. What we need is a finely tuned, highly standardised, average industrial worker with just the right subnormal intelligence.

LALEE

And DTT Mark II...

VIJENDRA

Mark II gives us just that. It's an absolute marvel. If you can just think about it – supercharged babies perfected to perform the most intricate, complex tasks with speed and accuracy... without thinking about them, without the capacity to think about them. Diversion into thinking is so... unproductive. *(Leela and Lalee are awestruck.)* The end of all thinking!

LEELA

(With parental concern) Vijendra, you must keep a tight lid on this. Nobody must ever take Mark II away from you. Tell us how we may help you. Command us.

LALEE

We are very good at helping when commanded.

VIJENDRA

Can you help me in court? Can you help me protect the copyright?

LEELA

Are there contenders?

VIJENDRA

Well... The Government of India claims that the Indian Administrative Service perfected the process long ago, even before Mark I.

LEELA

Vijendra, my son, you need help.

LALEE

(To Leela) We must help.

VIJENDRA
Can you? Will you?

LEELA
(To Lalee) No time to lose. We must speed up the proceedings in this court...

LALEE
Expedite things, as they say.

LEELA
Expedite things so that Vijendra's case can be taken up next.

LALEE
Taken up fast.

LEELA
Vijendra, Vijendra, you have had a long journey. You must rest a bit now, and prepare yourself for your turn coming up. Lalee, take Viju to the green room and make him comfortable. Make sure the backstage crew look after him well. Some hot chocolate or a tot of Triple X or something.

LALEE
Yes, dear.
Lalee leads Vijendra out. The lights fade in at the courtroom area, and with them the voices of the characters. The Judge raps the gavel several times. Silence.

LEELA
Didida, didida, didi DAAA! Nice!
The Judge rises. So do the others.

JUDGE
Court adjourned.
He steps down, looking spent. The others remain in their places as he makes a circuitous exit, passing Leela. He stops, peers into the basket, straightens, and speaks to the baby.
Court adjourned. Until further notice! Indefinitely!!
He leaves quickly. So do the other characters. Leela watches them leave. A beat.

LEELA
The end... of the beginning!
Blackout

Close of play

Home Movies

Second to None
Vijay Padaki

FOR

BHAGIRATI NARAYANAN

CHARACTERS IN THE PLAY

DHANU .... *Ambuja Seetaram. Well read, well informed, articulate, sensitive. A writer and mother of two. Heavily built, with a strong voice.*

DULARI .... *Daughter, in her late teens, in Junior College, affectionately called Dilu. In transition between puppy fat and campus slim.*

DEVEN .... *Devendra Seetaram, husband, wage earner. A secure job, a vaguely senior position. Defies further description.*

DASH .... *Adarsh, younger brother of Dulari. Self-sufficient, seen little, heard even less. At the age of rapid vertical growth at the expense of girth.*

HARI .... *Close friend of the family. Warm, unobtrusive.*

INTRODUCTION

The play, on completion, appeared to be the third in a trilogy that fell into place largely by itself. The other two plays would be *Family Albums*, written in the late 'eighties, and *Arrowheads*, written in the early 'nineties. The basic idea of *Home Movies* was brewing at the back of my mind for a long time, the characters revealing themselves as snapshots or comic strips every now and then. A period of forced rest in the middle of the year helped in drawing the bits and pieces into a mosaic of scenes that could be called a play script.

What *Home Movies* has in common with the other plays is the focus on the family, rather than on individual personalities. There is an emphasis on the characteristic process in the family, rather than on a plot or story line. This follows the writer's observation in his professional work that the character of a person cannot be separated from the character of the larger human interactive unit of which one is a part. It seems relatively easy to write a play around a strong, recognisable personality type. It appears to be a greater challenge, to this writer at least, to attempt a characterisation of that larger unit which must include the dynamics of interactions across individuals. These individuals have, of course, personalities of their own. But these are influencing the character of the larger unit all the time. At the same time, each of them is being shaped by it too. A multi-sectional view of the family seemed to offer interesting dramatic possibilities.

The character of the mother in *Home Movies* is dominating. It would be natural for a performing group to see the play as Dhanu's story. All the more reason for the group to rethink this and see themselves as an interesting *family* first, of which Dhanu is one element. The character of Dhanu is actually not too difficult to sketch. The consequences of unfulfilled ambition are not too unusual. On the other hand, every one of the others in the cast can make very interesting character sketches in themselves, each with an inner uniqueness.

As with the first two plays, *Home Movies* has been developed with a case study platform. The specifics of characterisation and the dramatic content, however, are necessarily fictional. The performing group is expected to engage in the usual rigorous research and improvisation to flesh out the characters by themselves around the minimal descriptions provided in the script. It is too easy to put 'clinical' labels on the characters in the play. These may be useful and even valid, but internal consistency and credibility must be regarded as more important than academic neatness. In *Family Albums* there is indeed a violent and tragic reaction to labelling.

There are three main acting areas in the play: a spacious sitting room in the Seetaram home, a smaller room occupied by Dash, and a space with a round table and chairs that serves both as the Seetarams' dining room and a café. Differences in level for the three areas, stage and budget permitting, would be nice.

With seamless scene changes and a brisk pace maintained, the play should have a running time of less than two hours. A single intermission should do, at the place indicated.

Language Notes

Ambuja: A Hindu goddess, a classical-orthodox name
Dulari: Darling, lovable
Guddi: From gudiya, doll. Nickname, like Dolly
Band-baaja: Hired processional band, common in weddings
Mandap: Canopy, gazebo-like structure. Enclosure for ceremony
Pujari: Priest. (From puja/pooja, ritual worship)
Baraat: The groom's party arriving in a procession
Dabba: Box, can
Sethia: Merchant
Shamiana: Decorative canvas enclosure for special occasions
Kanyakumari: Southern-most point of Indian sub-continent
Pooja: Worship. Also religious festival
Hungama: Hullabaloo
Dry days: Days on which bars and wine shops are closed
Chota: Small, as in chota peg
Shrimati: Title to address a (married) lady formally, respectfully
Yehi toh hai: This is it. From popular ad jingle 'This is it, it's the right choice, baby.'
Chaturvedi: Master of all four Vedas. A Hindu (Brahmin) surname
Bharatanatyam: A classical dance form
Lakshmi Kaki: Lakshmi aunty. (Kaki - paternal aunt)
Idli: Common breakfast food in South India
Sambar: Broth that goes with idli
Ravi Varma: Turn of century 'classical' painter
Semiya: Vermicelli
Payasam: Milk-based dessert
Galli cricket: Street-corner cricket
Vrindavan: Mythical/idyllic forest associated with Krishna
Lota: Metal tumbler-like container for water, liquids
Gundu: Nickname, affectionately meaning plump and naughty

FIRST PERFORMED

Performed by Kahe Vidushak at the VP@80 Festival in association with Bangalore Little Theatre and Deccan Herald July 2019

Dhanu .... APARNA JHA
Deven .... ASHISH ATHAWALE
Dilu .... ANKITA JAIN
Dash .... ADITYA NAIR
Harini .... SANGITA NAMBIAR
Ganganna .... SIDDHARTH SS
Guitarist .... SHREY CHAKRABORTY, AMIT SINGHA
Waiter .... TANUJ KAPOOR
Set Design .... ANKITA JAIN AND SRINIVAS BEESETTY
Sound Design .... ANKIT AGARWAL
Lighting Design .... SRINIVAS BEESETTY
Costumes .... ANKITA JAIN
Photography .... AHMED KHAN (ZAVIA)
Backstage .... TANUJ KAPOOR, ANKIT AGARWAL, MAULIK PANDEY, VAISHNAVI, SWAMI, SHUBHAM KHANNA
Assistant Director ANKITA JAIN
Directed by SRINIVAS BEESETTY

There were two changes to the script in this performance:

1. The family friend Hari was played by a woman and called Harini.
2. Non-speaking parts of a servant, a waiter, and a guitarist were introduced

PART I

[1]

In the dark, we hear a chorus of voices over the audio system, all women, singing a group song usually heard in a wedding. (The song could be in the language representing the location of the play in the production.) As the song fades out over the system, we hear the voices of Dhanu and Dulari continuing with the song. At the end of a stanza, only Dulari continues. The lights come on revealing mother and daughter concluding a doll's wedding on the floor in one part of a sitting room. The song ends. They both clap hands in childish glee.

DHANU

Only the best for Guddi at her wedding.

DULARI

The best band-baaja in the city.

DHANU

The grandest mandap.

DULARI

The richest ladies and gentlemen in attendance.

DHANU

The finest jewellery, the biggest diamonds, set in the purest gold.

DULARI

The yummiest wedding lunch.

DHANU

The best cooks from all over the country.

DULARI

The fattest pujari!

DHANU

Oh, look, the baraat has arrived! Oooh, look at the groom!

DULARI

The most dashing, the most charming...

DHANU

They are all so jealous, all those other girls and their mothers who couldn't snare him.

DULARI

The most eligible, most sought after, most handsome young man in the land.

DHANU

For our most talented, most sought after Guddi *(Dulari claps)*.

No dabba-wallah groom for our Guddi.

DULARI

Only the best.

DHANU

No government-wallah babu, no bazaar-wallah sethia.

DULARI

A prince for a princess.

DHANU

The best for Guddi. *(She sobs. Dulari comforts her.)*

DULARI

Mama, why do we always cry at weddings? *(No response. Dhanu continues with the wedding ceremony quietly.)*

Do they cry in the boy's family too?

DHANU

You can toss the rice. *(They both do.)*

The flowers now. *(They complete the ceremony.)*

DULARI

Are they married now? Can we serve the sweets?

DHANU

Wait. We must pray for the couple.

DULARI

What do you want for them, Mama?

DHANU

What would you like for them?

DULARI

A comfortable life. Lots of money.

DHANU

They have lots of it already.

DULARI

Lots of children!

DHANU

How many?

DULARI

Eight. Four boys and four girls. No, four. No, sorry, two. Only two.

DHANU

A boy and a girl?

DULARI

A boy and a girl, yes. Mama, can I serve the sweets now?

DHANU

I suppose so. Don't you want to pray for their children too?

DULARI

They will be smart!

She busies herself, serving sweets to imagined guests.

DHANU

Guddi will have a daughter first. She will be first. She will be known as the first in many things. Like her mother. She will be the cleverest girl ever.

DULARI

First in class, always.

DHANU

In school, in college, in everything she does.

DULARI

She will be pretty, I hope.

DHANU

Pretty, of course, in a special sort of way, in her own special way.

DULARI

The whole world will love her.

DHANU

There will be envy too. There will be many who will be envious, even jealous. They will have good reason to have their bile churning. There will be gossip behind her back. They will try to trip her on her every move.

DULARI

Mama...

DHANU

The poor idiots, they don't know her. They know nothing. Each time they think she is down, she rises again, defiant, strong, more beautiful, radiant. They can't understand it. They don't know what she is made of. She ignores them. They scowl. She smiles back. They bare their fangs, the handles of their daggers bulge under their sleeves. She knows, but doesn't care. She holds her head high.

DULARI

Mama, the guests...

DHANU

Announce dinner! Tell them to get their dinner. They can carry on with their backbiting gossip in the shamiana. We shall join them later. We must prepare a counter attack.

DULARI

They won't start without us. They can't start without the bride and her mother.

DHANU

Where is the father? He can accompany them.

DULARI

He is busy with...

DHANU

Send them home!

DULARI

Mama...

DHANU

My head hurts. Tell them I am not well. I must be excused.

DULARI

Mama, they will think...

DHANU

They will think what they want to think. They will say what they have been saying all the time anyway. As if we don't know what their dirty, vicious minds are full of. Let them walk out of here. Let them fall into the gutters and get sucked into their hell holes. Let them go back where they belong.

DULARI

All right, Mama. I'll send them away. I'll be back soon.

DHANU

Wait! Stay here. Sit here, next to me. *(She does. Dhanu lies down, resting her head on Dulari's lap.)*

They'll be all right. We will join them soon.

DULARI

(Gently massaging Dhanu's forehead) Guddi will be happy, won't she?

DHANU

She will be.

DULARI

And her prince? Will he be happy too?

DHANU

She will make him happy. She knows how to make him happy.

DULARI

Men are so hopeless on their own!

DHANU

Every girl has something to make a man happy. Her secret weapon. You should know that.

(Dulari giggles) She is the best.

DULARI

We have a great responsibility.

DHANU

Will you sit by me a little longer?

DULARI

As long as you wish, Mama.

DHANU

It feels good, having you here.

DULARI

I can sit here as long as you want me to.

DHANU

Love me?

DULARI

Mmmm.

DHANU

Is that yes or no?

DULARI

Yes, of course.

DHANU

How much?

DULARI

Oh, lots and lots and lots.

DHANU

How much is that?

DULARI

From Kashmir to Kanyakumari.

DHANU

Nut case!

DULARI

It's always so lovely, having our dolls wedding.

DHANU

Always.

DULARI

We must make it an annual thing. Fix a date and all.

DHANU

Same date every year. Great! Better than some of our stupid pooja festivals.

DULARI

Once a year, every year.

DHANU

Like an anniversary?

DULARI

No, not an anniversary. That's like going back to the same wedding. Guddi must have a fresh wedding each time.

DHANU

Of course! Guddi deserves a new husband each time.

DULARI

Mama, when was the first time we had a wedding for Guddi?

DHANU

Oh, you must have been five then. You got Guddi as a birthday gift when you were four. When you leave this house some day, maybe Guddi will stay back with me!

DULARI

I'm always with you, mama.

DHANU

You and I. We stick together.

DULARI

We make a great team, don't we Mama?

DHANU

You are very good with your hands.

DULARI

Close your eyes, mama. Close your eyes and take a nap if you want to.

She continues to stroke Dhanu. After a while she gently slips a cushion under her head, rises, and turns on some music, keeping it soft. She watches her mother from a distance as the lights fade out.

•

[2]

The music is continuing. When the lights come on, Dhanu is still lying down, alone. Deven enters, sees her, and goes to turn the music off.

DHANU

Don't.

DEVEN

It's past six.

DHANU

Are we going? Must we?

DEVEN

They wanted you a little earlier, didn't they? A little before seven, they said.

DHANU

What if we don't go?

DEVEN

Don't go early... ?

DHANU

What do you think they'll do?

DEVEN

Or don't go at all? You're not saying...

DHANU

(Rising) You go.

DEVEN

Without you?

DHANU

Go and see what they will do. Put on your best mingling face. Like the king who walked the streets after sunset, dressed as a beggar.

DEVEN

Dhanu, this evening...

DHANU

Beggar thief. Go and find out if they are happy or sad, what they are saying behind our backs, what they really think.

DEVEN

Why should they be saying anything different?

DHANU

Because it is much more fun. It is boring to be saying the same thing all the time.

DEVEN

In any case the actual awards function is not likely to...

DHANU

It is not an awards function. Fe-li-ci-ta-tion is what it's called. And our going early is meant to be a fa-ci-li-ta-tion, so that they know what to say in the speech-making.

DEVEN

In any case it is unlikely to get going before half past seven, what with a minister-type for a chief guest.

DHANU

And a platoon of office bearers for sundry incantations.

DEVEN

I wonder if they will put all of them on the dias from the start.

DHANU

Dais. Not dias. Rhymes with lace. The decoration.

DEVEN

Can you imagine the hungama when the awards function itself takes place?

DHANU

What hungama? It will all be quite stale by then. It's not even going to be in this city.

DEVEN

There has to be some write-up anyway.

DHANU

They will have a little mention in the city tit-bits section. About a column and three inches. About the same as an obituary.

DEVEN

A photograph or two.

DHANU

If it has been an exceptionally uneventful week, and if the staff photographer chooses to observe a dry day and can be located, they might include a picture of one award being given. Or received. Depends on how you look at it. They just might include a picture of Mr Ganesh Krishnamurthy. *(Pause. Deven looks anxiously at Dhanu for a moment and turns away. Dhanu continues.)*

And why ever not? Mr Ganesh Krishnamurthy, or GK, as he is called in artiste circles, or Jigs, as he is called in artsy circles, is the winner after all.

DEVEN

Yes, but look at the stuff he is turning out – the so-called genre he is driving.

DHANU

There was a jury, a distinguished panel.

DEVEN

We've talked about this before.

DHANU

When has talking between ourselves ever helped?

DEVEN

Dhanu, I've told you. What you bring to your work is special. There is depth, sensitivity...

DHANU

Substance beyond packaging, that's what you keep saying. Content beyond form.

DEVEN

Not form for form's sake.

DHANU

Empathy beyond indulgence. So, what's new?

DEVEN

Nothing new at all.

DHANU

Packaging wins.

DEVEN

Nothing new in that either.

DHANU

He has fans.

DEVEN

So do you.

DHANU

Devoted fans.

DEVEN

Also myopic. Fans around fads. *(Pause. Dhanu turns away, does not know what to say. Deven moves to comfort her.)*

People who matter know better. They know what you are capable of. You know that, don't you?

DHANU

I know that you are good for me.

DEVEN

People like GK come and go. They are little flashes with limited life.

DHANU

Who is GK? Nobody knew him till a couple of years ago.

DEVEN

They are also very narrowly set. They can't think beyond their in-things. They can't last. You are not one of them.

DHANU

I must be mad.

DEVEN

Mad not to see that you are different. You paint. You write. You sing. You have an appreciation of artistic traditions as they evolved over thousands of years, in so many different cultures. GK has none of this.

DHANU

Is he a fraud?

DEVEN

You showed me once long ago how the various arts in any culture must give and take among themselves – a co-evolution you called it.

DHANU

Is GK a fraud?

DEVEN

Dhanu, you know very well that...

DHANU

I know that you know that he's a fraud. You know that I know that he's a fraud. But what about all those unfortunates who know not and know not that they know not?

DEVEN

Bliss.

DHANU

Their birthright.

DEVEN

Ignore them.

DHANU

They are the majority. In the vibrant democracy in which we find ourselves, they shape the minds that shape the vibrant democracy.

DEVEN

You should go early as suggested by them and be interviewed. They should get to know you.

DHANU

Will it make a difference? They will write what they want to anyway.

DEVEN

So, are you saying, you are not going?

DHANU

Am I saying I am not going?

DEVEN

If they don't meet you...

DHANU

They will write anyway.

DEVEN

How can they?

DHANU

Because, it is the first law of human adaptation – to cover up ignorance with expert opinion.

DEVEN

You can at least minimise the error.

DHANU

You really want us to go, don't you?

DEVEN

I want you to go.

DHANU

You'll come with me?

DEVEN

Of course!

DHANU

All right. We'll go.

DEVEN

We'll need to hurry.

DHANU

I'll tell you what. We'll do a test. I will keep count of the number of times people refer to me as the wife of da da da, and you keep count of the number of times you are introduced as the husband of you know who.

[3]

Dash is at his desk, which is an amply-equipped computer workstation. It may be his own room or a room shared by Dulari and Dash. He is alone, absorbed. Deven enters, watches him from a distance. He goes up to the desk to talk to Dash, changes his mind, steps back, finds a seat for himself, and watches him at work. There is no response from Dash. After a while Deven rises to leave. Dulari enters.

DULARI

Dash! Guess what happened in school today... *(She stops, takes in the scene)* Oh, I'm sorry. I didn't know you were in the middle of... sorry to disturb you.

DEVEN

No disturbance at all. I was leaving. Dash and I were just...

DULARI

Bonding. One chota bout of bonding.

DEVEN

You could say that. He was so absorbed in whatever it is he is doing. I was just watching him. Absorbed. I was just watching him – admiring his concentration.

DULARI

You've never seen him like that?

DEVEN

Of course, I have.

DULARI

Has he ever been less absorbed?

DEVEN

That is him, isn't it?

DULARI

Do you think he is listening? Is he aware that there are two persons in the room talking about him?

DEVEN

I hope you are not making fun of him, Dilu.

DULARI

Of course not, papa! Dash, did you think I was making fun of you? Of course not!

DEVEN

Good.

DULARI

You didn't really think I would do that, did you?

DEVEN

No, I didn't.

DULARI

Thank god, the two of us are what we are – different, that is. Can you imagine Dash jabbering as much as me, the two of us switched on together?

DEVEN

I can't.

DULARI

Stereo surround sound.

DEVEN

Three hundred watts per channel.

DULARI

Non-stop.

DEVEN

Anyway, I was just leaving. And you were going to say something to Dash.

DULARI

Was I?

DEVEN

No?

DULARI

Oh yes, it was about the Pre-University essay contest.

DEVEN

They announced the results?

DULARI

I was coming down to tell you and mama too. No, not the final results. But I was informed that mine is in the short list.

DEVEN

That's great!

DULARI

There are six chosen for the finals, and mine is one of them.

DEVEN

How did you find out?

DULARI

The Princy told me. He saw me in the corridor near the notice board, called me over, and told me himself.

DEVEN

He is really fond of you, isn't he?

DULARI

He's so sweet.

DEVEN

Always been fond of you, I think.

DULARI

Such a pet.

DEVEN

Not without good cause. It's not everybody who has a track record like yours.

DULARI

It is not to be talked about. Strictly, strictly no. We are not supposed to know. He asked me to keep it to myself.

DEVEN

Have you told Mama?

DULARI

Not yet. You are the first to know. You and Dash.

DEVEN

Maybe you should have told her first.

DULARI

I was going to, but I saw the two of you first. Anyway it is only the four of us who will know. Strictly within the four of us.

DEVEN

Let's go and tell her.

DULARI

You go ahead. I will be there in a minute.

DEVEN

I won't say anything. You tell her yourself when you come. (*Deven leaves the room.)*

DULARI

Dash... you heard what I said, didn't you? Nobody must know about this. Nobody. You know how difficult it is for me not to talk about it. But I am not going to. Not to anybody in the whole world.

DASH

Not even Dabbu?

DULARI

Not even Dabbu. You promise you'll keep this to yourself?

DASH

OK.

DULARI

Thanks. I knew you would. See you at dinner.

She leaves the room. Dash continues with his work for a while, stops, rests his head on his arms on the desk.

[4]

The Seetaram family members with Hari. Deven is connecting a VCR to a TV set. Dash and Hari help in various ways, mainly by not getting in the way. Dhanu and Dulari are setting up coffee, drinks, and snacks.

Since this scene will slip into a television interview and slide back to the same scene, the director and actors can choose the stage business best suited to aid the transformations. What is given here should be treated as illustrative.

HARI

I thought the Reddys were joining us.

DHANU

Not this evening. This is just for us.

HARI

Just the family?

DHANU

Just the family.

HARI

A very special family!

DEVEN

And a very special friend.

HARI

The illustrious D-4!

DHANU

Sounds distinctly Enid Blyton.

DULARI

So what? The fact is that we are the celebrated D-4.

DHANU

I wonder why they chose Hari to interview me. What do you think, Hari? Why do you think they chose you?

HARI

Oh, I don't know. I suppose...

DEVEN

It is well known that he is a good friend. He knows you well, he is close to the family.

DHANU

Those would be reasons not to have him do it. He would bring in a lot of bias.

HARI

Dirty, four-letter word.

DHANU

Well, prejudice, if you'd rather have a dirty, nine-letter word.

DEVEN

The producers didn't seem to fear bias in Hari.

HARI

What about you? Did you think I would be biased in interviewing you?

DHANU

To be dishonest, I didn't think about it then.

HARI

Were you surprised?

DHANU

Not really.

HARI

Disappointed?

DHANU

No, I wasn't disappointed.

DEVEN

Let's say she was pleasantly apprehensive.

HARI

Oh? You didn't reveal this before.

Dulari is helping Dhanu touch up her makeup before the interview. Deven is settling down in front of the TV with Dash. Hari is setting up the interview space. (Also used in later scenes as the dining area and the café.)

DULARI

My, you are sweating. Here, use this pad. Are you nervous?

DHANU

I don't know. Do I look nervous? I shouldn't be. It's our Hari, after all.

DULARI

Keep the pad with you. With all those lights you might sweat some more.

DHANU

And dab my nose in front of the camera?

DULARI

You'll know when the camera is turned away, when it is only on Hari uncle.

DHANU

Ready?

DULARI

Set.

DHANU

Shall I go on?

DULARI

Go! You are looking great. Give it to them! *(She kisses her.)* I'll wait here.

Crossfade. Dhanu walks into the interview area, which has a round table and two chairs. Hari seats her, gives her a lapel mike, and helps her with it and the various preparatories. When ready, they 'face the camera'. Hari begins.

HARI

Good evening. And welcome to the Friday Evening Profile. We have in the studio today a person who has enriched the cultural life of our city in very many ways, but has managed somehow to remain out of public gaze so far. It is not going to be easy for her to maintain that low profile, not after the announcement of awards by IFPA, the Indus Foundation for Promotion of the Arts, in which she and her work were featured prominently. Ladies and gentlemen, Shrimathi Ambuja Seetaram, better known widely as Dhanu. Welcome to the programme, Dhanu. It's nice to have you with us.

DHANU

Thank you, Hari. It's nice to be here.

HARI

As you know, Friday Evening Profile is like Friday dressing. It is informal and warm and...

DHANU

Then you will not be addressing me as Shrimatiji, thank goodness.

HARI

Not at all. Dhanu should be fine, I suppose.

DHANU

Yes, of course.

HARI

We can start right there. How did Ambuja get the name Dhanu?

DHANU

Well, it is a long story, but I'll try and make it short.

Crossfade. Deven, Dash, and Dulari are watching the interview.

DULARI

Here we go again!

DEVEN

Shhh!

DULARI

They all ask.

DEVEN

So, what's wrong? It is a natural question.

DULARI

But Uncle Hari knows! Why wouldn't he... ?

DEVEN

Shhh!

DULARI

Don't worry, the VCR is on.

DASH

We can watch it a hundred times.

DULARI

Get on with it, Mama, get on with it!

Crossfade. Hari continues with the interview.

HARI

You have won many awards over the years. Tell us about your first reactions when you heard about the Indus Foundation award.

DHANU

It was my daughter who took the phone. She covered the mouthpiece and said to me that it was a very serious voice. It sounded like somebody had died. So when the caller announced who she was and what she was calling for, my first reaction was one of relief. At that moment I don't think I caught all of what she said.

HARI

Except that you had won the second prize in the Indus Foundation awards.

DHANU

Except that I had won some award, one out of several announced.

HARI

You happen to know most – if not all – of the other artists honoured by IFPA. Do you have any comments on them? On their work?

DHANU

Every artist has his own calling, his or her own pair of spectacles, with its own special lenses. Some have binoculars, some microscopes. You need to go up a very tall mountain to understand why they see the same things in so many different ways. As long as we are on the ground, it's best to accept the differences beyond the similarities. There is great beauty in the diversity. Why spoil it with analysis and wordplay?

HARI

Have you been up that mountain?

DHANU

We all know the mountain must exist somewhere. Nobody knows where it is. Nobody has climbed it yet.

HARI

Nobody?

DHANU

Little mole hills, yes. Some people find the view breathtaking.

HARI

Would it be correct to say that you are sharing with us your philosophy of the arts?

DHANU

A very personal philosophy. I don't expect everybody to subscribe to it.

HARI

Since you have displayed your abundance of talent in many different forms of expression, would you say...

DHANU

I don't particularly care for that word – Talent. It has a commodity like sound to it. To be commercially exploited.

HARI

But there is such a thing as talent, is there not? Some have more of it, some have less.

DHANU

How do you know this? This difference in heights that you suggest – what instrumentation have you come across to assess 'talent', and to say that I have more or less of it when stood next to another person?

HARI

I wasn't referring particularly to you or anybody else. It was...

DHANU

Were you not? I thought questions like these were always posed with particular persons in mind, with some purpose in mind. Didn't you have something in mind, Hari?

HARI

Well, yes and no. Not what I think you believe to be the purpose.

DHANU

What do you think was my reading of it?

HARI

(To the camera) Dear viewers, you have just seen a bit of pure Dhanu repartee. If I had not been prepared for it, this programme would surely have slipped into Dhanu interviewing me instead.

DHANU

That was clever of you, Hari, avoiding my question like that.

HARI

Back to the discussion, then.

DHANU

Back to your question, then.

HARI

Right, we will accept that you would rather not get into a discussion on the subject of talent, on the grounds...

DHANU

Please don't get me wrong. I'm not avoiding any discussion. It's just that the assessment of talent cannot be free of our assumptions of what talent is – or ought to be – in the first place.

HARI

Isn't that true of all qualities, all human attributes?

DHANU

Possibly true. Quite probably true.

HARI

So, is it futile, even meaningless, to try and assess talent?

DHANU

Not if all are agreed that we are only looking for something that we are all agreed upon already.

HARI

The rules of the game.

DHANU

Carved in stone.

HARI

The old dictum – we see things not as they are, but as we are.

DHANU

Every language and culture has a saying that means the same thing.

HARI

And yet...

DHANU

I know you are going to say that the fact is the beast exists. It must be somebody's job to spot it, harness it, get everybody else to notice it.

HARI

Who should do this?

DHANU

Only those deemed to be already talented shall be deemed qualified to recognise others as deemed talented!

HARI

I am not sure you mean that seriously.

DHANU

Of course, the more objective alternative is to have a totally disinterested cadre of professionals, who have no talent at all themselves, to pick and choose the talented as they wish.

HARI

Are you referring to any particular... ?

DHANU

You will need outstanding talent to move this extraordinary body to give you due recognition. If you get the recognition, well, you have proved that you had what it took.

HARI

Are you suggesting, Dhanu, that awards and titles have no real value in the life of artists?

DHANU

I don't think I said that.

HARI

That they have little value in your own life as an artist? (Pause)

DHANU

I will not disagree with that.

HARI

Thank you, Dhanu, for your views on the subject, although you wished not to discuss it.

DHANU

Clever Hari!

HARI

Moving on, then, what in your opinion is the secret of success in artistic pursuits? If we put aside the talent factor, what other factor accounts for the track record of achievements that some seem to have, and others don't have?

DHANU

You have answered the question yourself.

HARI

Have I? I didn't know. What is that answer?

DHANU

Momentum. Nothing succeeds like momentum.

HARI

But surely it begins with some movement, somewhere.

DHANU

The push. The boost.

HARI

Where does that come from?

DHANU

All movement requires a push, the force for which must necessarily be located outside the body itself. Your son's middle school physics text would tell you that.

HARI

How does that translate into human endeavours?

DHANU

A godfather. Godparent, if it is important to appear politically correct. Call it by any name – patron, well-wisher, sponsor, contact, godfather – it is the right person at the right place at the right time that makes or breaks your momentum.

HARI

In your own experience...

DHANU

It is not the same as an agent or impresario. Not even the editor. They do mere face-lift jobs. Sure, they are street smart. They can get you a quarter page coverage in the local newspaper if they move on it. And then what? You are left with that cutting in your scrap book. No, the difference between an agent and a godfather is not always understood.

HARI

In your own experience, who have been the persons most responsible for your success?

DHANU

You mean a godfather?

HARI

As you said, called by any other name.

DHANU

Not everybody has one, you know. Not everybody has the configuration of heavenly bodies to have one. You are born to a godfather, it seems. You cannot acquire one just like that.

HARI

In your own life... ?

DHANU

No such luck.

HARI

What about Ganesh Krishnamurthy? What would you say about his role in your work?

DHANU

GK? Good Heavens! He was just a good friend, that's all.

HARI

Was?

DHANU

Well, we don't seem to be meeting as often as we used to. I can't remember when the last time was.

HARI

Ten years ago, when you first made a mark in the critique of contemporary cultural movements, you acknowledged an intellectual debt to GK.

DHANU

I did. It was a newly emerging field of writing then, highly multifaceted. They were exciting times.

HARI

It is well known that GK arranged for your fellowship in the National Academy.

DHANU

It is widely believed to have been so.

HARI

Most recently, he is on record saying how happy he was that you were chosen for the second place in the prestigious Indus Foundation Award. After all, you are both from the same circle of artists, he said.

DHANU

Are you by any chance suggesting...

HARI

Suggesting what?

DHANU

No, of course not. Look, you might like to have something to quote from me too – as my having gone on record, so to speak.

HARI

Go ahead, Dhanu.

DHANU

Awards have a way of dropping into people's lives and changing the scenery all of a sudden.

HARI

This is not the first award to come your way.

DHANU

No, it is not.

HARI

And not the last, we hope.

DHANU

That we can never say. Nor should we waste time thinking about it. We just get on with our work.

HARI

(To camera) Ganesh Krishnamurthy, I hope you are watching the programme, and that the words of Dhanu Seetaram strike the right chords. *(To Dhanu)* Now, a question that every viewer must be wanting me to ask you.

DHANU

What was your first reaction when you were informed that you had won the second place in the Indus Foundation Awards? *(A pause)*

Crossfade. Deven, Dash, and Dulari are switching off the TV/VCR system. Dhanu sweeps in, but stops at a distance. She is visibly agitated. Deven notices and goes up to her.

DEVEN

Welcome back, Dhanu!

DULARI

You were great, mama! You looked good, you sounded good, just like the last time you were...

DEVEN

We just ran the tape to see the whole interview once again. I thought you were staying back at the studio with Hari... to meet GK.

DHANU

I was tired. I wanted to get back.

DEVEN

You didn't stay for the second part of the programme? The interview with GK?

DHANU

No. No, I didn't.

DULARI

We have it on the tape. Shall we...

DHANU

No. Not just now.

DEVEN

No, not now... we can always... maybe Dash and Dilu should get the dinner going. It's quite late, really.

Dash and Dulari start to move, Deven ushering them out.

DHANU

No need. The three of you just go ahead. I'm going to relax for a while. I'm tired.

DULARI

Do that, mama.

DEVEN

All this studio-wudio business can be quite taxing, I suppose. We will join you after dinner.

DULARI

Then you can tell us all the stories!

DEVEN

All the things the camera didn't catch for us.

DHANU

Go, get your dinner before it gets cold.

Deven, Dash, and Dulari leave. Dhanu sits motionless for a while. She moves to the TV, takes out the tape cassette from the player, and walks around the room playing with the cassette. She gets an idea, she picks the tape out of the cassette, plucks the end free, and starts pulling it out of the cassette, dropping it all over the floor as she walks about, her mood lifting, but controlled. She then picks up the end and starts to wrap the TV set with the tape. The wrapping done, she returns to the seat with the cassette in her hand, with the other end of the tape in it. She sits watching the TV set with the 'reins' in her hand.

[5]

Dhanu has dozed off, the cassette on her lap. Dulari is standing next to her. She gently takes away the cassette from Dhanu and begins to unwrap the tape from the TV set. Midway through the task Dhanu stirs.

DHANU

Is that you, Deven?

DULARI

No, Mama, it's me.

DHANU

Have you eaten?

DULARI

Yes, mama, all of us. We have cleared up.

DHANU

Come and sit next to me.

DULARI

Shall I get you something? A hot chocolate?

DHANU

No, just come and sit here.

Dulari has finished the unwrapping. She stands next to Dhanu, cassette in hand with the tape all over the floor.

DULARI

You were good, mama, you really were.

DHANU

What are you going to do with it?

DULARI

I don't know. It's probably better on a CD anyway. Hari uncle said he could...

DHANU

Hari uncle is a busy man.

DULARI

I know, but he did say...

DHANU

A very busy man.

DULARI

Yes, but he always makes time for us.

DHANU

Even if he has to shoot two interviews the same evening sometimes.

DULARI

(Mischievously) Busier than Mrs Seetaram? Readings, receptions, cocktails, autograph events! Oh, and some interviews too!

DHANU

In a bookstore, or on Mrs Narayan's terrace.

DULARI

With the right people in attendance.

DHANU

Not in the banquet hall of the Taj, not on Mrs Wadia's lawn.

DULARI

The wrong people.

DHANU

Now you're telling me.

DULARI

Wrong place, wrong people, wrong reasons.

DHANU

Wrong caterer.

DULARI

Wrong wine.

DHANU

Wrong cheese.

DULARI

Wrong reading, wrong lines.

DHANU

Wrong necklines, wrong hemlines.

DULARI

Wrong gossip, wrong scandals.

DHANU

Wrong husbands, wrong wives.

DULARI

Yehi toh, yehi toh, yehi toh...

DHANU

Yehi toh hai wrong choice, baby!

A high five, and then together to tune.

DHANU

Ataka lataka, Guddi lost her bataka,

DULARI

Nataka khataka, Guddi found her phataka.

DHANU

Rataka sataka, Guddi lost her mataka,

DULARI AND DHANU

(Together) Gataka jataka, Guddi found her man! *(They laugh, hug, kiss, and generally enjoy themselves.)*

DULARI

Guddi feeling good?

DHANU

Mmmm, good!

DULARI

Guddi eat something?

DHANU

No!

DULARI

Guddi play some more?

DHANU

Yes!

DULARI

Guddi have hot chocolate, then play some more. No hot chocolate, no play.

DHANU

Okay, hot chocolate.

DULARI

Good girl, Guddi. You wait here. Hot chocolate coming.

Dulari leaves. Dhanu watches her go. She picks up the tape lying on the floor and starts to wrap it up on the cassette, humming and dancing a gentle step as she does so.

[6]

The interview area is now a café. Deven and Hari are at the table there.

HARI

What did you mean by that exactly?

DEVEN

I can't explain much more. You know it's not easy. It is a very...

HARI

I know that. A very difficult situation – for you at least. But I still don't understand why I should be given this treatment.

DEVEN

I am sorry.

HARI

Dulari is like my own daughter. Remember what she said once? 'Hari uncle is the only one here who can call me Dilu.' That was in front of all the guests in her last birthday party. And this year – you have to meet me like this to give me a personal dis-invitation.

DEVEN

You know I am sorry.

HARI

You know I am hurt.

DEVEN

I can only say Dulari – Dilu – she still thinks very highly of you.

HARI

Dhanu... it's Dhanu, right? *(Deven does not reply)* All right, Deven. It's all right, I understand. You have my word. I will not be there on Dilu's birthday. *(Pause)* I won't cause any embarrassment. I promise.

DEVEN

It's not just the birthday.

HARI

That follows logically, doesn't it? No, don't worry. I will not be a visitor in your lovely home any more.

DEVEN

I knew you would understand.

HARI

I do, believe me, I do. But do you understand what you are doing? You and Dhanu – do you see what is happening in your lives?

DEVEN

It's not the best of times...

HARI

It is in the worst of times that you could do with the warmth and comfort of good friends. But where are they? They have not left you. No, you have dropped them, one by one, with seasonal regularity.

DEVEN

I wish you wouldn't...

HARI

I wouldn't normally, not earlier. But now I think I should. You and Dhanu might have struck me off your list, Deven, but I have not struck you off mine. You are still a friend of mine, and by my book of rules it is okay to hold a mirror to one's friends now and then.

DEVEN

I suppose you are entitled to your point of view.

HARI

About both things – the friendship and the mirror. Deven, do you think the outside world doesn't notice these things? Your ever-changing circle of friends? In today, out tomorrow?

DEVEN

What about you? You have been a permanent fixture, have you not?

HARI

A bit longer than some others. I must have been an accident, some freak. But even that was not forever. All good things must end.

DEVEN

I am sorry.

HARI

There you go again. Don't feel too badly about it, Deven. As long as it lasted – which was really a long time – it was a wonderful friendship. And it was with the whole family – you, that perpetually chirping bulbul of a daughter, the quiet but frightfully perceptive Dash – god, he is terrific – the whole family, yes. And Dhanu...

DEVEN

She has never hidden her thoughts about you.

HARI

Could there be a gap, perhaps, between thought and feeling?

DEVEN

She has often referred to you as a friend, philosopher, guide.

HARI

Pleased to be of service.

DEVEN

I also believe that she has gained a lot from your presence. You have influenced her in many ways. You might not realise it, but you have been something of a counsellor too. She has grown in your company.

HARI

Then it must be time to phase out. When people find themselves growing, they take out their anger on the counsellor! *(Pause)* Somebody will take my place.

A long pause. Hari extends his hand. Deven takes it. They smile warmly.

HARI

Is it all right to send a greeting to Dilu through you?

DEVEN

Why, of course!

HARI

A little gift maybe?

DEVEN

Maybe. Why not?

HARI

And a greeting with compliments of the season for Dhanu?

DEVEN

I'm meeting her soon, in about half an hour.

HARI

Here?

DEVEN

No, not here. Another café.

HARI

Café hopping today, are we? You could have met here. I'm leaving now anyway.

DEVEN

It just happened that way.

HARI

Do we have another minute or so? *(Takes out an envelope.)*

DEVEN

Sure, go ahead.

HARI

GK was making kind enquiries...

DEVEN

Nice of him.

HARI

You know that MetroBiz has had a long relationship with him?

DEVEN

The TV company?

HARI

That's right. Well, GK proposed to MetroBiz that they should consider dramatising Dhanu's award winning novel into a TV serial. *(He looks at Deven for a response.)*

Does that come as a surprise?

DEVEN

Yes... but no, not really.

HARI

And GK being Ganesh Krishnamurthy, there was no need for a second opinion. MetroBiz said okay.

DEVEN

That was nice of him.

HARI

Not just that. He even suggested a format for the serial. A unique piece of work deserves a unique format, he said. The serial is to have Dhanu as a narrator, providing links between scenes, and reflecting on her writing experience – her writing in general and the creation of this novel in particular.

DEVEN

How far has this idea gone?

HARI

Far enough to be turned into a proposal. They are thinking of a 13-part serial. Here – this is a letter of invitation from MetroBiz to Dhanu. It contains the broad proposal, and has an invitation to meet the Chief Producer in MetroBiz for a discussion on how Dhanu and the company may proceed further.

DEVEN

Do you have any... ?

HARI

A carrier-pigeon service, pure and simple, and nothing more. Here it is. I must now request you to kindly pass it on to her.

DEVEN

Thanks. *(Pause)* Thank you, Hari.

HARI

Pleased to be of service. *(Pause)* I liked her as a lovely person. Who knows? Some day she may win a first prize, and it won't be the same any more.

[7]

The living room. Dulari is alone, watching TV. The telephone rings. She picks up the receiver (or cordless unit).

DULARI

Yes? Oh, Hi, Hari uncle! How come, at this time? Are you... No, he's not back... I have no idea... Do you want me to... Okay, but let me tell you what happened in class today... Why later? Gosh, you sound like our PT master today... Okay, okay baba, later. See you!

[8]

The cafe area again, but it is another restaurant-café. Deven and Dhanu are at the table. The opened envelope and the papers are on the table.

DHANU

Just like that? MetroBiz sent this invitation and letter just like that?

DEVEN

It is a good proposal, is it not?

DHANU

How did it get to you? You said it was delivered by hand. Who gave this to you?

DEVEN

Somebody from the Company. That is not so important, Dhanu. It's the proposal that is important. The idea of the proposal – that is important.

DHANU

Is there something you are not telling me?

DEVEN

All I know is that we have a letter from the Chief Producer of MetroBiz. It has a proposal. There is an invitation. It is for you. They seem keen on meeting you and working with you. That is all I know.

DHANU

MetroBiz did a 26-part serial with GK's whatever it was he wrote. Okay, that's GK there, and this is Dhanu here. It's not the 13-parts in the serial that I am thinking about, but why would MetroBiz want to do this in the first place? I smell something. It is too much like the smell of a sewer rat.

DEVEN

Take it easy, Dhanu. Just think about the letter before us now – whatever it might be that made MetroBiz write to you.

DHANU

It was GK, wasn't it? Tell me the truth. You know about it! Tell me now – it was GK, wasn't it?

DEVEN

Well, maybe it was. So what?

DHANU

We don't need this patronising shit. What is GK's claim to fame anyway?

DEVEN

He has been around a long time. His work is well known... whatever we might...

DHANU

His only claim to fame is his fame to claim. What does he mean by this now?

DEVEN

He admires your work. That's all it means.

DHANU

I wish GK would drop dead! He should drop dead! Drop dead!! *(A long pause. Deven seats Dhanu, comforts her.)*

DEVEN

Are you okay?

DHANU

What do you think?

DEVEN

I just thought...

DHANU

It is not menopause! *(Deven manages a weak laugh)* I'm okay, thank you. Are you? You must be. Everybody is supposed to be okay, right? Everybody, everywhere, okay every bloody minute of their lives.

DEVEN

Amazing how your sense of humour never fails you. *(Pause)*

DHANU

Time to write that letter.

DEVEN

The letter to... you think we should?

DHANU

We should have done it long ago. You should have listened to me. The Indus Foundation needs to know.

DEVEN

Isn't it too late to write to them? You know that GK is now on their Programmes Committee.

DHANU

No, not to the Foundation. It's time to alert the media, it's time the public got to know.

DEVEN

GK may deny everything. He may retaliate.

DHANU

He will not. We know him well enough. Anyway, he'd better not.

DEVEN

But if he does?

DHANU

Then everybody will get to see how unoriginal he really is. They will see why he is not what he is not.

DEVEN

Dhanu...

DHANU

They will see the nothingness between his two ears, and the nothingness between his two legs.

DEVEN

Right now, can we just decide on the MetroBiz letter?

DHANU

Who knows, even MetroBiz may sit up and decide to do something about it.

DEVEN

You've made up your mind?

DHANU

What do you think?

DEVEN

Well, if it has to be done...

DHANU

Write, then.

DEVEN

You want me to write?

DHANU

Better you than me.

DEVEN

Would be best if it was neither of us – a third party – somebody seen as detached and objective.

DHANU

It can still be somebody else, detached, a third party.

DEVEN

Who do we know who'd be willing to write a piece like that?

DHANU

You. Why not? You've written letters to the editor before, haven't you? And you know you write well. That series you wrote on sex and violence in Indian cinema made pretty good reading. The name you used was clever too. Chaturvedi, Hrishikesh Chaturvedi. Commanded respect.

DEVEN

That was for fun, Dhanu.

DHANU

Serious writing on a fun topic. This time it will be some fun writing on a serious topic. So, when will you get down to it? Okay, you can decide in whose name you write – vedic or epic or plain Seetaram.

DEVEN

Give me some time?

DHANU

Five minutes? We can order a second round of coffee by then.

DEVEN

Okay Dhanu, let's do it. I will need your help though.

DHANU

We can jot down the main points now – if you're up to it, that is – and you can give it body and shape when we get home.

DEVEN

(Taking out a scribble pad and pen) What is a good way to start?

Hari enters cautiously, sees the two of them together, and tries to get the attention of Deven.

HARI

Deven...

DEVEN

Oh, hello Hari. What a surprise! What brings you here?

HARI

Sorry for the intrusion... Hello, Dhanu... I called home. Dilu... Dulari told me you might be here, so I took a chance.

DEVEN

Sit down Hari. Shall we order a coffee for you?

HARI

No, thanks. I have to rush... just wanted to see you for a minute.

DEVEN

What is it, Hari?

HARI

Bad news. Terrible, terrible news. GK is dead.

DEVEN

GK? Dead? Are you sure? How did...

HARI

Very sudden. Just an hour ago. He complained of pain in the chest. Gowri was with him. She went to the phone to call their family doctor. GK walked to the bathroom to clear his throat. He collapsed there. When Gowri returned... he was... it was all over.

DEVEN

Oh, my god! Oh, my god...

HARI

Please excuse me now. I am going back to his place. I had to find you and tell you.

DEVEN

Thanks, Hari.

HARI

Will you come there? Both of you?

DEVEN

You go ahead, Hari. We will...

Hari leaves. Deven rests his forehead in his palms. Dhanu remains still, staring ahead.

PART II

[9]

A spot picks up Deven and Dhanu in a downstage corner. They are in whites and dark glasses, standing, solemn, motionless.

Crossfade to Dulari and Dash in their room, playing a computer game, fully absorbed. Dulari hums to herself as she plays. Dash observes her moves quietly.

Crossfade to Deven and Dhanu. They raise their cupped hands and drop flowers in front. They remain standing for a while, heads bent, and then file out.

Crossfade to Dulari and Dash. They are still in front of Dash's work station. He is showing her how to operate a programme.

DULARI

Cool! That's really cool! You did this all by yourself?

DASH

Sort of.

DULARI

How did you think of something so fantastic? It's really way out, man. It's way, way out there.

DASH

Well, I saw so many people struggling with the same problem. Me too. Then I thought if there can be a programme to tell you if your spelling is right or wrong, there should be one for your physics syllabus too.

DULARI

Is it only for physics?

DASH

For now, yes. Chemistry is next. I'll start on the biology texts after that. That will take a little longer. Of course maths is the easiest. I'll do that at the end.

DULARI

I can tell my friends now, right? It's not a secret anymore?

DASH

Just your best friends, nobody else.

DULARI

Okay, so this is what you did. You first fed the text book through the scanner to the belly of your PC. Then?

DASH

That's where the programme comes in.

DULARI

It digests the stuff and burps.

DASH

It breaks down the total into single, indivisible bits of information.

DULARI

Then you feed in a question. Can it be any question? From anywhere?

DASH

As long as the info is available in the text, any question – from your homework, from exam papers, from anywhere.

DULARI

You feed in the question, press the little button here, and whammo-bingo! The correct answer!

DASH

You can choose the length of the answer. A maximum of 100 words per question. That's more than enough for all science subjects.

DULARI

Fill in the blanks? Multiple choice questions?

DASH

Just say how many words, and you have it.

DULARI

When will you do one for my English and sociology texts?

DASH

No go. The programme works only with facts. It can't handle bullshitting.

DULARI

You can't take it into an exam hall, can you?

DASH

Not yet. Maybe they'll allow it some day. It's good mainly for doing your homework. And studying for your exams.

DULARI

Has it ever given you a wrong answer?

DASH

Never.

DULARI

Like, 'What is the formula for measuring the heat generated inside the boys' room from the noise levels escaping from the chimney?' And the answer churned out is 'Earthworms.'

DASH

The programme is foolproof. But you can still get a wrong answer.

DULARI

It can happen?

DASH

It can happen under two conditions only. You can have a cheap textbook which has factual errors printed in it. Or you can have a question which has been worded incorrectly.

DULARI

Shit! That's more than half of our question papers. 'How many boys' brains are needed to make one earthworm?' And I thought my kid brother was a genius!

DASH

Here, let me show you something.

He takes out a large envelope from a drawer and gives it to Dulari.

DULARI

What is it?

DASH

Open it. (*She does, cautiously. There is a medallion that looks like a CD, laminated on a certificate. She looks at it in surprise and awe.)*

DULARI

Wow! Holy mother of all creepy crawlies on earth! This is yours? A citation and a medallion! For this programme? When did you get it?

DASH

Some time ago.

DULARI

(Reading) Outstanding Young Achiever Award instituted by ISIS, the Indian Society for Information Sciences... The first prize for the Pre-graduate category... Wow! Wow! Wow! My kid brother is a genius after all! Was there anything else? A cash award?

DASH

A small amount. I upgraded my system.

DULARI

Mama and Papa don't know about it?

DASH

As if they'd notice... (*A pause. Dash moves away and sits by himself. Dulari goes up to him.)*

DASH

Dilu, you'll keep this to yourself, right? Promise?

DULARI

How can this be kept a secret? It will be out everywhere – if it isn't already.

DASH

Only in the computer magazines.

DULARI

People out there know about this? (Pause) And nobody here...

DASH

Nobody.

DULARI

Why not? Why haven't you told us?

DASH

Who is interested in computers? Who reads computer magazines?

DULARI

That's not the point. This is an All-India prize. A first prize.

DASH

It will get to be known some time – by and by.

DULARI

Dash, Dashy, please... What is bothering you?

DASH

I am scared... Don't look at me like that...

DULARI

Like what?

DASH

Like mama... you know what is bothering me... but you must look as if you don't know... you are beginning to...

DULARI

I'm sorry, Dash, I'm really sorry.

A long pause. A quiet moment, a moment of closeness.

Tell me what you want to say.

DASH

When was the last time I won a prize?

DULARI

I don't know. I can't remember.

DASH

It can't be very important anyway. But I remember. You want to know? It was in that on-the-spot painting competition on Independence Day at the club.

DULARI

Oh, yes, I remember that one! I carried your sandwich box and juice for you. You were five then.

DASH

I was six.

DULARI

And what excitement there was in the evening when the prizes were given away.

DASH

On that evening I lost all interest in painting. Forever.

DULARI

That's right. I remember now. Mama tried so hard to get you to take painting seriously.

DASH

She must have been... disappointed?

DULARI

She tried a tutor. He came home for your painting lessons.

DASH

Later it was for music lessons. I couldn't stand it!

DULARI

Why, Dash?

DASH

I didn't know then. I think I know now. At that time I was just scared that I couldn't stand it.

DULARI

Scared?

DASH

My memory of the details – the things as they happened – is near zero. But my memory of how I felt is as strong as ever. It was a strange sort of fear, something that had me pinned down. I was scared, but I didn't know what it was or why.

DULARI

You were scared – you? You were not even afraid of the dark. I was. I had to ask you to put on the light in the bathroom.

DASH

It returned. It was the same fear I felt when I won this award. Exactly the same feeling, down here in my belly. Except, this time I knew what was behind it, why I was scared. I think I knew.

DULARI

I think I know what you mean Dash.

DASH

Do you?

DULARI

Is that difficult to believe? I will try, Dash. I will try really hard to understand. I promise.

DASH

I know you will. I think you do know.

DULARI

Hey, I've always known you were different.

DASH

Different?

DULARI

Of course, different. Even the way you speak – like some professor-type. Don't look at me like that! I didn't mean different in any odd way. Just different.

DASH

Uh-huh.

DULARI

You remember the stories we made up? You made up. Mama used to ask me to look after you, to tell you stories to keep you occupied. But you would just take over and do all the storytelling! All your own. I really loved looking after you!

DASH

Thank god, mama didn't find out. She would have sent me to some drama classes. My little Dash is a great actor, you know!

DULARI

Like I was a great Bharatanatyam dancer, you know!

DASH

Among other things. *(A pause. They look at each other)* Funny how these things stick.

DULARI

What if I'm not really a great dancer, but believe deeply that I am?

DASH

Desperately.

DULARI

Desperately. What if I'm not any of the things I am supposed to believe I am? How will I know?

DASH

Outgoing, full of life, loving...

DULARI

How will I know?

DASH

'I love meeting people', 'I love helping out... '

DULARI

Okay, okay, stop throwing it at me. What about you? Quiet going, in a world of his own...

DASH

Cold, withdrawn... Dilu, do you sometimes get the feeling you are not really you? That you are doing something or saying something – you don't know why?

DULARI

I want to tell you something. Your turn to promise you'll keep this to yourself.

DASH

Go ahead.

DULARI

Pukka secret, okay? You remember when Lakshmi kaki died? We were there the whole day, we got home only at eleven that night.

DASH

Mama and you did a lot of work in their house that day.

DULARI

Okay, we all pitched in and all that, but what I wanted to tell you was this. I don't know how to say this, but I didn't feel anything. I kept thinking about it, asking myself why am I not feeling sad like everyone else, why am I not feeling anything...

DASH

And you loved Lakshmi kaki so much.

DULARI

Of course I loved her. I loved her a lot... I think. That's what I kept thinking. Don't I love Lakshmi kaki, don't I? I knew I did. There didn't seem to be any doubt about that. But she was gone, and I wasn't feeling anything. I was not crying, there were no tears... so strange.

DASH

Nobody could tell.

DULARI

I remember thinking, what do I do, how do I behave... I just kept myself busy, doing something or the other all the time.

DASH

All the time, till we got home. You and mama – so many people talked about it.

DULARI

Actually... here's another thing, don't make fun of me, please... actually, every now and then I'd be thinking, when do we get away, when do we go home.

DASH

You are not supposed to think thoughts like that!

DULARI

I thought of that too! You know, I never got to ask you – what did you do when we reached Lakshmi kaki's place? You were silent right through the car ride. As usual.

DASH

I remember the first sight of the body when we got there.

DULARI

Laid out in the verandah, with the lamp at her feet.

DASH

She was covered completely with flowers. Only her face was visible. Flowers all over.

DULARI

What did you do? How did you feel?

DASH

My turn. I went up to the terrace. I sat down and cried. I was there for nearly half an hour.

DULARI

God, you never told me.

DASH

I think I had a crush on Lakshmi kaki.

DULARI

You little devil, you!

DASH

You didn't know this, but it was she who got me interested in maths and electronics... and computers.

DULARI

And here you are, winning the Young Achiever award and all.

DASH

Making that programme work was more fun than winning.

DULARI

What if you didn't win? What if you were a runner-up?

DASH

I don't know. Maybe the prize for the second place would have knocked out the fun. And knocked in something else.

DULARI

You'd become...

DASH

The runner-up syndrome, they call it. They say that those who come third are disappointed, but happy. Those who come second are unhappy and bitter. *(A long pause)* And it is habit forming.

DULARI

Anyway, you are numero uno. And one of these days you'll be in Who's Who.

DASH

You've got to be kidding.

DULARI

My kid brother in Who's Who.

DASH

No, thank you.

DULARI

Why not? It will be great to keep it in the drawing room, next to the marble Ganesha.

DASH

Dilu, I don't think you know how it works. Who's Who thrives on the vanity of people. You have to pay to get yourself included. It is a business, that's all. Plain and simple.

DULARI

How do you know this?

DASH

I found the papers on mama's writing desk. It came in the post. It is made to look like an invitation. Then the amount you pay is mentioned. A nominal service charge, they call it. Neat. You want to be noticed? Pay for it.

DULARI

A lot of people want to, I guess.

DASH

There must be. That's how it runs.

DULARI

Getting yourself into the City Times is more honourable, I guess.

DASH

More cool.

DULARI

But the need to be written about is the same, isn't it? *(A pause)*

DASH

Why are we talking about all this?

DULARI

Because... it just came. Maybe...

DASH

Maybe we had something on our minds.

DULARI

Some people.

DASH

Ourselves too, maybe.

DULARI

Maybe.

DASH

Tell me, what does mama want from us most? How would she like the world to see us?

DULARI

I've never thought about that. There could be many things.

DASH

What virtue?

DULARI

I don't know. Humility? Like herself? She is always saying how important it is to remain humble.

DASH

Yes, she is very proud about her humility.

[10]

The living room. Deven and Dhanu enter. They are dressed well, returning from a public engagement. Dhanu tosses her handbag on a sofa and drops into it. She remains motionless, staring ahead. Deven has a programme brochure in his hand when he enters. He busies himself through the following speech, pouring himself a drink, trying a TV channel, and so on.

DEVEN

I thought it was too long. Too many speakers. The programme mentions only five. They had to go and accommodate nine more. All basking in GK's shadow – after he's gone. All claiming some intimacy or the other, some so-called little-known facts or the other, knowing there would be nobody contesting them. Not just then, anyway. Not GK himself, anyway. They did a good job on the publicity though, so many heavyweights on the dias. Sorry, dais. Starting with the Governor himself, ADC and all. Mercifully short and sweet. Mustn't have known who the hell GK was, never read him! Good speechwriter anyway, short and sweet. The Chief Minister – what a contrast! He just went on and on and on, as if he owned GK's ghost. You know, I thought it was extremely wise of you to decline a slot in the speechifications. That would make it fifteen! You did it with such quiet grace. I think one of the TV cameras caught that. It should be there in the nine o'clock news round-up. Let me see, that's channel eleven, right? I thought the best part of the evening was the way the evening ended. The end of the evening, too, of course. But the announcement just before the end. It was a magnanimous gesture of the State Government to make the first contribution to the Memorial Foundation. But the idea of an annual award in GK's memory was a bit hackneyed, I thought. They could have thought of something original, something more exciting. There was a fair sprinkling of the foreign media, wasn't there?

DHANU

Did you invite Rajiv Mehta home?

DEVEN

Who? Oh, Mr Mehta, the new editor of...

DHANU

We should have him over. He appeared a nice person, very balanced.

DEVEN

Anyway, GK's name will be more widely known now. His fame will spread...

DHANU

Rapidly and wide.

DEVEN

There's a word for that... Spread like...

DHANU

Like an epidemic.

DEVEN

No, not that.

DHANU

Like the AIDS virus.

[11]

The café area is now the dining area of the house. Deven and Dash are seated. Deven is reading a newspaper. Dash is sipping his orange juice.

DULARI

(Off) Hot idlis and chutney coming up!

DEVEN

No sambar? We'll have to note that in the report card.

DULARI

As if you'll ever have sambar made by anybody else but mama!

DEVEN

So idli-chutney.

DULARI

Idli-chutney is easy. Sambar needs a special touch.

DEVEN

How long did she say she'd be out?

DULARI

(Entering with dishes on a tray) No idea. She left soon after she took a phone call. Just when she was coming down to the kitchen after her bath.

DEVEN

We have to be satisfied with the chutney, then.

DULARI

You have to finish it too. No wastage, and no leftover chutney at lunch time. Just leave a little bit for mama. Dash, some more for you?

DASH

No.

DULARI

That was to the point, thanks!

DASH

The idli is nice and soft. You got it right.

DEVEN

Yes, they've come out well. Good show, Dilu!

DULARI

Dashy, you want to...

DASH

I have to rush.

DULARI

You think it might be time to ...

DASH

Not today. Please, Dilu, not today.

DEVEN

What are you two... ?

DASH

Dilu wants me to clear up and do the dishes.

DULARI

Is that what I want you to do?

DASH

I know – Gangamma hasn't come in this morning. But not today, Dilu, please. I have a lab project today. I have to be there early.

DULARI

Okay, another time, another day.

A door is heard slamming.

DEVEN

That could be mama.

DULARI

Good! The idlis are fresh and hot.

DASH

Tell her about the ill-effects of skipping breakfast.

DULARI

'Never, never skip your breakfast. It's the most important meal of the day!'

DASH

Tell her about the research in Cornell University – about the nutritional properties of idlis.

DEVEN

It takes a Western scientist to tell us things about Eastern wisdom. Always.

Dhanu storms into the room. A moment of silence.

DHANU

So, where was I first thing in the morning even before breakfast?

DULARI

Where were you, mama, first thing in the morning even before breakfast?

DHANU

I gave it to them good! How could they stoop so low? The pits, I tell you!

DEVEN

Who, Dhanu? Where are you coming from?

The rest of the scene has Dhanu in a state of agitation matched by moves and business.

DHANU

Your Principal, who else? First he tells me – on the phone, mind you, talking like a railway station master, without the minimum courtesy – first he tells me Dilu has won the second prize – with all that oily, hypocritical bunkum about her talent and how highly he thinks of her, and so forth. And then he goes on to say that the boy who is being given the first prize is such a nice chap, the son of such a nice, decent family, and all that crap.

DEVEN

Who got the first prize?

DHANU

Almost got! Some unheard of nice chap from a nice, decent family, some Chatterjee or Batterjee or something.

DULARI

Debashish?

DASH

Dabbu...

DHANU

Could be – yes, I think it was Debashish. Anyway, it's all been set right now.

DEVEN

Set right? Of course! They couldn't possibly go ahead with that.

DHANU

Of course not! They couldn't possibly go ahead with that asinine decision. How could they? How dare they! And what sort of panel was that to judge the essays? The convener – a retired art teacher, myopic, who can't see an inch beyond Ravi Varma. The chairperson – a journalist who claims to be a feminist and an activist, and god knows what else – anarchist, mad cow in a China shoppist – all body, no soul. All that savvy stuff about being a woman and rediscovering your body. But what about the heart? What do these people know about a woman's heart?

DASH

I have to go. *(Starts to leave.)*

DHANU

You stay right here! You need to know about the real world out there. A wicked world, a crooked world – a world full of crooks. You should open an online guidance centre called crooked.com.

DEVEN

You went to the Principal's office?

DHANU

To his house first. I picked him up from there and then we went to his office. He had called the panel of judges for a meeting. I insisted on meeting them. The fourth member couldn't be there. He is attending a Rotary conference in Kathmandu. That's the panel for you! I mean, the whole thing is... ohh, calling it dumb is paying a compliment!

DASH

I'm sorry, but I can't be late for the lab.

DHANU

Go, if you have to.

DASH

Bye everybody. Dilu, tell me about it in the evening. Bye. *(He leaves.)*

DULARI

Bye Dash. See you.

DEVEN

Bye. Leave the gate open.

DHANU

(To Deven) Do you have a lab to catch too?

DEVEN

I can stay a little longer. Go ahead, tell us what happened.

DULARI

You said it was set right. Does it mean...

DHANU

It means everything is on hold. Mr Smatterjee cannot walk away with the prize just like that.

DULARI

But mama...

DHANU

Your Princy showed me the so-called prize winning essay in his office. It was pure drivel. Awful syntax, terrible grammar, all cleverness, all froth, not an ounce of substance. 'A refreshing style,' the judges are supposed to have remarked.

DEVEN

There's a lot of that going around nowadays. Newspaper columnists seem particularly prone to the infection.

DHANU

Substance, substance, substance! Are we all turning into mute witnesses to the death of substance?

DULARI

Still, Debashish is considered a very...

DHANU

Still, he is considered a smart and intelligent student! You wrote more intelligently when you were ten!

DULARI

Mama!

DHANU

But you are not the child of the Managing Director of a clutch of cement factories.

DEVEN

But she is the child of a famous writer!

DHANU

And that seems to be a problem. It seems to be a disqualification.

DEVEN

They should have concealed the names of the writers.

DHANU

That's exactly what I told the Principal. There was a clear bias in the ratings. The honourable members of the panel might not have realised it, but they were working with preconceived ideas about the entries. But then, what could you expect from a panel like that?

DEVEN

They agreed to withhold the results?

DHANU

They didn't dare go ahead.

DULARI

What next? What do they do now?

DHANU

That's their headache.

DEVEN

Are they thinking of a re-evaluation?

DHANU

Maybe. One of them has admitted anyway that he just went along with the other's opinions – that's the worthy Rotarian. The journalist has asked to be relieved, as she simply doesn't have the time to do justice to the task. So...

DEVEN

There may be a fresh panel, you mean?

DHANU

Maybe. Maybe not. That's their headache. But they simply cannot go ahead with the present choice of winners. No way!

DULARI

Did you...

DHANU

Did I what?

DULARI

Nothing. Will you have your breakfast now?

DHANU

Yes, I will. Of course, I will. I feel a great appetite coming on.

DEVEN

And I had better...

DHANU

If you leave straight away, you may just about beat the nine o'clock traffic jam.

DEVEN

I may be late this evening. I have to stand by for a late conference call. I'll see you at dinner time. Bye Dilu.

Deven leaves. Dhanu is ready for her breakfast. Dulari brings in a fresh batch of idlis. She serves Dhanu and then stands aside, watching her eat.

DULARI

Mama...

DHANU

Do you know this Debashish boy?

DULARI

Yes, mama.

DHANU

Who is Dabbu? *(Dulari does not reply)* Dabbu is Debashish, then. *(No answer)* Dumb charade? You can nod your head in the North-South axis if the answer is yes, and in the East-West axis if the answer is no. *(Pause)* Well, are they the same, then?

DULARI

Yes, mama.

DHANU

Good girl! Never the one to hide anything from mama.

DULARI

No, mama.

DHANU

You love your mama, don't you?

DULARI

Of course, mama.

DHANU

Good.

DULARI

Mama...

DHANU

The idlis are good. You've got the hang of it now. Good... *(She continues with her breakfast, Dulari remains at her place)* About Dabbu...

DULARI

I know, mama.

DHANU

Good. I knew I could trust you to be sensible. *(She smiles at Dulari)* Come and press my forehead. It could do with your touch.

A pause. Dulari picks up the dishes and leaves.

[12]

Dash is in his room, immersed in a book. Dulari enters. He does not see her. She goes up to him and sits beside him. He puts the book down. They look at each other. Dulari is holding back tears. Dash notices and reaches out affectionately, awkwardly. Dulari smiles, rises, and leaves the room.

Crossfade to dining area. Deven is at the table. He is working on his laptop, papers and folders on either side of him.

Crossfade to living room. Dhanu is surfing TV channels with the remote. Not happy with what she gets, she switches off, picks up a magazine, flips a few pages, and puts it aside. She walks over to a table, picks up a large writing pad and pen, and returns to the seat. She opens the pad to a page and stares ahead.

[13]

The dining area. Dulari and Deven are in the middle of a discussion.

DEVEN

Well, if you must...

DULARI

That's so much like mama! 'Well, if you must... You know what I think about it. Now you do whatever you feel like doing... '

DEVEN

I'm sorry. I didn't mean anything else except that...

DULARI

That, too! No, papa, I think you really meant it in a different way. But, gosh, you sounded so much like her.

DEVEN

How is one to interpret that?

DULARI

As mama might say, it's up to you to see whatever you want in it!

DEVEN

I suppose we are all influenced to some degree or the other by mama, in one way or the other. She is like that – that's her.

DULARI

You are right. That's her.

DEVEN

You, too, you know. You may not know it, sweetie, but when you are talking on the phone you sometimes sound just like her.

DULARI

How is one to interpret that now?!

DEVEN

As mama would say... *(Pause)* We are straying from the main point.

DULARI

I suppose we are. It's the third time. Maybe we don't really want to discuss it.

DEVEN

Let's give it another try. I will get back to the first question, but put it in a slightly different way.

DULARI

I know, 'why do I really want to go?'

DEVEN

Or – what will you really get from going for this course?

DULARI

You have a theory?

DEVEN

I asked the question. Your job is to reply.

DULARI

You have a theory about Dabbu?

DEVEN

The thought did cross my mind.

DULARI

And mama's mind?

DEVEN

And mama's mind. She knows that he has enrolled too.

DULARI

So have twenty-two others! Twelve boys and twelve girls altogether. And the twenty-four selected are from over eighty applications. It means something to me!

DEVEN

But this interest in indigenous socio-economic systems – isn't that what the course is called – it's so sudden.

DULARI

Socio-ecological systems – from the subject called social ecology.

DEVEN

You never talked about it before. When did you get interested in it? How did it come about?

DULARI

I told you! Maybe you didn't take it seriously then. It was during the trekking camp last summer in the Western Ghats. The preservation work being done in the rainforests was so impressive. They didn't have a certificate course then. Ours will be the very first batch.

DEVEN

But six months! You will lose the year in your junior college. I don't suppose you will be able to catch up half way when you return.

DULARI

That's okay. I have my whole life ahead of me. What is one year of junior college?

DEVEN

And the remaining six months?

DULARI

I'll find something to do. I won't waste the time away. I promise. I will do something useful.

DEVEN

Another course, maybe?

DULARI

I hope you are not being sarcastic, papa.

DEVEN

No, no, not at all. I was trying to be helpful.

DULARI

I may even continue with the Western Ghats project on some short-term job.

DEVEN

It means a lot to you, does it?

DULARI

Yes, papa! I knew you'd understand.

DEVEN

And Mr Debashish Chatterjee... Where does he figure in all of this?

DULARI

He happens to be one of the twenty-four selected.

DEVEN

Was he – how do we put it – was he a factor in the decision to sign up?

DULARI

Maybe. But not a major factor.

DEVEN

Was he a factor in your decision, or were you a factor in his decision?

DULARI

Papa, you are investigating!

DEVEN

Or a little bit of both?

DULARI

Or neither?

DEVEN

Neither?

DULARI

You remember your mini-seminar to us at the dining table two months ago? Dash said something about how Carnegie Mellon happened from a merger of Carnegie Tech and Mellon University and it led to this long and never-ending discussion on the great Indian brain drain.

DEVEN

Yes, I remember, but I don't see how that comes in.

DULARI

You made a point about two types of factors – the pull factors and the push factors.

DEVEN

Are you saying... ?

DULARI

There is absolutely no doubt that this course has some great pull factors. But there could also be...

DEVEN

That you are...

DULARI

A little bit of push somewhere.

DEVEN

And Dabbu... Something that he also is trying to get away from?

DULARI

Don't look at it that way, papa! Don't make it sound like a Bollywood family drama.

DEVEN

Okay, it is a Star Plus comedy, if you want to call it that.

DULARI

It's National Geographic, if you want to call it that.

DEVEN

It is a difficult script to follow, that much I can say.

DULARI

Papa, you and mama have always talked about the nest that must get vacated some day. I have to fly now.

DEVEN

Are you sure you're ready.

DULARI

I have enrolled for the course, haven't I?

DEVEN

Don't hurt yourself, sweetie.

DULARI

I can only try.

DEVEN

(Taking Dulari's face in his hands) It's not a push factor after all.

DULARI

You could give it another name. *(Pause)*

DEVEN

What do you know about Dabbu?

DULARI

He's cute!

[14]

Dhanu and Deven are in the living room, she is seated on the sofa. He is standing. A moment of silence.

DEVEN

She is capable of looking after herself, Dhanu. Quite capable.

DHANU

I don't need that verdict from you – neither the assessment, nor the verdict. I know what my Dulari is capable of.

DEVEN

She called as soon as she reached the project site, didn't she? She seemed to like the place.

DHANU

She seemed happy.

DEVEN

She is moving on.

DHANU

That sounds distinctly clinical. Moving on from what?

DEVEN

What I meant... It doesn't have to be clinical... I meant that she is moving ahead. We must all do that, right? Get on with our lives, milestone to milestone

DHANU

And all that.

DEVEN

You know what I mean.

DHANU

I know exactly what you mean. A male syndrome. They will discover the genes for it one of these days. Erase the past, get on with it. A male syndrome. What do you know about the female of the species? What have you learned in all these years? Well, I'll tell you. We don't work that way. Are you surprised? We don't work that way. We are special. And Dilu and I are special within the special.

DEVEN

I know. You can be sure I know that.

DHANU

Steadfastness is not a male virtue, never has been. Trouble with the laptop? Trade it in for a new one. Bored with the food? Change the cook. Tired of your friends? Find new ones. Had enough of the wife?

DEVEN

Get another! You manage to make it sound funny too.

DHANU

Work place getting tiresome? Change the job. What progress on that front?

DEVEN

Well, I have sent in a formal application. They seem interested. It will take some time, they say.

DHANU

Getting on with it. Moving on.

DEVEN

You could call it that.

DHANU

Some people move on. Others stay back and fight.

[15]

The living room. Dhanu is alone, seated, sorting out photographs in a large collection and rearranging them in albums. An audio system is playing softly in the background. The music is faintly recognisable as an album for children. Deven enters and watches Dhanu for a while.

DEVEN

(Going up to Dhanu) What's going on?

DHANU

You are, in years.

DEVEN

Oh, yes, of course, but I was asking about...

DHANU

In light years. You will soon be a fossil older than the planet itself.

DEVEN

Is that what we are celebrating?

DHANU

Do you sense a celebration?

DEVEN

I smelt a celebration – as soon as I got out of the car. Gangamma confirmed it was the semiya payasam.

DHANU

Dilu's favourite payasam.

DEVEN

That's what I thought. And here you are, listening to that old album. God, I haven't heard that since Dilu's twelfth birthday.

DHANU

When she insisted on having her friends perform a play in the verandah.

DEVEN

The Prince Who Lost His Laugh. Wasn't that a cute play! Do you remember the stage that was set up?

DHANU

I remember stitching the four bed sheets together for the front curtain.

DEVEN

These pictures... the music... It's not Dilu's birthday, is it? Of course not. It's only October.

DHANU

She is coming home today.

DEVEN

Coming home? But she doesn't finish until next February.

DHANU

It is a long weekend, she says in her letter. There are two holidays next week. And she could do with a long, leisurely oil bath, she says.

DEVEN

She wrote? We haven't had a letter in over three months.

DHANU

Four months and fourteen days.

DEVEN

Ever since she went back to the project. Back from the course for a week, and off to the project for another six months.

DHANU

Back from the project today.

DEVEN

When is she expected? How is she coming? Do we go and pick her up?

DHANU

No need. There is a jeep coming into town. She will be dropped off. As a matter of fact... I hear the gate. That could be her.

DEVEN

Let me see! *(He rushes out)*

Dhanu remains seated. She quietly places a framed photo on the TV, an album on a table next to it, and puts the other pictures away. She waits seated. Presently we hear the voice of Dulari.

DULARI

(Off) Gangamma, Gangamma! *(In the vernacular)* How are you? How are things at home? How's that brat Kittu? Still bunking classes to play galli cricket? Papa, look at that! Gangamma has made semiya payasam. For whom, Gangamma, for whom?

DEVEN

(Off) For whom, I wonder.

DULARI

Naughty Gangamma!

DEVEN

Let's go in. Mama is expecting you.

Dhanu picks up a magazine and opens a page. Deven and Dulari appear and stop at the entrance.

DULARI

(Loudly) Papa, mama is busy reading. Let's not disturb her. We can come back later!

DEVEN

(Going along) Let's go out for dinner and get back in time for the payasam. There's a new restaurant that serves great Afghan cuisine.

DHANU

Vegetarian, of course.

DULARI

Oh, my god, she has heard us! We've had it now!

DHANU

(Stentorian) You may now approach!

Dulari approaches Dhanu in mock obsequiousness and kneels before her. Dhanu condescends to bless her with a few rhythmic taps on her head. Deven turns off the music and stands by.

DULARI

I await your command

DHANU

Ae, get up yaar!

DULARI

Oh, mama!

Joy and celebration. Deven decides to leave the two of them alone.

DEVEN

I'll put Dilu's things in her room. Shall I get some tea going?

There is no response. He shrugs and leaves.

DHANU

You've lost weight, silly girl! And tanned too.

DULARI

You are saying that just because you've put on weight!

DHANU

Have I? Is it showing?

DULARI

Anyway the average between us is steady.

DHANU

When did you bathe last? When it rained last?

DULARI

Come on, mama! We bathe everyday, everyday in the evening. Hot water twice a week.

DHANU

Deforestation project for hot water for the afforestation project staff!

DULARI

We use only dry twigs and fallen branches. No cutting. The rules are very strict about that.

DHANU

Okay baba, so you are clean. And you are eating well too. A balanced, nutritious, vitamin-rich diet, in tune with mother nature. Your bowels are regular, and so are your chums, I hope. The visit to the city will be tiresome. You will be longing to return to Vrindavan.

(Pause. Dulari smiles faintly) When do you have to get back?

DULARI

I don't have to. I quit.

DHANU

Quit the project? *(Dulari nods)* You're back for... you didn't say that in the letter. You never... you quit! Was there any... ?

DULARI

No, there was no problem. It was all quite – what's the word – amicable. They said I was always welcome later if I wanted to go back.

DHANU

So, will you?

DULARI

No. Not for some time, anyway.

DHANU

What happened?

DULARI

Nothing. I just...

DHANU

It's not like you. It's not like you to quit. A quitter you are not.

DULARI

I was tired.

DHANU

I was tired... now, that sounds like a people problem. Was it by any chance... Dabbu?

Dulari hugs Dhanu and buries her face in her lap, sobbing. She is quick to control herself, and pulls herself up.

DULARI

So... semiya payasam with raisin and cashew nut. The raisin for me and the cashew nuts for Dash. What time does he get back? I'm dying to see him. I'm dying to eat! When will Dash be back?

DHANU

You'll have to wait a bit. The three of us can go ahead and have dinner – whenever you feel like it.

DULARI

We can wait. When is he expected back?

DHANU

We don't know – no point waiting.

DULARI

Mama...

DHANU

His turn. He left a month ago.

DULARI

Left? What does that mean? Where to?

DHANU

We don't know. When you took off – took flight – we knew where you were landing, where you were going to be. Dash just... took off.

DULARI

He left home? Is that what you are saying? What did he say when he was leaving?

DHANU

Not much. That is the point. He didn't leave in the middle of the night, good-bye message on the dining table, and all that. No, none of that. That's not Dash. He came up to papa and me in the living room, right here where we are sitting now, and simply told us that he was going out next morning after breakfast, and was not sure when he would be back. We thought oh, well, he has a late evening assignment or something like that. Next morning he comes down for breakfast with a bag in his hand, and a haversack on his back, and...

DULARI

And he was off! Did you ask him where...

DHANU

Didn't have his breakfast. Papa did ask him. He said something about a design workshop, somewhere near Pune. Ask papa, he may be able to tell you more.

DULARI

He's taking part in a workshop! That's different... I thought you meant he had run away or something.

DHANU

Isn't that what it is? Doesn't tell us what he's doing, where he's going, just takes off, just like that.

DULARI

That's Dash, mama! He'll be all right. He is all right, isn't he?

DHANU

I don't know. Ask papa. I am completely in the dark. I never know what's going on. I never know if I'm supposed to know. We don't understand, you see.

DULARI

He'll be all right, mama.

DHANU

You won't understand, anyway. That's what he said. This is the third time in the last nine months.

DULARI

Oh? And the first time?

DHANU

He won some prize. It was soon after that.

DULARI

The prize... You know about that?

DHANU

Can't remember what it was. He was gone for eight days then.

DULARI

He'll be back, mama. Don't worry about him.

DHANU

What does it mean, coming back? Come back for what?

DULARI

For the favourite pillow in bed, for the oil bath sitting on the same stool, using the same brass lota.

DHANU

And take off again after refuelling.

DULARI

(Snuggling up) And come back again!

DHANU

Welcome back!

DULARI

You missed me, didn't you?

DHANU

Is this the time to ask you about Dabbu?

DULARI

(Breaking free) If you want me to take off again!

DHANU

Oh! That bad, was it?

DULARI

Mama, you are not going to get anything out of me!

DHANU

Except that you don't want to talk about it.

DULARI

That's right.

DHANU

And that it's all over between you two.

DULARI

That's right. Ohh that was cheating! That's it! We close the topic straight away! *(She has become more serious.)*

DHANU

It's all right, Dilu, mama understands. Don't get upset, sweetie. Here, come to mama. *(Dulari moves to her, but with restraint.)*

You'll be fine, Dilu. You are no ordinary jelly-belly female number. You are Dilu! You are made of sterner stuff, even if that is a cliché. You are tough, you are tempered steel.

DULARI

I'm fine, mama.

DHANU

You are special. Always remember that. Very special.

DULARI

The most talented, the most sought after Guddi.

DHANU

No dabba-wallah groom for our Guddi.

DULARI

Only the best.

DHANU

No government-wallah babu, no bazaar-wallah sethia

DULARI

A prince for a princess.

DHANU

Only the best for Guddi.

(From under a seat cushion, Dhanu takes out an elaborately dressed pair of dolls with a platform on which they are to be stood. She speaks to the dolls.) You have visitors.

DULARI

Guddi! Guddi and her prince!

DHANU

Straight from the pooja room.

DULARI

Visitors for me! I'm honoured!

DHANU

One on either side of fatty Ganesha bambalatti. His best friends ever since they set up home in the pooja room.

DULARI

So nice to see you, Guddi! You look happy. And this gentleman with you – he is your prince, isn't he? How do you do, your majesty? I am Dilu, Dulari, Guddi's best friend.

DHANU

(Joining) Pleased to meet you, dear lady. Guddi has told me so much about you. She speaks very highly of you.

DULARI

Oh, your majesty, she exaggerates. You must know that about her by now.

DHANU

Of course, my dear. All girls do. But even with two pinches of salt you seem to be quite a package.

DULARI

Are you happy, sir, your majesty? You and Guddi...

DHANU

You may call me Gundu. That's what your dear friend Guddi calls me. She is a total nutcase, your friend, but a lovable nutcase.

DULARI

She must make you very happy, sir – Gundu, sir – she knows how to make you happy.

DHANU

Men are so hopeless on their own, especially those of royal upbringing.

DULARI

Every girl has something to make a man happy.

DHANU

Her secret weapon. You should know that.

DULARI

Guddi, look at this smarty pants prince of yours! Is he always so audacious? Keep an eye on him, Guddi. I think he is a flirt.

DHANU

Your friend Guddi is a very sensible girl.

DULARI

Right, and it's time for the royal couple to retire to their royal chamber. *(She makes the two dolls lie down and covers them with her hanky.)*

Good night, Guddi. Good night, your majesty, Gundu, sir.

The lights begin a slow fade out. Dulari snuggles up to Dhanu, this time more easily, comfortably. They sit still, close, watching the two dolls. The wedding song at the start of the play fades in. The lights fade out.

Close of play

Footprints

The future of the past

Vijay Padaki

FOR

SUDHIR VOMBATKERE

CHARACTERS IN THE PLAY

THE WRITER .... *In his late fifties.* *A light frame, carried straight, but with ease. Careful in choice of company and choice of words.*

HIS WIFE .... *Just a little younger, but older in style.* *Devoted. The manager of the household and the writer's work life.*

MAN 1 .... *A social activist in the earnest age of early to mid-thirties. An atypical combination of willingness to act with readiness to learn.*

MAN 2 .... *His companion, a comrade in waiting. Some induction accomplished, some renunciations pending, the obvious preoccupations.*

THE AGENT .... *Late thirties to early forties.* *Alert, agile, committed. He has seen good action, is on the upward in the service. The Agency is not explicitly revealed.*

THE WOMAN .... *His senior, perhaps the boss.* *In control. Just a little older, but not in appearance.*

MEMBERS OF THE COUNCIL .... *As described in the script.* *Out of the ordinary, but real and credible. A surrounding dignity. The last member, the newcomer, does not speak.*

INTRODUCTION

A sub-title to the play might be, *'All good things must begin'*. At the end of an early reading, a good friend suggested that it might be, *'The future of the past'*.

Beginning in the late 'sixties, as a psychologist committed to a career in applied research (later in policy research), I was constantly concerned with the process of science as much as the products of science. I realised soon enough that this formed an unseen undercurrent in a lot of my work in several spheres. The work of two philosophers of science fascinated me and, I am sure, influenced my work in one way or the other. One was Robert Rosenthal, a clinical-social psychologist, who was later chosen for the Lifetime Achievement Award by the American Psychological Association and felicitated by the American Academy for the Advancement of Science (AAAS). From a huge body of work on the process of science, Rosenthal demonstrated how human beings are very likely to prove by research what they want to believe. The other was DG Garan, whose prolific writing consistently carried the message of our sciences being ruled by human prejudice. A trilogy of three books developed the thesis of a species-specific predisposition for vicious cycles in which the acts of seeking positive experiences are driven by the exhaustion of negative experience caused by the positive experience itself. The substance of Garan's third book *(Against Ourselves)* is in fact referred to in the play. People who have read *Footprints* or seen it on stage have recognised the connection to the central idea in the play – the unsustainable life of the human species being the Great Mistake. I had only a brief correspondence with Rosenthal as part of a research programme. I had a longer correspondence with Garan, exchanging notes on several matters of common interest.

The characters in the play *Footprints* are not placed in any specific city or country. The play can be located anywhere. Any performing group can produce this play with appropriate adaptations in the style of speech of the characters. However, the structure and construction of the script should be left intact.

Following from the above, none of the characters has a name in the script. Only two characters need to be named – the writer and his wife. The performing group can choose the names for them. In the script, their names are given as *Mr Writer and Mrs Writer* (in italics) when they are spoken to by others.

In the council scenes, the members can be any combination of men and women. The new member (gardener) is a man. There are thumb-nail sketches of the Council members gathered by the Agency in the play. Every one of them is based on real persons I have been privileged to know.

The play has a string of eighteen scenes, with an estimated running time between 100 to 110 minutes, depending on the business the performing group wishes to put into the scenes. It can be done in one stretch. If an intermission is desired, it can be at the end of Scene 8.

Descriptions of the physical layout in the three principal acting areas are kept to the minimum in the script. The performing group is free to design the stage, décor, and property according to its vision of the play. There is only one suggestion from the author – not to cross the line and give it a science fiction look.

One of the oldest 'truth serums', sodium pentothal (thiopental sodium), was also used in psychiatric treatment, especially for uncovering repressed experiences. Although largely discontinued in the clinic, variants of the drug are known to be in use routinely in undercover operations. This information is given for the benefit of the performing group for one particular scene. The scene itself is best played in a matter-of-fact way and not unduly highlighted.

The play was conceived through the late 'eighties, written at the end of 2001, and first produced towards the end of 2003. WWF (Worldwide Fund for Nature, not the wrestlers) produces a report every four years based on their research called the *Living Planet* series. By a strange coincidence, and coming as a pleasant surprise, the 2004 report echoes the theme of this play and is called *Ecological Footprints.*

There are references to a palmtop that the Agent uses. In a contemporary rendition of the play, this may be taken to be any hands device such as an advanced smartphone.

FIRST PERFORMED

First performed at the **Season of Theatre, Anderson Theatre**, Gustavus Adolphus College, Minnesota November 2003

The Writer .... NATHAN SUURMEYER
His Wife .... KAYLA MARIE THORSON
Man 1 .... JOSHUA BOERTJE
Man 2 .... JESSE RAY
The Agent .... KEVIN HANSEN
Pater .... NOAH MIROVSKY
Mater .... CATHERINE SCHOENECK
Council Members .... DAVID ENGELHARD, TURA FOSTER CHARLOTTE SEIBEL, MATTHEW LEDDER
The Gardener .... KOFI NUM
The Woman .... KIRSTEN KUIKEN
Field agents .... CHRIS BACON, KRISTIN KOPERSKI, NATE BORKA
Set design .... STEVE GRIFFITH, M MARIA LOPEZ
Lighting design .... JULIA GORDON
Costumes design .... ELIN ANDERSON
Sound design .... JADON PECK
Poster design .... EILEEN HOLZ
Stage management .... M MARIA LOPEZ, NATE BORKA
Technical director .... TERENA WILKENS
Costume shop .... JAN JENSEN
Movement coach .... MARIA TIERNEY
Props master .... JESS HELLER
Electrician/Light board .... ERIC OLSON, NICHOLAS DILLENBURG
Sound .... SARAH PEDERSEN
Backstage .... KRISTIN KOPERSKI, EMILY SIEDSCHLAG, NATE BORKA
Video and photography .... ASHLEIGH PENROD, JADON PECK, TERENA WILKINS

GILLIAN DAWSON, KRISTIN KOPERSKI

Harmonica music .... PETER BLOEDEL
Directed by .... ROBERT GARDNER

Scene shop .... BETTY APPLETON,
KATRINA HESTERMAN, ERIC RUSER,
TAMMY LIS, MATHEW SWENSEN,
MICHAEL BOHNETT, KENDRA WILSON,
SCOTT ERNST, KATHERINS MACHOWSKI,
ERIC YOUNG, CARL FERKINHOFF, KRISTIN MULL,
NICK FOX, ELIZABETH OBERG, LIV ROQUE,

Costume shop .... BECKY ARBIN, MOLLY GATZLAFF,
GRETA HOFFMAN, TURA FOSTER, SARA GIVEN

Performed at the **VP@80 Festival in Bangalore Jagriti Theatre**, July 2019

Mrs Writer .... CHITRA B

Mr Writer .... ABHINAV UNNIKRISHNAN

Man 1 .... RATNESHWAR BANERJEE

Man 2 .... RAHUL SAPRE

Agent .... VARUN KAINTH

Woman .... HARSHITHA BHASKER

Pater .... MANOJ CHAUDHURY

Mater .... SHIVANI SHAH

Council Members .... DIMPI SAKIA, LAVANYA NARAYAN,
SANTOSH PATIL, SAKET GUPTA,
DIVEY GAMBHIR, MEGHNA SHETTY

Gardener PRASAD BRAHMA

Agent on Video 1 .... MOUMI GUHA

Agent on Video 2 .... PRITESH BHANDARI

Agent on Video 3 .... LABAN TP

Videography .... PRITESH BHANDARI

Lighting Design .... REBECCA SPURGEON

Technician .... BINOD BIHARI MISHRA

Sound Technician .... J MANOJ RAJKUMAR

Costumes .... SANKEERTHI

Stage Manager .... RIDDHI BHATT

Assistant .... ANUSHA SARATHY

Production Coordinator .... SHATARUPA BHATTACHARYYA

Directed by .... ARUNDHATI RAJA

PART I

[1]

The Writer's living room. The sound of a telephone ringing in the dark. The scene opens to reveal the Wife in her night clothes going up to the phone. She picks it up.

WIFE

Yes... That's right... He is in, but he is not... Oh, I see... Well, I could, if you don't mind holding the line a while... Who shall I say is calling... I understand. You can talk to him yourself. Please hold on.

She puts the receiver down. By now the Writer has entered the room. He is in his pajamas. The wife goes up to him.

WIFE

It's a long distance call – somebody from the Greenwich Foundation. Says she'd like to talk to you directly.

WRITER

Greenwich? Oh my god, this could be... *(He picks up the phone)* Writer here... Good morning... No, not at all, go ahead... *(A long pause)*

Yes, I am here, please continue... Well, thank you very much for calling... I feel deeply honoured... Yes, I will wait for the formal communication... I would be delighted to... Yes, of course... Thank you... Good day.

He hangs up and sits down.

WIFE

What was that all about?

WRITER

Good day!

WIFE

Thank you. And a very good day to you.

WRITER

Vanishing Species.

WIFE

Vanishing Species? Your novel? Don't tell me...

WRITER

Yes, that's what it is. Vanishing Species has won the Greenwich Foundation Award!

WIFE

That's wonderful! *(A long tight hug)* Fully deserved too. I told you it was good. I told you long ago.

WRITER

You did. I remember. You read the first draft.

WIFE

You're the one who wanted to put it aside. If it wasn't for me, it would still be an unfinished manuscript lying under a pile somewhere. In longhand, and on sheets of varying sizes and colours.

WRITER

You are right. The award is really because of all that you did to keep me writing.

WIFE

Well, it's six in the morning. We are up and chirping. I should get the coffee going.

WRITER

I could do with some coffee.

WIFE

And then we will make a few calls.

WRITER

No!

WIFE

Not even... ?

WRITER

No, we can't talk about this to anybody until we get an all clear from the Foundation. They seemed very particular about that.

WIFE

Okay. I'll go by that. I can whisper to the coffee pot, can't I?

A peck. She leaves. The Writer sits still for a while, pleasantly dazed. He picks up the receiver of the phone. After a hesitant pause he dials a number.

WRITER

Francis? Yes, it's me... Is it coming along? *(The sound of the front door opening)* Hold on a minute...

Two men burst into the room and go right up to the Writer. Man 1 has a pistol, which he places at his temple, Man 2 puts the receiver back and disconnects the line.

WRITER

What's this? How did you get in here?

MAN 1

No talking. No screaming. No tricks.

WRITER

Who are you?

Too late. Man 2 has gagged him and is tying up his hands behind his back. The two men lead him out. The sound of the front door closing. The Wife enters with the coffee service.

WIFE

Did I hear the front door? *(She notices he is not there, speaks in the direction of the front door.)*

Are you there?

She keeps the tray down and sits at the telephone table. She is tempted to make a call but holds herself back.

[2]

The Wife is seated at the telephone table. The Agent is standing.

AGENT

Let me summarise. It was about six in the morning yesterday. There was a phone call. You don't know who the caller was. You went in to make coffee. When you returned, he was not there. The front door was shut, but not bolted. The night latch key was in its place in your husband's key wallet.

WIFE

That is correct.

AGENT

Does he take a morning walk sometimes?

WIFE

No. Not in his pajamas.

AGENT

Had anybody come into the house at that time?

WIFE

It was six o'clock.

AGENT

It might be unusual, but please think about it carefully. Did you hear any voices? Any sounds?

WIFE

I was in the kitchen. I had the BBC news on over the system. The only other sound was from the kettle on the stove.

AGENT

Why did you wait so long to report this?

WIFE

It was just yesterday.

AGENT

It is past 9 pm now. That makes it two whole days.

WIFE

I didn't think there was anything to panic. He could return any time.

AGENT

From where?

WIFE

From anywhere. I just expected him to be back sooner or later. From somewhere.

AGENT

Does he do this often? Go out without telling you?

WIFE

Sometimes, yes. We have separate keys to the front door.

AGENT

Do you always know where he has gone? Do you know every place he goes to, every person he meets?

WIFE

I can't be absolutely sure, but I suppose I do. We've been married a long time, you know.

AGENT

Who is Francis?

WIFE

Who?

AGENT

Francis. Who is Francis?

WIFE

I don't know. I don't think I have...

AGENT

Think about it very carefully, Mrs Writer. It might be very important. It could help in finding him. It could save his life.

WIFE

Do you think his life is in danger?

AGENT

When a man is reported missing, anything is possible. Who is Francis?

WIFE

The only Francis I can think of is the Saint.

AGENT

The Saint?

WIFE

St Francis of Assisi.

AGENT

The patron saint of the environment. I see.

WIFE

He has been a source of inspiration. There is a reproduction of an etching from the original Franciscan monastery in the last book of his.

AGENT

Vanishing Species.

WIFE

Yes. You know about the book?

AGENT

I am not much of a reader, but I know about the book. Is there something else you want to tell me about the book?

WIFE

No, not really.

AGENT

When do you think the announcement of the award will be made?

WIFE

How... What award?

AGENT

The award that your husband Mr First Name Writer is to get from the Greenwich Foundation for the book.

WIFE

I don't know what you are talking about.

AGENT

Come on, Mrs Writer, of course you know what I am talking about.

WIFE

Who are you?

AGENT

You called for help, didn't you?

WIFE

I called the police.

AGENT

Not exactly. You called a retired Commissioner of Police who is a family friend. You didn't want to attract unnecessary publicity. You need have no worry on that count. The case is being handled with the utmost care.

WIFE

Who else knows?

AGENT

Difficult to say. I can only assure you that we will not allow the news of your husband's disappearance to get out before the Foundation announces the award. And as long as possible even after that.

WIFE

Are you not from the police department, then? Where are you from?

AGENT

From very much higher. You could say we look after the police force. The case is being pursued by the body, most competent to handle it. Because of its significance, it is being given the highest possible priority.

WIFE

What significance? It is just a case of a missing person. My husband. All right, he won an award. Yes, he did. But please understand that the Foundation wishes to be the first to make it public. I really don't know how you got to know about it, but that's all there is to it.

AGENT

Mrs Writer, you are very modest. Your husband is a great man, a great mind. Soon he will be a very famous man too. The work of people like that cannot remain a secret.

WIFE

He just wrote a book.

AGENT

Now, once again, please think very carefully. Who is Francis?

[3]

Surround sound. The gentle but permeating sound of the surf on an ocean shore. A dim light reveals a group in a circle in deep meditation. The sound fades out. In time, the members of the group rise one by one and leave. We cannot see their faces clearly, but their attire, still dimly lit, suggests a transcultural bind in the group. One of them is seeing the others off. He is a father figure in the group. He remains at the exit till all but he and one other have left. Nobody speaks.

The lights brighten to reveal the other person, still seated, a maternal figure. They are both in loose gown-like dresses that transcend all cultural stereotypes. She speaks from her place.

MATER

Are we seeing the candidate today?

PATER

That is the plan.

MATER

Should we meet him together or separately?

PATER

It shouldn't matter.

MATER

The Council should see him – one at a time or all together or both. It is a very important decision.

PATER

They have copies of your report, all the findings.

MATER

Still...

PATER

A final presentation can be combined with the admittance and installation.

MATER

The need to move faster must be obvious.

PATER

Yes, the announcement... the award...

MATER

Vanishing Species. We all knew he would get it. It was only a matter of time. With the award announced, the Entropic Theory of Ecological Intelligence, also known popularly as the Writer Principle – it will become the topic of discussion in every gathering in every corner of the planet where books are still read.

PATER

We shouldn't let it bother us.

MATER

It shouldn't bother us?

PATER

It doesn't matter too much, really. First of all, almost all of the discussion will be simply because of the award. It will be the done thing, the flavour of the month. It will fade out of the chatter menu as soon as another treat comes along. The average life of a buzz is less than two months.

MATER

In that period, our work will be the focus of attention of all kinds of people in all kinds of buffoonery.

PATER

Not our work, the work of the author of an award winning novel, Vanishing Species.

MATER

Can you imagine the consequences of this sudden interest in Vanishing Species? Viewing the human condition through the eyes of the writer?

PATER

That was the second point I was making. With so much of the buzz all around, with so many cults and crackpots mouthing the so-called Entropic Theory of Eco-Intelligence, there will be no danger of attention being drawn to our programme.

MATER

I hope you are right. I am sure you are, but I can't help feeling uneasy about it.

Pater is seated before her, he places his hands on her head, the thumbs over the eyes, and the first two fingers on the temples.

PATER

Close your eyes... Restore the breathing... Recognise the source of the unease... The possessiveness of human intelligence... It is difficult to accept that another mind, in another body, has a unified theory... very similar to ours... different in detail... but in essence the same... He is with us, but not one of us... It might be said – he is one of us, but not with us.

MATER

(Relaxed) Thank you. We must simply press on with the programme.

PATER

The most important phase of the programme begins only now.

MATER

The question remains. How did he arrive at it?

PATER

Probabilistically amazing, but not impossible.

MATER

How did he choose this as the centre piece for a novel?

PATER

A fertile imagination, a rare coincidence. He came to it singly. We converged to it from our separate spheres.

MATER

It is a question he will be asked hundreds of times. In TV interviews, in the lecture circuit, in the award ceremony.

PATER

He is a writer. He will have the right answer.

[4]

The sound of a harmonica playing a soulful melody. When the lights come on we see Man 2 on a stool playing the harmonica. Next to him is a bench on which the Writer is seated with his head in his hands. He is in his pajamas, with a jacket on top that has seen much service. Next to the bench is a WC with an old style thunder cistern on top. There is a chain from the Writer's right wrist to the steel pipe that connects the cistern to the commode. Man 2 finishes his song, looks at the Writer, claps in applause, takes a bow, and speaks to him.

MAN 2

Any requests? From the Top Ten? Oldies? *(No response)* Perhaps the gentleman would like a potpourri of sacred music. A Gregorian chant? The Hawaiian war chant? A chant from the Sufi whirling dervishes? *(A groan.)* Perhaps the gentleman has a complaint. Too much salt in the tea? Too much tea in the spaghetti? No complaints? We can go on then. *(He takes out the harmonica again.)*

WRITER

No...

MAN 2

Ah, the gentleman speaks!

WRITER

Please, no more.

MAN 2

Your wish, my command. *(He pockets the harmonica.)* I can sing too. Three tenors in one, brought to you in a concert by the loo. But we can't have crowds breaking into the building and rushing to the basement for autographs. Not while I'm on duty. We can't have them asking questions about you. What can I tell them? Ladies and gentlemen, behind every tenor there is an alto, behind the harmonica, a mouth organ. It is my privilege to present to you...

WRITER

Stop it. Please... I beg you. Just leave me alone for a while. Go out and have a smoke. Get yourself a drink, or a coffee, or anything. I'll be right here when you get back.

MAN 2

No, sir. Doctor's orders. I can't let you out of my sight.

WRITER

Just ten minutes. Please.

MAN 2

Not one minute. What do you want to do all by yourself anyway? We're all grown-up boys here. We don't mind others being around.

WRITER

I just want to lie down... close my eyes... lie down and stop my head spinning.

The sound of a steel door opening and closing is heard.

MAN 2

You know, I'm tempted to let you do that. Maybe you'll come to your senses and see things properly and all.

WRITER

I just need to close my eyes.

MAN 2

I might even get a special reward for bringing you to your senses... *(He stops. Man 1 is in the room.)*

If you don't come to your senses on your own, we'll have to think of ways... *(They both look at Man 1.)*

MAN 1

It's out. *(To the Writer)* I told you not to make it more difficult for yourself. *(He takes out a two-page document)*

Putting your signature here before the announcement would have been the best thing for all. For you, for the movement, even the Foundation.

For a change, the award would have balls to it – your statement coinciding with the announcement.

MAN 2

You see? All your own making. You wouldn't listen.

MAN 1

Now it's out that you are missing.

MAN 2

Who all know?

MAN 1

The whole of the world that watches TV or reads newspapers knows. It leaves out two-thirds of the people on the planet, but what the hell do they care? And who the hell cares about them?

WRITER

Mrs Writer... where is she?

MAN 1

At home. Safe. Fully protected. Nobody can get within rocket launcher range without being picked up on a screen and tracked.

MAN 2

The Agency?

MAN 1

The Agency has stepped in.

MAN 2

We're big time!

MAN 1

It's an even bigger responsibility now.

MAN 2

Do we move out of here?

MAN 1

We stay right here. We move only with his signature on this.

MAN 2

He'll sign.

MAN 1

That might not be enough now. Mister Philosopher Writer, sir, the whole of the one-third of the world that matters is sleepless with suspense. They want to know where you are. They want to see you, they want to hear you. Will you do them the honour? And help yourself too? You can be back in the warm embrace of Mrs Writer within twenty-four hours of your statement. A simple three-minute video shoot. The same matter as the testimony you will sign. The copies will reach the TV networks at exactly the same time. No channel will be able to claim a scoop. We will present you a copy – unedited.

WRITER

I don't see how it will help. Nobody will believe it.

MAN 1

They will. Believe me.

WRITER

I can always disown it. I can tell them what happened.

MAN 1

You won't. Believe me.

WRITER

I don't know what to think. I'm too tired, weak. I can't keep my eyes open.

MAN 1

That's what you need. A little bit of rest. A good hot meal.

(To Man 2) There must be a sheet and a pillow in the transit room. Get him something nice from the take-away.

MAN 2

If it's not too much trouble, may I have my jacket please? I don't like to be seen outdoors without my jacket.

The Writer takes off the jacket and gives it to Man 2, who puts it on and starts to leave.

MAN 1

Tell him it's for me. Be careful with your tongue.

MAN 2

I'll keep it locked in. *(He leaves.)*

MAN 1

We can talk when you are feeling better.

WRITER

Why are you doing this?

MAN 1

We really do care, you know.

[5]

The Writer's living room. The telephone desk now has a monitor, two headsets with microphones, and a pair of speakers. The Wife is seated. The Agent is connecting a palmtop and configuring the system as he speaks.

AGENT

Safer than the President's living quarters, Mrs Writer. There have been cases of clever intrusions there, but even a fruit fly entering your kitchen is spotted on our security screens here.

WIFE

I'm not really worried about myself. My husband, what about him?

AGENT

He will be found.

WIFE

When? Do you have news?

AGENT

Sooner rather than later. We should know in a little while. There are two concentric rings of the electronic cordon thrown around the city – at a thirty-mile radius and at seventy-five. Nothing gets out or in without full identification. Your husband must be within the city still.

WIFE

By himself somewhere?

AGENT

We have reason to believe he has company.

WIFE

Are you saying he is... ?

AGENT

You see, Mrs Writer, there is a very good chance that you had visitors here who persuaded your husband to join them for a little outing.

WIFE

Who would do that? For what?

AGENT

A celebration drink, perhaps. Old friends who cared.

WIFE

You mean there were others who knew about the award? Other than you?

AGENT

The telephone that doesn't talk hasn't been invented yet. *(The Wife is speechless.)* Two world wars and a hundred local ethnic wars have been lost by the nakedness of the telephone.

WIFE

Please don't beat about the bush. Give it to me straight. What is it about my husband that is getting all this – you know – special treatment?

AGENT

He is a very special person. He has written a book that is a very important piece of literature. He has won a very special award.

WIFE

There must be something more. You are not telling me.

AGENT

Perhaps. But I can assure you that I will tell everything that needs to be told. In good time, as soon as we are ready for it.

WIFE

I hope that will be soon.

AGENT

Meanwhile, I have the day's round-up of headlines from all the major news agencies in this part of the world. Would you like to listen?

He hands her the headset. She puts them on and listens intently. The Agent tunes the reception through his palmtop. Soon her face registers a vacant stare. There is a short convulsive move of her shoulders. She is still. The Agent waits a while, carries her to a couch, and sets her down. He returns to the table and operates the palmtop again. A woman's face appears on the monitor. The Agent speaks into the headset mike.

AGENT

Come in Central Ops. Ready for report and review.

WOMAN

(On monitor) Uplinked. Can you read me?

AGENT

Loud and clear.

WOMAN

Commence report.

AGENT

Subject has no knowledge of intrusion. No knowledge of links to Schedule A suspects.

WOMAN

Abduction probe status.

AGENT

Surveillance category Alpha X-ray on seven societies. No spikes in transcripts. There is an explosion of new societies in the last seventy-two hours.

WOMAN

No go. Stay on course.

AGENT

Advice on subject.

WOMAN

Assessment.

AGENT

Zero. Either completely in the dark, or completely rehearsed.

WOMAN

Pento probe?

AGENT

Option. Subject prepared.

WOMAN

Proceed pento probe. Report on the hour. Over.

AGENT

Over and out.

The Agent switches off the system. He then takes out a small pack from a briefcase. From the pack he takes out a sealed hypodermic syringe. He breaks the seal, sits next to the Wife and administers the content intravenously. He talks to her as he does this.

AGENT

Mrs Writer, I promised you more information. Here it is. We are friends. I trust you. You must trust me in return. I will tell you what we know about your husband... After that you can tell me what you know about him... Are we agreed?

WIFE

Thank you, yes.

AGENT

Good. Mrs Writer, you are a kind and gracious lady. An honest and god-fearing citizen of a great country. Together, we can solve the mystery of your husband's disappearance, can we not?

WIFE

We can find him.

AGENT

We must make a list of all his friends. Tell me about his friends.

WIFE

His friends.

AGENT

Who are his friends?

[6]

An elaborate ceremony, with Pater seated in the centre. The other members of the council take their places on either side of him forming an arc. Mater leads in a new member. The colour of his gown suggests he is not fully admitted into the group yet. He bows to the members one by one and takes his place in front of the arc. Mater stays by his side. There is a set of potted plants kept in the area.

Mater presents a folder to each of the council members and takes her place beside the new member. The members ask questions or make comments.

PATER

You may begin.

MATER

The reports are with you. You will see that he clears all twelve of the recommended primary criteria with scoring reliability in excess of the stipulated levels of statistical confidence. A rare phenomenon. We, the members of the Council, have between six to eight criteria each to our credits.

MEMBER

The tertiary criteria.

MATER

The cross criteria correlations are such that the factorial distinctions between the primary, secondary, and tertiary criteria are dissolved.

MEMBER

Occupation.

MATER

He is a gardener.

MEMBER

Recommendation.

PATER

There is a background.

(To Mater) You may.

MATER

He has been a gardener all his life. Attached to a family that prided in its garden. The garden has won prizes regularly over many years.

MEMBER

Is the gardener well known? A celebrity?

MATER

Fortunately, no. He is unknown. The family and the prizes are well known.

MEMBER

What does he bring to the garden?

MATER

Language.

MEMBER

Many gardeners speak to their plants.

MATER

Here, the plants speak to him in turn. It is a highly developed language, far beyond normal human comprehension, that relies entirely on visual symbols or audible sound patterns and some combinations of the two sensory stimuli.

MEMBER

Is it only with one person, this gardener?

PATER

The language has always been with us, all around us. Our surmise is that, it is at least twenty million years old, emerging about the time the hominid Ramapithecus shifted his dwelling from tree tops to the ground, evidently in the land that is now called Kenya, perhaps in the Indian subcontinent too.

MATER

There is also reason to believe that plant life had developed the language before the human species had one of its own. They reached out to man at the first footprints on their soil.

MEMBER

This must mean an altogether alternative basis to language, the means of communication across species, orders and forms.

PATER

We have called it Metacom.

MATER

Some have it. Most don't. A dormant potential is not ruled out. The estimated probability is one in twenty-four million.

MEMBER

Recorded cases.

MATER

None. However, the fragmented and anecdotal evidence from historical documents suggests the recognition of Metacom at various points of time. Among those who might have displayed the gift are an American Indian chieftain, a native scientist in British colonial India, and the founder of the thirteenth century order, St Francis of Assisi.

MEMBER

The gardener.

PATER

Yes.

MEMBER

Validation.

MATER

We have considered two categories of evidence, the documentary and the experimental.

PATER

The documentary is anecdotal, nevertheless significant. In the family garden, there were specimens rejected for display by the owner. They withered rapidly in spite of routine attention and care, but recovered dramatically under the care of the gardener, some of them even going on to win blue ribbons at exhibitions.

MEMBER

Nature of treatment.

MATER

A form of non-verbal counselling – entirely by Metacom.

PATER

Perhaps we are ready for the experimental validation.

MATER

There are six potted plants before us. They have been chosen randomly from the nursery at Central Park. The folder with you contains a detailed profile of each of the plants – age, parentage, nurturance, and so on. Only you have this information. Nobody else. The candidate member does not know from which nursery the plants have been brought. He is seeing them for the first time. He shall now report to us the content of his communication with the plants, one by one. You may verify the facts either from the data already with you, or from fresh investigations at the nursery. Are we ready?

PATER

Proceed.

Mater picks up one of the plants and places it before the new member. He caresses the plant lightly with the tips of his fingers, and then allows the plant to caress his cheeks, his hair, his neck. He stops. He then leans towards Mater and whispers into her ears.

MATER

The keeper at the nursery is kind but careless. He has a problem with his right wrist from an old accident injury. He is often looking at people passing by while he is tending, causing spills and wastage. Yesterday he took a shortcut, putting the plant in sunlight before lunch instead of after.

She places the second pot before him. The conversation with the pot is completed. He whispers to Mater.

MATER

There was a visitor. She was young, soft-spoken, and earnest. She suggested an experiment to the keeper. Keep one group of pots under direct sunlight, another set under the branch of a tree. The sunlight through the leaves on the branch is like a sprinkle and is superior for photosynthesis. This pot was one of those kept in direct sunlight.

She places the third pot before him. The conversation with the plant is completed. He whispers to Mater. There is a moment's hesitation.

MATER

The plant was the third one to be picked. It was not chosen at first, but picked up later. The plant left behind was knocked down by another visitor. It was a man in heavy grey clothes. His face was not clearly visible. He followed us from the nursery. He watched us from a distance after we came out of the park.

[7]

The living room of the writer. The Wife is lying still on the couch. The Agent is moving quietly about the room making entries into his palmtop. He sits at the system, connects the palmtop to it, switches on, and speaks into the microphone.

AGENT

There are six main circles of friends. A few overlaps, but largely separate circles. Almost all of them in our records. One exception. It is a group that meets on the last Thursday of each month. Location unknown, may be rotated. Exact membership unknown. Never seen in Writer home. Five possible names from stray references. Request profiles ASAP. Joint involvement in charity, social work. Address book and phone entries keyed in. Commencing transmission.

He punches a key in the palmtop and sits back.

[8]

The Writer is looking better, rested. He is in the middle of a relaxed conversation with the two men while being given a shave by Man 2.

WRITER

Surely you are aware that there are large sections of opinion makers who do not agree. They think the book is an insult to human intelligence.

MAN 1

Needless to say, most of them have not read the book.

WRITER

My signature on that piece of paper will confirm their choicest suspicion – that I belong to the lunatic fringe.

MAN 1

They don't need the signature for that.

WRITER

And the piece of paper being waved about by your group – what do you think they will make of that?

MAN 1

What do you make of it yourself? Do you think our demands are lunatic?

WRITER

I asked you first. How will my endorsement help your cause?

MAN 1

You are an important man. Right now, a very important man, a somebody. An opinion maker yourself, if you didn't know already.

WRITER

There are others – hundreds of them – more important and more famous. Far more weighty in opinion making.

MAN 2

You must run the razor when the lather is fresh. When it dries up it's useless.

MAN 1

Your signature will make a difference today. It might not have the same impact a year or two from now. Sure, it's the opportunity we are exploiting. But you know we also want people like you to join us. We are hoping you'll see we are serious, and become part of us.

WRITER

You'll give me the job of kidnapping next year's Greenwich winner?

MAN 2

You can give him a shave when he's locked up.

MAN 1

Don't you believe in what you write?

WRITER

Believe in what?

MAN 1

What you have written to win a prize.

WRITER

If you separate the two things, the writing and the prize, does the writing seem worth the fuss? It must look like nothing more than a content but illegitimate baby from a one-night stand – the product of a fertile imagination in an idle mind.

MAN 2

Is he making fun of me?

MAN 1

He's making fun of me, I think. Making fun of all of us.

WRITER

I'm sorry. I didn't mean to give you the impression... but you see, there is a difference in the way we see things.

MAN 1

I'll try again, start at the beginning. You must try too, for your own good, unless you're mighty keen on a long sabbatical in this waterless loo.

WRITER

That must apply to all three of us. Go ahead.

MAN 1

People talk about different things that they find exciting in Vanishing Species. Which of these is the most important for you?

WRITER

Exciting? Do they really find it exciting?

MAN 1

Provocative, disturbing, tickling, troubling – words like that have been used.

WRITER

I was imagining an interview by the media with questions like these. I had not imagined the intimacy of the venue.

MAN 1

Yes?

WRITER

It is a novel, not an academic thesis. It should not be taken on an empty stomach.

MAN 1

All the same, it should be taken seriously.

WRITER

I suppose the central idea is what matters in any book.

MAN 1

And that is about the Great Mistake?

WRITER

Yes, that, the mistake.

MAN 1

You don't think the dinosaur and the dodo were mistakes. Only man is a mistake. Why is that?

WRITER

Through over three and a half billion years of the evolution of life forms there have been many misfits. They've come and gone. Man is the only evolved life form which is a mistake. Nature is equipped to deal with misfits, to eliminate them, and restore balances. There is no power, no capacity in nature to deal with the mistake. *(Pause)*

MAN 1

Go on.

WRITER

Except in man himself.

MAN 1

The fittest survive, right?

WRITER

You could say that. But who is the fittest?

MAN 2

Who? The ones who have the staying power.

MAN 1

The toughest.

WRITER

The humblest? The ones who submit?

MAN 2

Oh, come on!

WRITER

Fitness to submit to nature's demands – humble, but intelligent fitness. Accepting death, not prolonging life...

MAN 1

That's why you should be with us! That's what the movement is all about – using human intelligence to clear the ecological mess we have all round us.

WRITER

Created by human intelligence.

MAN 1

That's right!

WRITER

It does not remove the mistake. It cannot. The mistake can only compound itself. A little gain here, a little success there, these are not without huge damages somewhere else in the system.

MAN 1

There must be a way.

WRITER

There is. Eliminate the mistake. Eliminate...

MAN 1

Eliminate... ?

WRITER

Yes, the species.

MAN 2

That's a solution? Cure a headache by putting a bullet through it?

WRITER

No more headaches, ever!

MAN 2

(Aside, to Man 1) He's crazy. You sure you want him with us?

MAN 1

Hold on. Let's listen to him.

MAN 2

I say we dump him.

MAN 1

Go on.

WRITER

Have you ever been in a train with a compartment full of nice people, sharing their food, sharing their jokes? They all have their places reserved, but they change seats readily. Suddenly a couple of bullies come along, push people out, park themselves in their seats, put their luggage on top of theirs... What is your first reaction to this intrusion?

MAN 2

They have no right to be there in the first place. *(He checks himself.)*

WRITER

The continued imposed presence of one species – the mistake – is at the expense of the peace, the joy, the harmony of... do you have any idea of the numbers?

MAN 1

You know, I don't like what you're saying. I don't like it one bit. I can smell something burning. But I can't help thinking you're okay. You, I like. There must be something god-awfully wrong in my thinking like this.

MAN 2

He's okay, I guess. He should just learn to talk like a gentleman. He chews with his mouth shut. He must learn to talk with his mouth shut.

MAN 1

And the solution?

WRITER

There are only two ways to end a play – a blackout or a slow fade out.

MAN 1

Is a blackout possible?

WRITER

A formidable challenge, but not impossible.

MAN 2

And the fade out?

WRITER

Easier on the mind, but it could be agonizingly long drawn out.

MAN 2

Do you have a preference? Is it in the book?

WRITER

Have you read it?

MAN 2

Do you know the price of the book? Have I read it!

MAN 1

Is a slow fade out possible?

WRITER

The sixty-four million question.

MAN 2

God, a quiz show on the end of the human race!

MAN 1

Wait a minute. *(To Writer)* Go on.

WRITER

Every sixty-four million years there is known to be a mass extinction process. Nature purges itself. Entire classes of animals and other life forms disappear from the face of the earth.

MAN 1

Every sixty-four million years?

WRITER

Plus or minus a couple of millions.

MAN 2

Great! Nice to be prepared.

WRITER

Yes, indeed.

MAN 1

What's special about the number?

WRITER

Nobody knows. There is no established scientific explanation yet for the cycle or the sixty-four million years. But there is much evidence that the cycle does occur.

MAN 2

And when is the next visit? *(Pause)*

MAN 1

You're not saying...

WRITER

Maybe.

MAN 2

Okay, that's nature at work. What about Man? Can there ever be a slow fade out designed by Man?

WRITER

Perhaps.

MAN 1

There's been a lot of talk about a big bang end in the last thirty years. The power of the nuclear arsenals, for instance. Enough to destroy all human habitation twenty times over.

WRITER

It could happen by accident.

MAN 1

Or by design, if we go by the characters in your book.

WRITER

The big bang doesn't have to be from bombs. It doesn't have to be noisy. Anything that acts on the whole species in a short space of time is on.

MAN 1

The book has a listing of eleven possible big bangs, including a super virus.

WRITER

And a neurotoxin that produces complete asphyxiation.

MAN 1

Like strychnine to put dogs to sleep.

WRITER

The important thing, of course, is that every one of these is a completely sound technical proposition. Not fantasy, no supernatural stuff.

MAN 2

You've seen these things yourself?

WRITER

You see them all around you. At a small scale just now, but the technical principle is well known. Intelligence agencies in the top echelon employ devices like these routinely to eliminate people they don't want around.

MAN 1

Upscaling must be just a matter of a computer programme, a new algorithm.

WRITER

Do you think they are waiting for your permission? Do you think the capacities are not there already? Every time they want to stamp out some other country's fledgling capacity, it is a sure sign they have the capacity themselves.

MAN 2

If you ask me, the only question is – who'll press the button?

MAN 1

Nobody is going to press the button.

WRITER

That's the point. That's the weakness in the big bang plan. The people around the button, watching it, are not going to press it.

MAN 1

Unless...

WRITER

Go ahead.

MAN 1

There's some way to get it pressed from the outside. Under their noses.

MAN 2

Boom! Blackout.

MAN 1

The only thing remaining would be the button.

WRITER

Close of play.

Pause. The two men look at each other. Man 2 stands the Writer up.

MAN 1

What do you think?

MAN 2

Looks very serious.

MAN 1

Will he turn around?

MAN 2

I thought maybe there's a chance. But he is too far gone. Completely bonkers!

MAN 1

We need him. He's got to join us. He doesn't know it yet, but he needs us too.

MAN 2

Can you imagine the march to Parliament with him in the front row, the crowds jeering, pelting us all with condom balloons filled with piss?

MAN 1

I think it's time to get him some breakfast. He likes a thick porridge with chopped bananas on top.

Man 2 packs up the shaving things and leaves.

WRITER

You have something on your mind.

MAN 1

How does the slow fade out work?

WRITER

It is making something spent. Used up. It comes to an end by itself, and there's no more to it.

MAN 1

You want all of us to fade out? Just like that?

WRITER

Nice and gradual. A few thousands per day. No replacements.

MAN 1

You mean no more children? That's stale wishful thinking gone rotten! Just look at them sprouting all around you, all sizes, all colours, all shapes. How do you stop that?

WRITER

The poor and the wretched will find ways to stop it by themselves. They don't need help. The rich and the contented will need a bit of pushing. Their worst impediment is the negation of death.

MAN 1

I remember a clipping in a magazine. It was about a race of aboriginals who had taken a community oath not to have any more children – to make themselves extinct.

WRITER

It sounds racist when you put it that way. It was a decision that came from great farsightedness, if you stop to think about it. It must be emulated, not sensationalised.

MAN 1

What about the unfortunate better off?

WRITER

Do you know what the alligators in the Everglades of Florida have in common with the human population all around them?

MAN 1

Red meat with every meal, very rare? No, tell me.

WRITER

A steady decline in the sperm count of the males.

MAN 1

That's what we are talking about. Man-made environmental disasters that are rebounding on us. We must find solutions.

WRITER

Yes... a solution. Technology may indeed help.

MAN 1

The Titanic is going down. The engine room is flooded...

WRITER

And there is a heated argument on. They disagree on the exact depth in feet to the ocean floor. *(A pause)*

WRITER

We have to find a nice, intelligent way to speed up the process. Selectively. Only for one species. The play will have a happy ending. Exit man. Enter alligators in festive mating dance. Slow curtain. Thunderous applause from a million frogs on toadstools.

PART II

[9]

The living room of the Writer. It is beginning to look like an operations control room. There is more instrumentation, more wiring, more intensity. The Wife remains stretched on the couch. There is now a set of wires connected to various points on her head. They lead to an instrument on a trolley next to the couch. The Woman is in the room, examining a length of printout from the instrument. The Agent is at the console speaking into the headset.

AGENT

Come in Sector six. *(A face appears on the monitor.)*

FACE

Sector six report negative. Procession group investigated. University office. Professor spokesman. Harmless. Over.

AGENT

Keep up scan. No let up. Over and out. *(The face goes off the monitor.)* Come in sector seven. *(Another face on the monitor.)*

FACE

Sector seven report negative. Poor attendance at the Mayor's Town Hall lecture. Listed cars zero. Over.

AGENT

Keep up scan. No let up. Over and out. *(The face goes off the monitor.)* Come in sector eight. *(Another face on the monitor.)*

FACE

Sector eight report negative. Low traffic. Food court thin. Mainly delivery orders, take-aways. People staying indoors. Over.

AGENT

Keep up scan. No let up. Over and out. *(The face goes off the monitor. He switches off.)*

WOMAN

We're getting nowhere with Mrs Writer either.

AGENT

They have remained married thirty years. Every anniversary celebrated together. Every vacation together. She must know something more about him than his collar size.

WOMAN

Does your wife know where you were last Friday night?

AGENT

That's different.

WOMAN

Do you know every little thing she does when you are out of town?

AGENT

I tell you they are different.

WOMAN

There must be parts of their lives that are their own. They are not always together, all the time in their charities and their fund-raising groups.

AGENT

She'll come around. Take it from me, she will.

WOMAN

Anyway... here's another charity group he gives his time to. *(She takes out notes.)* The Thursday group you asked about has no place of its own. It is an informal get-together, a voluntary set-up. The people who meet once a month are... well... here it is.

Profile 1. Catatonic schizophrenia. Onset suspected early childhood. Seen frequently in adolescence in contorted states lasting two to twelve days. Episodes average three to four per year in adulthood *(The agent punches in key words in his palmtop.)*

Profile 2. Epileptic. Low income family, early record not available. Institutionalised at age fifteen for florid speech and alien behaviour pattern after epileptic fits.

Shall I go on?

AGENT

Since you've started...

WOMAN

Profile 3. Fits description of autism. Withdrawal behaviour first noticed age three. Autistic fantasy revealed in junior school art. Fear of company. Interpersonal relations severely limited.

Profile 4. A slight departure. A junkie. A PhD scholar who dropped out of the system. Experimented with drugs in University lab. Graduated to hallucinogens. Spent three years in drug culture communes in the Himalayas. Disowned by family. Found by de-addiction centre on their doorstep in severely disoriented condition.

AGENT

Different but same. Some sort of support group in a rehab programme.

WOMAN

There's one more.

Mentally retarded. Suspected secondary condition from early child abuse. Day care programme at Institute for Mentally Challenged since age ten. Occupational therapy in gardening. Engaged by homes in neighbourhood. Shows episodes of trance-like states.

AGENT

In the old days he might have been branded to exorcise an evil spirit. *(He connects the palmtop to the system and punches a command.)*

WOMAN

Or stoned to death. It didn't seem to matter whether you were possessed by the devil or by god.

AGENT

There was no way to find out.

WOMAN

It's important, isn't it? To know who has you possessed?

AGENT

Not god or the devil, but what is good and bad, what is right and wrong.

The system beeps. The agent goes up to attend to it.

WOMAN

It's more important to separate the harmless and the unfortunate from those who can be disruptive.

AGENT

This might interest you. Do the five cases have something in common, besides being unfortunate wrecks in a rehab group?

WOMAN

What is it?

AGENT

The multivariate analysis on their case data shows that all of them have a statistically significant probability of having at least one common feature. It is called Alternative Configuration of Cognitive Vectors. In earlier literature, with limited understanding of cognitive processes, it was called altered states of consciousness.

WOMAN

You mean, like telepathy and things like that?

AGENT

Not quite. It says here that in an alternative configuration of consciousness, a person experiences new meanings and new insights, transcending the common connections between sensory data and knowledge formation.

WOMAN

Interesting. Find out more. *(The Agent punches keys.)*

AGENT

Look at this. Catatonia, or catatonic schizophrenia. The divine revelations to prophets in several cultures might have come in catatonic states – extended hallucinatory states, often recorded by a close companion.

WOMAN

Entire civilisations may be built on the utterances of some catatonic prophets.

AGENT

Epilepsy. In the recovery phase after a convulsive seizure, known as post-epileptic furore, there have been rare cases of speech in a language or subject domain to which the patient has had no exposure in life. Recorded case of a fourteen-year-old boy who recited poetry in a language never learnt since birth.

Paranoiac dissociation. The isolation of an entire belief system from knowledge categories already established can lead to new truths. This is observed in the case of an order of monks who have produced valid mathematical treatises from an alternative number system, but who also believe that the earth is flat. It is highly probable that this cognitive state is associated with the accepted custom of imbibing the hallucinogic extract from a locally cultivated weed. *(They look at each other.)*

WOMAN

Do you think... ?

AGENT

It's not ruled out. There is more here. About autism, and...

WOMAN

There are two ways of looking at it. Either a group like this is the source of ideas for a book like Vanishing Species, you know, the writing exploiting the colourful but harmless outpourings of – what do they call it – altered mind states, or...

AGENT

Or there is really a group working on a master project of the type in the novel. This may be the biggest lead in the whole case.

WOMAN

Hold on. No need to rush. We may be running headlong into nothing. This is not what you were trained to do. Ask yourself the obvious questions. One, if our award winning writer is really a part of a vanishing act project of that type, why would he reveal it by putting it into a book that the whole world will read? Two, equally important, how is it connected to his disappearance?

AGENT

I don't know the answers any more than you do. But let me try. Your training again. One, Mr First Name Writer, the award winning writer, cannot be a fool. He could put the ideas into a bestseller for more than one reason. To make it so open that nobody thinks anything more about it. To make it so open that lots of people start thinking about it, and maybe start doing something about it, which might be part of the project design. He could also be doing this to throw people off the track – get them to follow the leads that are duds, while his project group remains on track.

WOMAN

Do you think there is a group?

AGENT

Your second question. He might have been abducted by the group. If the project has made headway, they might want to prevent further leakage.

WOMAN

So, you think there is a group.

AGENT

Maybe not. But there could be one.

WOMAN

Like this Thursday group?

AGENT

It could be a virtual group – like-minded people, wired and in touch, but not meeting anywhere, with no visible organization.

WOMAN

There is also the mushrooming of Save the Planet groups that has come with the success of the book.

AGENT

We can't take chances. We are keeping tabs on every one of them, as soon as we get to know. Mostly fads. Some cults. They come and they go. But they must be watched anyhow.

WOMAN

If there is a master project on, there must also be a technology developed – for the idea to be implemented. It is either developed already or in the making.

AGENT

Probably in an advanced stage of development, for upscaled implementation.

WOMAN

Good. You're doing fine. We have two priorities now. We must locate Mr Writer and bring him back without harm.

AGENT

We can intensify. I'll need more support from your office.

WOMAN

Done. Just go ahead. The second job must get the same top priority. We must locate the project group before anybody else does. The technology cannot fall into the wrong hands.

AGENT

Our own labs have acknowledged the theoretical feasibility. It is simply a question of who develops it first.

WOMAN

And owns it.

AGENT

Mrs Writer – should we... ?

WOMAN

We need her. We need to work together. You can continue to direct operations from here. She will be grateful.

The system beeps again. The Agent goes up to it, watches it by himself, and makes quick notes on his palmtop.

AGENT

It looks like she doesn't know much herself.

WOMAN

Bliss.

AGENT

She also doesn't know how helpful she has been. *(Switching off the system)* Excuse me, while I attend a call. It shouldn't take too long. Mrs Writer has asked you to stay for lunch. She should be coming round in another ten minutes. You can fix yourself anything you need in the kitchen.

[10]

The basement. The Writer and Man 1 are playing a card game.

MAN 1

You read and write a lot, but you are stupid with your cards. How come? Don't you play games on the computer?

WRITER

It's worse when I'm on the computer. Give me a nice big pad of foolscap size sheets and a pair of fountain pens any day.

MAN 1

You have something against computers too?

WRITER

Poor, innocent computers. Why pick on them?

MAN 1

You sound so superior. That's funny. You're talking about all that's wrong in people... They are people like yourself, you know.

WRITER

I wish you could see how much funnier it can get – when you realise that superiority is a comic curse. The more superior you get, the more inferior you really are.

MAN 1

It's still difficult for me to believe that somebody like you could actually write stuff like that.

WRITER

I'd like to believe you are saying something nice, but I don't think you are.

MAN 1

I mean, haven't we done anything right? Anything okay? Sure, a lot of technology has led to bad things. That's what we are fighting against. But there's a lot of the good too, you know. You see that, don't you?

WRITER

All technology, through all of human history, has had only one single motive in its creation – to eliminate the barriers to a selfish need being fulfilled. When the other fellow makes it, we call it greed and we say it is evil. When we make it ourselves, we say it is for quality of life, and our integrity is unquestionable.

MAN 1

How can you stop human intelligence from expressing itself? How can you stop knowledge?

WRITER

Why not? You need to question that.

MAN 1

What do you mean? Knowledge is the solution.

WRITER

Knowledge is the problem! There could be ways – it shouldn't be too difficult – to stop all further expansion in knowledge. There shall be no further new knowledge, and almost certainly no new technologies either. The naturally creative capacity of human intelligence can be allowed to remain. Its so-called inherent good quality will then have a chance to prove itself. It can do this by demonstrating a better utilisation of all existing knowledge.

MAN 1

Earthquake-proof housing, harnessing sea water for safe drinking water, cheap solar energy – these are the things we need. They are there in our charter of demands. We are against animal testing, for instance, for new products.

WRITER

All that can come later. The repository of knowledge in the species must be first turned to examine the problems it has created for itself. The consumption and hoarding...

MAN 1

The garbage produced!

WRITER

That too.

MAN 1

In the matter of garbage value, the intelligence of the earthworm is far ahead of ours, right?

WRITER

The consumption is senseless in the first place, inevitably at the cost of others, the inequalities created and the racism to maintain it...

MAN 1

Some people will think you are preachy – what's the word – didactic. Overdoing things.

WRITER

The massive edifices of scientific justification erected to perpetrate myths, the aberrant and unnatural social conduct...

MAN 1

And the violence.

WRITER

The violence against women... we could go on. These are the ugly truths about itself that the species must be willing to face.

MAN 1

So, you admit there is another way. We don't have to eliminate ourselves, wipe out the mistake. We can correct the mistake too. That's what our Green program is all about.

WRITER

What is your program really all about? Tell me.

MAN 1

It's about preserving the environment, even reversing the damage done over the years. It's about saving precious natural resources.

WRITER

All that for what?

MAN 1

For what? Because it must be done!

WRITER

Because then you can continue to enjoy the fruits of the earth, as it was always intended to be.

MAN 1

We must rest on a faith to drive our mission.

WRITER

Yes, indeed. All missions are driven by deep faith.

MAN 1

As they should be.

WRITER

And all missions manufacture truths to support what they want to believe. That is the nature of faith.

MAN 1

Tell me, do you or do you not have faith in the environment mission? *(A pause)*

WRITER

There are only two faiths in the entire human race. These faiths are far deeper than the religious faiths created by mankind over a hundred thousand years. Very simply, one faith says the Earth belongs to Man. The other faith says Man belongs to the Earth. Which faith do you belong to? *(A long pause.)* The house is on fire, and we are trying to put it out with a couple of mugs of water.

The sound of the steel door opening and closing.

MAN 1

People like us, you and us and many more like us, why should we pay for the sins of a few garbage producers? Of course we can correct the mistake. We must!

WRITER

If only we could. In a lot of things we do in our life, we realise we made a mistake. If only there was another chance, we say to ourselves, it wouldn't happen again! If only there was another chance... but we know deep within that it's too late. It's too late.

The Agent has entered the room with Man 2 held in front of him and a pistol against his head. There is a take-away pack in Man 2's hand.

[Optional: In the premiere performance the agent was accompanied by two men in commando attire carrying assault rifles.]

The Writer and Man 1 freeze.

AGENT

Don't do anything, you won't live to regret. We'll take it nice and easy from here. We don't want Mr Writer's breakfast getting messy, do we?

[11]

The Writer's living room. The couch is empty. The trolley with the instrument has been moved to one side. In its place is a tripod with a video camera. Man 1 and Man 2 are seated before it. They wear T-shirts with the slogan, ONE PLANET ONE WORLD. The Agent is behind the camera. He has a set of prompt cards with him. The Woman is watching from the telephone desk. The two men are handcuffed together. On the two free hands are wristbands from which lengths of wiring go to the desk.

MAN 2

It is our understanding that the need of the hour is cooperation.

Separate struggles do not achieve anything.

We must cooperate.

There is only one planet. This is our only chance.

There can only be one struggle.

Those who have the will must work together with those who have the ways.

We hope to see you soon. Thank you.

AGENT

Thank you. That was well done.

WOMAN

Pretty speeches, gentlemen.

AGENT

Very well put, even if I say so myself. The copies will reach the networks in less than an hour. All at the same time, of course. Would you like a copy yourself?

MAN 1

What if... ?

AGENT

Yes?

MAN 1

Nothing.

AGENT

Now, for the signatures. *(He goes to the table.)*

WOMAN

Wait. There's no great hurry. *(She moves the camera tripod, pulls up a chair next to the men.)* You do see we are on the same side, don't you?

MAN 1

Not as clearly as you do, I can tell you that.

AGENT

But gentlemen, you have just made a most convincing statement.

MAN 1

But sir... *(He raises his free hand to show the wiring.)*

WOMAN

Oh, those are mere formalities. You were agitated and snappy when you came in. Quite understandable. You needed to be calmed. You are now, aren't you?

MAN 1

Well...

MAN 2

I'm calm enough to know I need a drink. And a woman.

WOMAN

The drink – why not? How about you?

MAN 1

A little later maybe. Not just now. A coffee would be okay, thanks.

WOMAN

I am sure these can come off now, if it's bothering you. *(She looks at the Agent. He begins to disconnect.)* I'm sure we can trust you to... you can see we have no harmful intent. But please don't do something foolish, because the building is surrounded. We just have to see this through in a civilized manner.

MAN 1

We don't know what you're after. We are not interested. We are only working for a safe and clean environment.

WOMAN

We are on your side.

MAN 1

We want to expose the wolves in sheep clothing who are out to destroy the ecosystem.

WOMAN

You are on our side.

MAN 1

You are the establishment. You are part of the problem.

WOMAN

A dreadfully misunderstood, maligned establishment.

AGENT

You don't know it, but we actually support the kind of work you do.

MAN 2

Keeping us locked up?

AGENT

Keeping tabs on wolves in sheep's clothing, and protecting little Red Riding Hood and her grandmother.

WOMAN

Tell you what. You can change into your own clothes now. We'll get those drinks. And then we can talk about our work with just a little more cordiality.

The Agent goes out of the room. The Woman gives the men their shirts and jackets.

WOMAN

Do you want me to leave the room?

MAN 1

That shouldn't be necessary.

MAN 2

Not even if you want to change yourself.

WOMAN

(Laughing) I've been in the service too long.

The men put on their shirts over the T-shirts and look themselves again.

WOMAN

You know, you can tell a lot about a man's character from the way he puts on his clothes.

MAN 2

Oh yeah? Like I'm the shy, retiring type because I don't look down when I'm zipping up. But he, on the other hand...

WOMAN

Oh, just the opposite, I think. He is the sensitive one, I can see. *(To Man 1)* Aren't you? You put on a rough exterior, because your group expects you to. But you are really a deep thinker. You act firmly when needed, but only after a deep understanding of things.

MAN 1

Well, I don't know...

MAN 2

Hey, hey, hey! You started with me!

WOMAN

You? You are yourself most of the time. The people in your group know that. But there's another side of you that you keep for special occasions. Your honesty is infectious.

MAN 2

You have nice legs.

WOMAN

Thank you. They must have been nicer some years ago.

MAN 1

Can we... ? There are other things we have to... Why don't you... ?

MAN 2

Change the topic ? Sure.

MAN 1

Let's get on with it.

WOMAN

(Going over to Man 1, taking his hand in hers, and patting it) You will get over it. There are lots of nice people in the world.

The Agent comes in, carrying a large tray with an opened bottle of wine, three wine glasses filled, an empty wine glass, and a mug of hot coffee.

AGENT

Here we are. Compliments of Mr and Mrs Writer. Not too dry, not too sweet. Just right for this weather. And a nice, piping hot mug of coffee for you, sir.

MAN 1

Thanks. If you don't mind, I'll have a glass of that wine too.

AGENT

Of course! Here, let me put that mug away. *(He pours out another drink.)* Join us.

(He raises his glass.) Well?

WOMAN

To new beginnings!

They drink. The Agent and the Woman make the right noises about the wine. Man 2 joins them. There is a murmur from Man 1.

WOMAN

(Continuing) You were saying?

MAN 1

The wine is good. Thank you.

AGENT

There's lots more here. Please help yourself.

MAN 2

It can't be spiked. It's from the same bottle. *(He laughs.)*

MAN 1

It must be. That's why you don't know what the hell you are doing.

WOMAN

Can we talk?

MAN 1

Sure. *(To Man 2)* Can we?

MAN 2

Sure, sure.

WOMAN

There are some things you must tell us.

MAN 1

About the group, there's nothing more you'll get from us.

AGENT

We're not asking you about them. We respect your privacy.

WOMAN

It's about things that worry both of us. *(Pause)*

MAN 1

What do you want to know?

AGENT

You've spent a lot of time with Mr Writer here. What did you talk about?

MAN 2

Can he talk! *(Man 1 looks at him. He stops.)*

AGENT

Go ahead. What did he have to say?

MAN 1

You have to listen hard to catch what he says. You catch one thing, you've missed three.

MAN 2

Sounds like a school teacher at times.

AGENT

Made you listen, did he?

MAN 1

We asked for it, I think.

WOMAN

There must have been talk about his book.

MAN 2

Little else.

AGENT

What does the award mean to him?

MAN 1

I think the book means much more to him than the award.

AGENT

You think so?

MAN 1

I think so. The man says things from deep inside his belly.

WOMAN

Does he believe in the things he has written?

MAN 1

That's what we wanted to know. But we couldn't tell if he was speaking as Mr Writer himself or as one of the characters in the book.

MAN 2

At times it was like he was playing a game with us.

WOMAN

You felt he was leading you on?

MAN 1

At times, yes.

WOMAN

You felt he was making a fool of you?

MAN 1

Well...

MAN 2

He knew everything. He had something to say about everything

AGENT

Was he dogmatic?

MAN 1

I don't know

WOMAN

Did he sound fanatic?

MAN 1

No, no, he was just... he had opinions. You could say he was – what did you call it – didactic. Maybe it was an act.

AGENT

Some people are like that, aren't they? You never know where you stand with them.

MAN 2

A troubled soul, that's what he sounded like to me.

AGENT

Did you feel there was something troubling him when he was with you?

MAN 2

At times, yes.

WOMAN

You can see now how important this is, can't you? We must know if there is actually a group like the one in the book. Maybe there are more than one.

MAN 2

It could be some sickness in his mind. A loveless life. Maybe that's why he can see nothing but the end of mankind.

WOMAN

Did you get the feeling that he really wanted that? An end?

MAN 2

Sure. He certainly put it that way to us. *(To Man 1)* What do you say?

MAN 1

He thinks there should be an end to all lovemaking.

WOMAN

Sad.

MAN 2

Oh, much worse than that, if you ask me. Can you imagine what that means for anybody less than seventy? Looking up a pair of legs and not feeling a pulse in your pants.

MAN 1

Walking hand in hand in the park, and whispering intimate details of each other's bank accounts?

MAN 2

Being asked to take off your clothes so they can be pressed?

Man 1 and Man 2 jab each other in the ribs. Pause.

AGENT

How did Mr Writer think he could bring about such a...

MAN 1

Not himself.

MAN 2

He did.

MAN 1

He didn't.

MAN 2

He had all these ideas. Big bang ideas and slow blow ideas. His head was bulging with ideas.

MAN 1

They were ideas. Because that's what he is – a man of ideas.

MAN 2

He seemed to be damned sure they'd work.

MAN 1

Still, just ideas.

WOMAN

There were some big bang ideas?

MAN 1

Meaning a quick end. All of it happening at the same time.

MAN 2

If it must end that way, I vote for one great big bang lovemaking festival before the switch is thrown.

WOMAN

Did he seem to have a preference? Any favourite idea.

MAN 2

Yes.

MAN 1

(Over Man 2) No.

MAN 2

But he did.

MAN 1

He didn't. He simply said these things are possible.

AGENT

He said that?

MAN 1

In a hypothetical way. That's what he said.

WOMAN

Look, this is a very important point for us to get a fix on. It's important for all of us – you, us, all of us – who want peace and justice in the world. You must think very carefully about all the things you heard from Mr Writer when he was in your care. And you know, it wasn't just a half minute conversation in a public loo – looking down most of the time.

AGENT

You don't know this, but you have had the rare privilege of a long and detailed and, I might add, unrehearsed discussion with an extraordinary person who has an extraordinary view of the world. You have had this discussion with him before anybody else has. It is just possible that he might have said something to you that might never again be revealed in any other conversation with any other person.

WOMAN

It is very important for us to know two things as quickly as possible. Is there really a project group, somewhere, of the kind described in his book? It doesn't matter if it is a blackout plan or a slow fade out. Is there a project? And, of course, is Mr Writer in the know?

MAN 1

If you ask me, I don't think he has the balls for it.

MAN 2

You don't think so?

MAN 1

Writers and artists like him – they are all the same. All their crying concern for the fate of the earth and its suffering peoples – it's all in words and in fancy print. They dodge their way out of any job that's going to get their hands dirty, their good looks muddy. They have one eye on the till and the other on the company they must keep. The Honourable Mister Spellbinding Bullshitting Writer couldn't care a damn what happens to the last remaining rain forests, or the victims of chemical poisoning from translocated factories, or the starving guppies in your fishbowl.

MAN 2

Phew!

AGENT

And what do you think?

MAN 2

I think maybe I was wrong. I think he is right.

WOMAN

Would you be surprised if you found out that there actually are secret societies – dozens of them – who would like the world to end?

MAN 1

We've seen them too. Losers. They can't keep up, they can't face up to things, so they want out.

MAN 2

There's a crackpot cult around every loser with a gift of the gab.

WOMAN

There are some that are different.

MAN 1

They're all the same. Only the passwords are different.

AGENT

There are some that are different. They are new. Very recent arrivals.

WOMAN

They don't want the world to end. They just want the human species out.

MAN 2

They've been reading... ?

AGENT

Probably.

MAN 2

God!

MAN 1

Are they serious? Or is it just fun, a passing fad?

WOMAN

Difficult to tell. People take their fun so seriously. Even if it's a fad for one season, we need to keep an eye on it.

MAN 2

It's dangerous any way you look at it.

MAN 1

They are a danger to themselves.

WOMAN

You see what I mean when I say we must work together.

MAN 1

If you already know who the groups are and where they hang out, you can break them up any time you want.

MAN 2

Any way you want.

AGENT

Sometimes that's possible. Sometimes we could do with some help.

WOMAN

We can't do everything by ourselves.

AGENT

Here, let me show you something. *(He goes to the system, switches it on, and operates the palmtop.)*

This is a group we picked up recently on our scan. *(The group huddles around the monitor.)*

It's a small group. Not clear yet when exactly they started, but still a small group. They are adding new members very slowly, only one at a time.

AGENT

We have information on six of them just now. You might be interested in knowing who they are, what they do.

WOMAN

Without the names. For the time being.

AGENT

Later, perhaps. Here they are.

The four of them remain around the monitor. As the Agent profiles the members of the Council, he (or she) is picked up by a tight spot at the Council meeting place. The Agent continues.

AGENT

A physicist with path-breaking work in liquid crystals. Twice honoured by the International Academy for distinguished contributions. Influential book in meta-theory seven years ago. Took early retirement to promote energy projects from urban waste. Declined a Nobel nomination.

A cybernetician. Produced a computer programme for real time monitoring of the economy on the invitation of a socialist government. A recluse. Has written extensively on decision-making models of a societal brain. Signatory to a protest against patenting of life forms.

A clinical epidemiologist. International authority on tropical diseases and rapid action viral dispersion. Highly sought after as a detector of new and unknown viruses. Tours third world countries six months in a year. Collaborated with computer hackers to model drug-resistant viruses.

An architect turned engineer turned mathematician. From Operations Research solutions in public systems, he has shifted his interest to global remote sensing systems for natural disasters. Worked incognito as a volunteer in an African refugee camp. Is currently validating Vedic mathematics.

An anthropologist who has spent half a lifetime studying indigenous peoples in four continents. His theory of technological co-evolution has won wide academic recognition, but has remained outside mainstream policy. Foster father of thirty-two orphans in a global virtual family.

Finally, a philosopher of science. A three-book trilogy from the most prestigious publishing house. Has expanded on the consequences of deep cycling of human stimulus-seeking behaviours and their depressive aftermaths.

WOMAN

Deep cycling?

AGENT

It means that the need for stimulation is very special to the human animal – us that is. What gives us a kick today is boring tomorrow.

MAN 1

So we want more and more all the time!

AGENT

Not just that. Every high is sure to be followed by a low, a kind of exhaustion and depression. That's what makes us go for a bigger high. Then comes a bigger low. And so on, and the swings are getting bigger and wilder over time.

WOMAN

And wham! We lose control. Or something like that.

AGENT

Something like that.

MAN 1

Something more than that. The author of Vanishing Species, in there, thinks this is a genetic defect in the human species. Ours is the only species that has this craving for higher and higher levels of stimulation. *(They look at each other.)*

AGENT

Well, that's the lot.

MAN 2

You call that a crackpot cult?

MAN 1

They could still be just that, in spite of their highfalutin books and lectures and all. A bunch of losers.

AGENT

There is one more. He is not in yet.

WOMAN

A candidate. He is being considered.

MAN 2

Another head in the clouds type? Spent his life talking to sea turtles, did he?

AGENT

Not quite. He is a gardener.

MAN 1

A botanist. Isn't that what they are called?

AGENT

No, he is a gardener.

WOMAN

He talks to plants.

[12]

The meeting of the Council. An elaborate installation ceremony is on for the Gardener. It is entirely without speech. A subdued background music is the only sound through the scene. The performing group can set the moves and business for the ceremony in accordance with the overall design. However, an ambience of maturity and dignity must be preferred over the merely exotic.

At the end, the new member bows deeply, first to Mater, then to Pater, and takes his seat at an assigned place. The others sit after he does, in an arc, facing him. The gardener strikes a meditative stance methodically. The others follow.

[13]

The writer's living room. Man 1, Man 2, the Agent, and the Woman are still at the system table.

AGENT

He seems the odd one out in the group.

WOMAN

Or the odd one in.

MAN 1

What does it take to get in?

WOMAN

Patience, to start with. It's a long process.

AGENT

Here is a checklist used for a first screening. If you want to be a member, ask yourself the following:

Have you at any time seen a great, overpowering, dazzling, pure white light in front of you?

Have you had dreams in colour?

Have you ever had an out of body experience, especially one in which you could see yourself?

Have you ever had an olfactory hallucination? Especially foul smells?

WOMAN

That one is considered important.

AGENT

Have you experienced dissonance delight – ie. peace and contentment with the awareness of contradictions and divergence in your beliefs.

Have you had synaesthetic experiences?

MAN 1

What's that?

AGENT

Cross-sense experiences. Do you, for instance, see a sound? Or hear things when you look at a picture?

MAN 2

Some kinds of pictures do exciting things to me, I can tell you.

AGENT

There are other things in the checklist. If you've had a lot of those experiences, you could get through the first screening.

MAN 1

I had an uncle they would welcome with open arms.

AGENT

Your uncle?

MAN 1

My uncle. He had a lot of those things. People laughed, made fun. He was a quiet sort anyway.

AGENT

Where is he now?

MAN 1

He was a booking clerk in a packers and movers outfit. That was over six years ago. Maybe eight.

AGENT

He is... no more?

MAN 1

No more there as a clerk. A team from the University picked him up, took him from lab to lab, wouldn't let him go. They paid him though. It was good money.

WOMAN

Where is he now?

MAN 1

Don't know. Haven't seen him since. Maybe he retired and settled down in Tahiti. Maybe he's dead.

WOMAN

Why was the University interested in him do you think?

MAN 1

All those weird experiences – they are supposed to make you look at the world in a different way.

WOMAN

In what way?

MAN 1

I don't know. They had a name for it. They called it Altered State of Consciousness, or something like that. *(The Agent looks at the Woman.)*

WOMAN

We must act.

The Agent and the Woman turn towards the inside of the house to see the Writer standing at the far end. He has bathed and changed and rested. The Agent moves, but the Woman restrains him.

WOMAN

So nice to see you again, Mr Writer. You look well rested.

WRITER

I hope it's not a disturbance. I thought I'd peep in to see if you could do with another bottle of wine.

AGENT

How did you... Mr Writer, sir, you and Mrs Writer are not permitted to move about outside the areas clearly designated for you. This is for your own safety. Your life is not out of danger yet, you know.

WRITER

I shall return straightaway. *(To Man 1 and Man 2)* Good evening gentlemen.

MAN 1

Good evening.

MAN 2

And a very good evening to you, sir.

WRITER

I hope the hospitality in my humble dwelling properly reciprocates the courtesies you extended me not too long ago.

MAN 2

Good wine.

WRITER

(To the Agent) Do look after the two gentlemen well, please. And do please help yourself in the pantry and kitchen.

WOMAN

Thank you, Mr Writer. You are very kind.

WRITER

Pleased to be of service. If it's not too much trouble, could you let me know when you are taking a break in here. I will take a few minutes to rotate the pots in here for their sunlight. I'll get back now.

WOMAN

Wait. Mr Writer, sir, please do join us for a while. We were in the midst of an interesting discussion. You might have something to contribute. Please come in. Here, please be seated. *(He is seated on the couch.)*

WRITER

Thank you. What were you discussing?

WOMAN

You, of course. Your work, really. A most imaginative piece of writing that has received critical acclaim from all over.

AGENT

There were some interesting ideas emerging in our little group here. To start with, we had to agree that it was a great science fiction novel.

WRITER

Did you?

WOMAN

Of course. Is there any doubt about that?

WRITER

Well, there have been two points of view on that. Some think of the book as science fiction. Some others like to think of it as fictional science.

WOMAN

I see. And that means, I suppose...

WRITER

I suppose they have an understanding of the difference.

AGENT

What is your own view? In what category of writing would you put Vanishing Species?

WRITER

I've said this before. For me it's just a novel.

MAN 1

But on solid scientific ground. It's not cock-and-bull sci-fi, that's what you said to us.

WRITER

Did I?

MAN 1

Didn't you?

WRITER

I only said, these things can be looked at scientifically. We need to at least look at them seriously.

AGENT

Mr Writer, sir, I think you will agree that we, at least, are taking it quite seriously. It has come to our attention... *(The Woman restrains him.)*

WOMAN

We have been advised to give the highest order of attention to your safety. The security around the house will be tightened further. I am afraid the restrictions on your movement will have to be enforced rather strictly. A slight annoyance, I agree, but do think of it as a small price to be paid for remaining a free society.

AGENT

(To Man 2) You will stay here. *(To Man 1)* The two of us will leave immediately.

The Agent goes up to the system and unplugs his palmtop. He and Man 1 leave. The Woman indicates that the Writer should be escorted in. Man 2 takes him in. She goes to the telephone table and switches on the system. Man 2 reappears, stays at a distance, looking at the Woman. She smiles. He goes up to the table, stands behind her, watching her at work.

[14]

The meeting of the Council. Mater is seated next to the Gardener. Each member has a potted plant in front.

MATER

All protein is of plant origin. *(Pause)*

PATER

Animal protein is derived primarily from plant protein. *(Pause)*

MEMBER

Human survival depends on protein. *(Pause)*

MEMBER

There is a dependence of human life on plant protein. *(Pause)*

MEMBER

Plant protein is a carrier. *(Pause)*

MEMBER

It is the ideal carrier. *(Pause)* As demonstrated in the pilot project.

The gardener gives Mater an envelope. She opens it, takes out a sheet, and passes it around the group.

MATER

Are we satisfied? *(The members nod.)* Those were the six sentences written by our new member on a sheet of paper, placed in an envelope, and sealed. None of us saw the written sentences. They were transmitted just now through a plant medium and picked up by you. This is Metacom at its simplest, most primitive level of operation. It is like connecting six computers in a tiny network within a limited geographical area.

PATER

It was the humble beginning. That connectivity has now expanded to a ubiquitous density, unimaginable at its installation.

MATER

The connectivity possible through Metacom has potentials far beyond current human comprehension. *(The Gardener whispers to Mater.)* It is not without dangers. The temptation of control and subjugation cannot be denied.

PATER

We have seen for ourselves the supreme naturalistic principle of Metacom. To submit is to gain. To want the gain is to lose.

The Gardener whispers to Mater.

MATER

The connectivity that already exists in the plant kingdom through Metacom exceeds the man made one by an order of two point five million.

MEMBER

Do we know the exact number of life forms on the planet?

PATER

It is a race against time. There is a global research consortium at work to document and classify every life form ever evolved.

MEMBER

A monumental task

PATER

Current estimates are unsatisfactory. They show an extremely wide variance, ranging from two million species to over forty million.

The Gardener whispers to Mater.

MATER

The number in the plant kingdom can be taken as known.

MEMBER

There are clearly two tasks before us, to be undertaken in parallel.

MEMBER

The scaling up of the human interface in Metacom.

PATER

And the scaling up of the protein carrier to reach widely distributed populations.

[15]

The Writer's living room. It is dark. There is a small working light on at the telephone desk. The system starts to beep. The Woman appears, switches on a larger lamp and attends to the system, plugging in her own palmtop. Man 2 appears and stands behind her.

WOMAN

(Speaking into the headset) Come in Delta four-two-zero. System open for Delta four-two-zero.

The monitor lights up. We see the face of the Agent.

AGENT

Delta four-two-zero reporting. Thursday group picked up. Search of all premises proceeding.

WOMAN

Where are they held?

AGENT

Transferred to a villa outside city, off Highway 14. Sponsored weekend outing by Sisters of Charity.

WOMAN

All in?

AGENT

All except one. The mentally retarded.

WOMAN

What's your reading?

AGENT

Same as yours. Permission to storm philosopher's den.

WOMAN

Granted conditional.

AGENT

Reading.

WOMAN

No force. Utmost care. Velvet gloves. There is a lot to be mined from the den. Most important, no leakage.

AGENT

Action immediate.

WOMAN

Immediate. Cover provided from sector twelve. I will direct operations from there.

AGENT

Going in velvet gloves. Over.

WOMAN

Over and out. *(She switches off, turns and looks at Man 2.)*

Sorry, I have to go now. We can continue later, okay? You have to stay. Don't let him out of sight.

[16]

The sound of the harmonica. It is early morning, a shaft of light in the Writer's living room. Man 2 is slouched on the couch, while the Writer takes a large potted plant out on a trolley and brings another in. He sits next to the plant on a footstool or low hassock. He meditates and tends the plant lovingly.

[17]

The Council room. The pots have been moved to a side. The members are in meditation. The Gardener stirs, opens his eyes. He moves quietly, going up to the pots and sitting beside them. He tends them lovingly, stops, listens carefully, rises, and leaves the room quietly.

Presently there are sounds offstage of a door being broken in, footsteps rushing up a staircase, banging on another door. The members come out of their meditative states but remain calmly in their places. The lights brighten suddenly.

[18]

The Writer's living room. It is morning. Man 2 is still on the couch, browsing a girlie magazine. The Writer is sitting next to the potted plant, but is looking at Man 2.

MAN 2

It's like old times, what? Only, I don't have to do all the dirty work looking after you. *(No response)* You have everything you need right here. All the comforts of home in captivity. Plus the security. What do you say, Mr Writer, sir? *(No response)* You are not very communicative this morning, sir. Anything the matter? Anything I can do to serve you better?

WRITER

They are not back yet.

MAN 2

Worried about them, are you?

WRITER

They could bring the morning papers with them.

MAN 2

Feeling lost with nothing to read? I could lend you this, but it's not your kind of dish, I should think. Not before the morning papers.

WRITER

Keeps you engrossed I can see.

MAN 2

It's a funny thing though. Here's a spread that's about as hot as it can get. I've been looking at it for – what – half an hour now. But that's all. I've just been looking. It's not doing anything to me.

WRITER

Is this the first time? The first time you've found yourself this way – unmoved?

MAN 2

As far as I can remember. Here, you want it?

WRITER

No, thank you.

MAN 2

Suit yourself. If you must get your kicks from the morning papers, so be it. *(Pause)*

WRITER

If it is all right with you, I might make just a short call to check on the papers.

MAN 2

Go ahead. Just make sure you keep it short.

The Writer goes up to the desk, picks up the phone, and dials a number.

WRITER

Francis?... Yes, it's me... Is it on its way?... Thank you. *(He hangs up.)*

MAN 2

And another thing. I can't say I know where this whole thing is headed, and when it's likely to blow over. But when I get out of here I'm going to find a way to buy that book of yours. I'd like to have you sign it for me, if that's not asking for too much.

WRITER

Why, I'm touched by your... Of course I'll sign it for you.

The Woman, the Agent, and Man 1 enter. The Agent goes directly to the telephone desk, connects his palmtop to the system, and punches a few keys. The Woman and Man 1 stay next to the Writer. The Agent joins them. They are looking down at the Writer.

MAN 2

What happened? Did you take them all in?

WOMAN

We took them in. All, except the gardener.

AGENT

The gardener is missing.

Fade out

Close of play

BANGALORE LITTLE THEATRE

Six Decades of Wholesome Community Theatre

In 1960, a small group of committed persons in Bangalore sought a theatre experience that could be a genuine alternative to the order of the day that was called BBC Theatre – British Bedroom Comedy. The group included the talented couple, Scott and Margaret Tod, and at least four other expats, along with a handful of Bangaloreans. They had a vision of a Community Theatre best described by the slogan invented 25 years later: *Think Globally, Act Locally.* Bangalore Little Theatre came into existence with a play reading in the last week of September that year. The first production on boards in December 1960 was Moliere's *The Prodigious Snob*, more commonly known as *The Would-be Gentleman.*

In 1962, within a year of inception, BLT arrived at a character and identity for itself: to maintain pride in its strictly amateur status, but to conduct its affairs in a thoroughly professional manner. The group gave itself a constitution and, through that, a participatory style of functioning. The group was seen as belonging to a membership, and therefore to be managed transparently by an elected management committee. The founding members were the first to give way to younger members to take the group forward.

Way back in 1963, BLT produced its first Indian play in English, an original adaptation of *Mrichhakatika* (The Toy Cart of Clay) by a founder-member, Prof B Chandrasekhara. Since then, the group has maintained the conscious policy of producing Indian plays periodically – translations, adaptations, original scripts, by its own members and others. Not surprisingly, two of the six awards for contemporary playscripts instituted for the first time by *The Hindu* in 1993 landed in BLT. The first prize was for the play by Vijay Padaki, *Credit Titles,* a political satire on intellectual property rights for patenting life forms. A Special Prize was awarded to another member, Ambika (Poile) Sengupta.

Old-timers of BLT have often been asked the secret of the group's long life when, in contrast, we see hundreds of cases of groups starting with a bang and dropping by the wayside in a couple of years. The difference, it seems, is in the simple fact that BLT is a community-based organisation and, therefore, a membership-driven group. From this fact has followed a number of guiding principles that appear to have served BLT well over the years. For instance:

- The participatory and transparency principles in management (with all financial transactions completely open and made available to the entire membership)
- The highly open leadership structure around an elected Managing Committee (rather than being founder-centric or personality-driven)
- The constant development of new talent, including new directors (rather than being dependent on the same old hands or breeding star complexes)
- The pursuit of the higher purpose, the constitutionally-enshrined objective of promoting the theatre and related arts in Bangalore (rather than the attitude of 'let's do another play')

All of this actually makes it far more difficult to 'manage' the organisation. It is so much easier to let a charismatic leader take charge and 'run' the group as he (or she) wishes.

The significance of these principles is understood better when we see that a sizeable majority of the theatre talent in Bangalore, including the more recognised names, has been in BLT productions, workshops and training programmes earlier. They continue their affiliation with BLT even if they perform under other banners.

Related to this point is one other indisputably important feature of BLT. It is the only English-language theatre group in Bangalore (perhaps anywhere in India) with strong links to the local-regional theatre, building bridges across language divides. Many of the stalwarts on the Kannada stage and screen have been either life members of BLT or have been prominently involved in some capacity or the other. After all, among the founders were personalities like Prof B Chandrasekhara, Nani, Shivaram, Seetharam, V Ramamurthy and S Ramaswamy. Then there were CR Simha, Vimala Rangachar, SG Ramachandra, KC Sekhar, Suresh Heblikar, Paddu, Shankar and Arundhati Nag, Ashok Rao…. And many many more – including some who went on to become Presidents of Karnataka Nataka Academy! Indeed, BLT has been a substantial support to Kannada theatre groups in their start-up stages.

BLT has invested heavily in training and outreach activity. In the late 1970s, BLT introduced for the first time in Bangalore a comprehensive introductory programme for newcomers to the theatre, based on the Stella Adler system. Since the mid '80, the group has made its Summer Project on Theatre (SPOT) a regular training event. It has come to be recognised as the most prestigious training event in the city, because of the quality of inputs provided. And it continues to be a part of BLT's social commitment. Other groups and productions snap up the talent from these training projects.

In 1993, the group initiated an annual Festival of Short Plays (SHORTS), aimed at promoting theatre activity among the college and youth population. With the audience response as enthusiastic as seen, the scale of the Festival may well be enhanced considerably in the coming years.

As a socially-responsible theatre society, BLT has readily taken on many a fundraising production for worthy causes. In 1970-71, BLT's production of the new play by Badal Sircar, *Evam Indrajit*, was the first fundraising event to contribute to the Prime Minister's Fund for the Bangladeshi (then East Bengal) refugee crisis. An original script, *Head Start*, by Vijay Padaki, was produced for CRY in January 1996. Since then BLT has made a constitutional commitment to dedicate one production for a charity every year. The group also provides various kinds of help to theatre projects in colleges, schools, clubs and other institutions.

With the high repute in training and outreach activity, it was only logical for BLT to set up an Academy of Theatre Arts in 2008. The stated mission of the Academy is to enrich the theatre institutional system through the thrust programme of *Theatre Education,* thus building the societal base for the true appreciation of the theatre and, indeed, all of the performing arts.

THE SERIES EDITOR

Vijay Padaki is a Theatre Educator based in Bangalore. He has worn two caps for most of his life with equal facility. He has been active in the theatre for sixty years. He has been a management professional for over forty-five years.

Vijay is a psychologist and behavioural scientist by training, and founder-director of The P&P Group, a management resource centre that has programmes of research, consulting and training in the areas of Organisation and Institutional Development. A good part of the work of The P&P Group is devoted to the effectiveness of large development programmes. Among his earlier assignments, he headed the Human Resources Division of India's oldest cooperative R&D institution, Ahmedabad Textile Industry's Research Association (ATIRA), which also helped set up the first Indian Institute of Management in Ahmedabad. Later, he was a member of the founding faculty at Indian Institute of Management, Bangalore, the founder of a Centre for Management for the textile industry in Ahmedabad, and a Visiting Professor at Indian Institute of Science, Bangalore to initiate a programme in R&D Management. He was a Senior Associate at the National Institute of Advanced Studies in its early years.

Vijay joined Bangalore Little Theatre in 1960, the year of its inception, and later served the company in many capacities – as actor, director, trainer, writer, designer and administrator, including two stints each as Secretary and President. In 2008, the institutional set-up was restructured. Bangalore Little Theatre Foundation was created as a Public Charitable Trust. It was done with the purpose of reinforcing the organisation's strengths in outreach activity, and thus *rededicating the commitment to social development goals beyond performance.* The Trust requested Vijay to provide the leadership to a newly-created Academy of Theatre Arts in its formative years. The Academy is developing a long-term programme thrusts to strengthen the institution of theatre education and practice in India.

Vijay has been responsible for institutionalising several activities of BLT, such as the annual summer workshop for newcomers to the theatre (SPOT), from which has emerged a large number of the theatre personalities in Bangalore, the History of Ideas programme of biographical plays, the Courtyard Theatre programme, and the Children's Theatre programme, which includes the annual flagship children's play as a partnership production to support a charity. Vijay conceived and initiated the highly successful Trainer-Training programme and the Directors Training programme in Bangalore.

He has forged several international partnerships with BLT over the years. The John F Kennedy Centre for Performing Arts in Washington invited him to serve as an advisor to the India Festival in 2011. The same year, he gave the Harold Clurman lecture at the Stella Adler Studio in New York. More recently, the Ministry of Culture invited Vijay to initiate a programme of Arts and Heritage Management in India.

Vijay has written over 50 original plays. He has also adapted or translated several play scripts. Seagull Books has published a volume of two Gujarati plays translated by him. In 1993, Vijay won the award for the best contemporary play script instituted by *The Hindu* for the play *Credit Titles.*

PUBLICATIONS IN THE SERIES

Volume 1: FOUR CLASSICS on the Indian Stage

Contains original English language adaptations of Indian classics. These include ***The Toy Cart of Clay,*** an adaptation of the Sanskrit Classic ***Mrichhakatika*** by Sudraka; ***The Anklet,*** an adaptation from Ilango Adigal's Tamil Classic ***Silappadikaram***; ***Kurukshetra Burning!*** based on ***Smashana Kurukshetra*** in Kannada by Kuvempu; ***The Echo,*** an adaptation of ***Chomana Dudi*** in Kannada by Shivarama Karanth.

Volume 2: THE HISTORY OF IDEAS Programme of new plays

From BLT's highly acclaimed History of Ideas programme, plays include ***The Prophet and the Poet,*** based on the Gandhi-Tagore exchanges; ***Finding Ananda***, rediscovering the life and work of Swami Vivekananda, with the Bengal Renaissance as the backdrop; ***Tiger! Tiger!*** revealing the humanistic side of Tipu Sultan; ***Monsters in the Dark,*** an original adaptation of the Pulitzer award book ***The Emperor of All Maladies*** by Siddhartha Mukherjee, sub-titled A Biography of Cancer; ***Einstein's Dreams,*** an original dance theatre adaptation of the novel by the same title by Alan Lightman.

Volume 3: CHILDREN'S THEATRE Programme of new plays

Containing plays from BLT's hugely successful Children's Theatre programme, this volume includes ***The Ungrateful Man,*** a tale from the Panchatantra; ***The Magic Drum,*** a collection of stories from the book by the same title by Sudha Murty; ***Ali Oh Baba,*** a retelling of the tale from the 1001 Arabian Nights; and ***The Court Jester,*** the tales of Tenali Rama.

Volume 5:
MANDAP and other plays

The plays included in this Volume represent two main periods of Vijay Padaki's writing. The first is when he was deeply involved in social-development programmes that had field projects in rural areas. They were all addressing the issues of human rights and social justice, although from different 'sectoral' perspectives. It was the absence of rights and justice that was coming in the way of development in real terms. Violence was not ruled out. ***Mandap*** is the play from that period. The dynamics of rights and justice are seen in the urban setting too. The next five plays in this volume represent a period of writing in which the writer was increasingly drawn to developmental issues in the urban setting. The plays form a set that came to be called ***Tales From the City***. They are grouped in this Volume as two double-bills and one play by itself. Violence is the recognizable undercurrent in all these plays. ***Second Shift Muster*** is the oldest of the play scripts appearing in this volume. The one-act play is included in this volume for a variety of reasons. As with the other tales, this play explores a lesser known city-based occupation in changing times. with changing value systems.

Volume 6:
SALT LICKS and other plays

The plays in Volume 6 reflect on the continued Western orientation of Indian communities till today. As a character in ***Salt Licks*** says: 'Go West, young man, to rediscover the East. And don't be in a hurry to get back'. The first play in this publication series refers to a peculiarly Bangalore society of elders fixated in the Raj, calling themselves the Empire Loyalists. If it was 'Great Britain' at one time, it was the American Dream later. In the pre-liberalized economy, young people went to extremes to get admission in American colleges and universities. Any university, any course, any location, it was only important to get there first. And yet... there was something so human in their dreams. The collection in this Volume can be called ***Vijay Padaki's early plays.*** The stories are set in the period early 'seventies to early 'nineties. The ubiquitous 2-in-1 music system in the plays creates a special place for itself. Two plays in the set need further explanation. ***Gold and Silver*** was written at the time of an exchange project with the Royal National Theatre celebrating India's Golden Anniversary of Independence. ***Evening Shadows*** is an original English language adaptation of *Sandhya Chhaya* by the Marathi playwright Jaywant Dalvi. The loneliness of an elderly couple is compounded by the son not returning from America.

